YALE CLASSICAL STUDIES

YALE CLASSICAL STUDIES

EDITED FOR THE DEPARTMENT OF CLASSICS

by

ADAM PARRY

VOLUME XXII
STUDIES IN FIFTH-CENTURY
THOUGHT AND LITERATURE

CAMBRIDGE
AT THE UNIVERSITY PRESS
1972

Published by the Syndics of the Cambridge University Press
Bentley House, 200 Euston Road, London NW1 2DB
American Branch: 32 East 57th Street, New York, N.Y.10022

Library of Congress Catalogue Card Number: 71–166948

ISBN: 0 521 08305 2

Printed in Great Britain
at the University Printing House, Cambridge
(Brooke Crutchley, University Printer)

Contents

v

Harry Mortimer Hubbell
1881–1971

Gladly wolde he lerne, and gladly teche

HARRY MORTIMER HUBBELL received his formal education in New Haven, Connecticut: a graduate of Hillhouse High School, he entered Yale to win his B.A., M.A., and Ph.D. But his progress to the doctorate was interrupted by periods of teaching in New York State and New Jersey. A combination of teaching and administrative authority in these positions is reflected in his career at Yale, where he was appointed in 1911; here, whether as instructor or Talcott Professor, a full teaching program never blunted his readiness to undertake academic committee work and finally the chairmanship of his department. It is not surprising that his delight in interpreting the values of classical literature led him in 1924 to introduce a course in Classical Civilization designed to interest those who had little or no Latin and Greek in the achievements of the ancient world. In this he was a pioneer, for few classical scholars at that time, not excepting colleagues, found such a program congenial or significant. He remained actively interested in this field throughout his life, and the proliferation of similar or derived courses in this country and elsewhere bears out his judgement. A man of such quiet energy as his could not settle into inactivity. On his retirement in 1950 a Visiting Professorship in the University of California at Berkeley was followed by a Fulbright Fellowship at the American Academy in Rome; he was one of the first John Hay Whitney Professors, joining the faculty at Goucher College, Maryland, where his enthusiasm raised a class of six to forty students. There were other appointments: at Princeton, Albertus Magnus, and in 1962 at Yale.

His special interest lay in Greek and Latin rhetoric; it showed itself in books, translations, and numerous articles on Isocrates, Cicero, Philodemus, St Chrysostom. But his wide-ranging mind could also investigate Ptolemy's Zoo, horse-sacrifices in antiquity, or a Christian liturgy found in an Egyptian papyrus; his knowledge of meteorology and astronomy could be valuable to such as might wish to fix the date of an eclipse in antiquity or know the prospects for a good day's sailing.

Harry Hubbell was known to his colleagues as 'Teacher'. No one could have deserved that friendly and respectful greeting more than he, not merely for his devotion in the classroom, but for his willingness to assist any who sought his advice: where he could give no immediate answer he knew where the answer might be found; and he might well, in his enthusiasm, anticipate his questioner, find, and offer the answer himself. He was, as one of his favorite authors might have said, not only σοφός, but φιλόσοφος, a wise man still seeking for knowledge. In temperament he was, as many testimonials attest, genial; one is reminded of Aristophanes' complimentary reference to Sophocles – εὔκολος. This is how we remember him – and he would like it: φιλόσοφος καὶ διδάσκαλος εὔκολος.

CHRISTOPHER M. DAWSON

Preface

THE ARTICLES in this volume are addressed primarily to the professional Classicist. Some of them, however, are much less technical than others. *E. A. Havelock*'s study of Aristophanes' *Clouds* deals with a fundamental aspect of Socratic thought; *A. T. Cole* introduces new distinctions into the conventional picture of Sophistic relativism; *A. Parry* infers from the *Archaeology* Thucydides' theory of history; *W. Sale* applies psychoanalytic concepts closely to a character of Euripides; and *G. S. Kirk* examines the definition of 'myth' in the light of Greek and other myths. All these articles deal with questions that are bound to be of interest to anyone concerned with the history of thought in the Western World; all are comprehensible to those who are not expert in Greek philology, and even to those who do not know Greek.

A middle ground in this respect is occupied by *M. McCall*'s solution to a perplexing problem in Sophocles' *Antigone*; by *H. Lloyd-Jones*' reconstruction of the plot and mood of Menander's *Samia*; by *M. Arthur*'s study of the independent role of the chorus in Euripides' *Bacchae*; by *D. Tompkins*' demonstration that Thucydides does after all adjust his style to individual historical characters, by *R. Brumbaugh*'s brief argument that Socrates, as portrayed by Aristophanes, used scientific models, and by *D. Claus*' interpretation of a key speech in Euripides' *Hippolytus*. These articles deal with more specific problems than the previous group, and mostly require a knowledge of Greek texts in the original language to be understood.

Finally, the articles of *B. Knox* on Euripides' *Iphigenia in Aulis* and *H. Lloyd-Jones* on Sophocles' *Trachiniae* are philology in an old sense. They apply technical expertise to the problems of the text.

The contents of this volume therefore cover a fairly wide spectrum in generality of interest and in degree of technicality. Such a spectrum is fairly characteristic of the present state of Classical studies, and, it might be argued, properly so. Without the ability to apply linguistic and stylistic learning to the details of a text, we shall ultimately lose contact with the substance of ancient thought. If we have not the ability to see the larger intellectual and literary significance of our texts, their value to us and those we teach will disappear.

The theme of this volume is fifth-century Athenian intellectual history. Some of the articles are obviously appropriate to this theme, especially those I have described as being in the more general category. Of these G. S. Kirk's consideration of myth extends furthest beyond the borders of the fifth century and of Athens; but we may not forget that myth is the subject of drama, and drama is the heart of Athenian literary culture.

The editor has judged that the more specific articles as well are concerned with intellectual history. If Tompkins' demonstration is accepted, the fifth-century Greek concept of what historical character is, as well as how it should be portrayed, may be different from what we had thought. McCall's paper deals with a specific problem, but his solution has far-reaching implications for the religious sense of Sophocles and his audience. Arthur's study of the chorus of the *Bacchae* suggests Euripides' concern with questions of the role of violence in society. Even a piece so textual as that of Knox entails consequences of a larger intellectual sort, since in defending the order of lines as they appear in our manuscripts, the author must argue that Euripides and his contemporaries possessed a far more flexible notion of what dramatic action is than what has been commonly assumed by scholars.

Lloyd-Jones' *Samia* alone leaves the fifth century to deal with a play of the early third. We included this article because this is the first literary treatment of a work which came to light again after so many centuries only a few years ago.

The authors of this collection other than E. A. Havelock wished originally to dedicate the volume to Professor Havelock, who has been a guide to us all, and a teacher of most. Since the editor, however, desired to include in the collection the essay by Professor Havelock himself, an essay which embodies so much of the insight and humanity of its author, the remaining contributors have chosen instead to express in this place their admiring gratitude, in the year of his retirement from the faculty of Yale University, to Eric Havelock, staunch fighter, bold thinker, wise counselor, good friend.

New Haven, 1971   A. M. P.

ADAM MILMAN PARRY

The Yale Classics Department suffered a grievous loss in the premature death of its chairman in a road accident at Colmar, France on 4 June 1971. He was in the forty-third year of his age. His wife Anne, herself at one time a lecturer in the department, was killed with him. A graduate of Berkeley and Harvard, Adam initially served the Yale department between the years 1955 and 1960 in the ranks of instructor and assistant professor. In 1962 he accepted an invitation to return on tenured appointment, and in 1968, on promotion to full professor, he also assumed the duties of the chairmanship which had just been extended for a fourth and final year at the time of his death. A fuller notice of his career and achievement will appear in a later issue of *Yale Classical Studies*.

New Haven, 1972 E.A.H.

The Socratic self as it is parodied in Aristophanes' *Clouds*

ERIC A. HAVELOCK

THE AMBIGUITIES surrounding what is called the Socratic Problem are reinforced by the fact that while Old Comedy has preserved a record of the philosopher which is contemporary, it also seems unsympathetic, whereas the testimony which treats him seriously and is also friendly to him is entirely posthumous. To be sure, the posthumous record is itself not consistent. The 'portraits' offered by Plato and Xenophon, and the doxographical notices in Aristotle, have received varying estimates in terms of their evidential worth. But scholarly differences in this area of the testimony can be accommodated and compromised, and in recent accounts they usually are.[1] A more challenging division in critical opinion separates all those who have preferred the idealized versions of either Plato or Xenophon and the accommodation built upon them, from those who have looked for possible clues in the cruder testimonies publicized in the philosopher's life-time.[2]

1. See K. J. Dover's commentary on the *Clouds* (Oxford 1968), where the combination of 'Plato and Xenophon' is thrice used (pp. xlv, xlvi, xlix; cf. also liv) to defeat any suggestion that the *Clouds* could contribute independent testimony. Norman Gulley, *The Philosophy of Socrates* (London 1968), assumes (p. 2) that the views of Socrates in the *Memorabilia* and Plato's early dialogues 'in most philosophically significant respects agree with those ascribed to him by Aristotle'. W. K. C. Guthrie, *History of Greek Philosophy*, III (Cambridge 1969), prefers for the Socratic contribution to philosophy (p. 349) 'to rely primarily on those who were themselves philosophers'; *viz.* Plato and Aristotle. But on p. 355 Xenophon, Aristotle and Plato are aligned as equivalent sources for Socratic ethics. There seems to be a recent consensus that Maier's demonstration (cap. 3, pp. 77–102), made over fifty years ago (below, n. 4), of Aristotle's close dependence on the *Protagoras* and on Xenophon can be ignored. But is it safe to do so?

2. The challenge was initiated by Plato himself, at *Apol.* 19c 2–5, where it is confined to the *Clouds*, though this was not the only play to notice Socrates, nor was Aristophanes the only playwright (see Guthrie, III, p. 360, who reviews the notices), a fact perhaps acknowledged at *Apology* 18d 1. In modern times the claims of Aristophanes first drew attention not from professional scholars but from a man of letters in the person of C. M. Wieland, the friend of Goethe, who in 1798 wrote an essay with the almost painfully judicious title 'Versuch ueber

The Socratic Problem is today quiescent.[3] It has perhaps been given up as insoluble.[4] The prevailing scholarly preference is clearly oriented towards Plato's authority, even though the extreme case for this preference has been rejected.[5] The *Clouds* viewed as a possible source of independent testimony fails to obtain serious consideration.[6]

die Frage ob und wiefern Aristophanes gegen den Vorwurf, den Sokrates in den Wolken persoenlich misshandelt zu haben, gerechtfertigt oder entschuldigt werden koenne' (reprinted in *Collected Works*, XXXIV, Leipzig 1840). In 1811, in his introduction to a translation of *Nubes*, F. A. Wolf championed the claims of the play to rank as the preferred historical record, thus launching not only the Homeric but also the Socratic problem upon the unquiet seas of scholarship. It is to be observed that both these pioneers were relatively untouched by German idealist philosophy, which, spreading beyond Germany's borders, has exercised so powerful a control over the scholarship of the Socratic problem.

3. It has been reviewed most recently by C. J. de Vogel, 'The Present State of the Socratic Problem', *Phronesis* vol. 1 no. 1 (1955), 26–35, and in the first chapter of J. Humbert's *Socrate et les petits Socratiques* (Paris 1967); also see Guthrie, III, pp. 323–4.

4. One may contrast the confident but quite diverse reconstructions of a previous generation of scholars: H. Maier, *Sokrates* (Tübingen 1913), A. E. Taylor, *Varia Socratica* (Oxford 1911), and *Socrates* (1932), Heinrich Gomperz, 'Die Sokratische Frage als geschichtliches Problem', *Historische Zeitschrift* 129 (1923/4), 377–43, with the skepticism of O. Gigon, *Socrates* (Berne 1947), and A.-H. Chroust, *Socrates, Man and Myth* (London 1957). De Vogel, 'The Present State of the Socratic Problem', notes some rejoinders to Gigon. Dover comments (*Clouds*, p. vi) on the modern literature that 'it is repetitious and verbose to a degree credible only to those who have sampled it' and concludes that time available 'was better spent in reflecting on what was written about him before 100 B.C. than in further reading of what has been written about him since then'.

5. De Vogel's extensive review of Magalhães-Vilhena, *Le Problème de Socrate* and *Socrate et la légende Platonicienne* (Paris 1952) (I have not seen these works), makes it clear that she shares with Magalhães-Vilhena a preoccupation with Plato as evidential source, while rejecting the 'Burnet–Taylor hypothesis'. See also Guthrie, III, p. 329, n. 2.

6. Partial exceptions are R. Philippson, 'Sokratische Dialektik in Aristophanes' Wolken', *Rh. Mus.* N.F. 81 (1932), 30–8, Wolfgang Schmid, 'Das Sokratesbild der Wolken', *Philologus* 97 (1948), 209–22, R. Stark, 'Sokratisches in den Vögeln des Aristophanes', *Rh. Mus.* N.F. 96 (1953), 77–89, and H. Erbse, 'Sokrates im Schatten der aristophanischen Wolken', *Hermes* 82 (1954), 385–420. Cornelia de Vogel notes of Magalhães-Vilhena's two volumes that 'Aristophanes is reserved for consideration in a future publication'. Humbert, after making a formal bow in the direction of Aristophanes (*Socrate*, p. 7), virtually ignores him: references to Plato, Xenophon, and Diogenes Laertius dominate his footnotes. Dover (*Clouds*, xlvi–l) firmly excludes Aristophanes from serious consideration; see also E. W. Handley, 'Words for "soul" "heart" and "mind" in Aristophanes', *Rh. Mus.* 19 (N.F. 99) (1956), 205–25. Presumably the last scholar to place central weight of authority on him was H. Gomperz (above, n. 4).

The present essay, while reviving the claims of the *Clouds* to some authenticity of record, does not aim to choose between contemporary and posthumous testimony, but rather to match the two, if perchance some congruities may become perceptible. My examination will limit itself to one possible item in the Socratic teaching, what has been called his doctrine of the soul,[7] as this is available for inspection in two documents, the *Clouds* of Aristophanes and the *Apology of Socrates* written by Plato. The available testimony covering this doctrine is more extensive, but, as I hope to show, is concentrated in these two works to an unusual degree.

The objectives sought by Plato's *Apology of Socrates* are twofold: to refute the charges brought against Socrates' activity in Athens, and to explain in positive and eloquent terms the general character of that activity. At a point nearly midway through the speech, the speaker envisages the one condition that would win him acquittal: a promise on his part to stop doing whatever he is doing. This is impossible; on the contrary, the proposal that the mission be abandoned becomes the occasion for stating as succinctly but also as positively as possible what precisely that mission is.

> So long as I have the capability and breath in my body, never, never shall I cease philosophizing...in my familiar language: 'Good sir, citizen of Athens, citizen of no mean city, a city famous for intellect and energy alike, as you concentrate on the maximum acquisition of money, and reputation, and social prestige, don't you feel at all guilty, when you give no concentration, nor indeed any thought at all, to thinking, and to truth, and to the maximum improvement of your ghost?' Perhaps one among you may reply, 'No, Socrates, I do concentrate'. If so, I won't let him go till he has been questioned and examined and tested...My sole activity as I peregrinate is to persuade young and old among you to avoid concentrating on the body or money, until you have given priority and energy to concentration upon the maximum improvement of your ghost.[8]

7. See below, n. 11.
8. 29d 4 sqq. esp. 'χρημάτων μὲν οὐκ αἰσχύνη ἐπιμελούμενος ὅπως σοι ἔσται ὡς πλεῖστα, καὶ δόξης καὶ τιμῆς, φρονήσεως δὲ καὶ ἀληθείας καὶ τῆς ψυχῆς ὅπως ὡς βελτίστη ἔσται οὐκ ἐπιμελῇ οὐδὲ φροντίζεις;' καὶ ἐάν τις ἀμφισβητήσῃ καὶ

The words are not less memorable for being familiar. If the Socrates of Plato taught anything, this was it. My translation may in some respects seem unexpected. The statement, however, is not unique in the *Apology*. It has counterparts, and cross-comparison may shed some light on the exact significance of the terms used.

The speech proceeds. The verdict of guilty is rendered by the jury. The death penalty has been assessed by the prosecution. It falls to the role of the accused to propose an alternative. But legal convention at this point is disregarded, in favor of the proposition that the activity in question, the target of the prosecution, should be not punished but rewarded. Why rewarded? Surely because its character, as already defined, calls for reward, and to drive home the point the definition is repeated:

> The course I have taken is to approach people individually as a benefactor, offering what, in my view, is the maximum benefit possible: I undertake to dissuade each one of you individually from concentrating on the things belonging to himself until he has first concentrated on the maximum improvement of himself and his maximum capacity for thinking.[9]

The response was adverse. To the majority who thereupon voted the death penalty the speaker addressed some last words which include the following:

> If you think that killing people is a way to restrain any criticism of your way of life, there is something wrong with your way of thinking. Riddance on those terms would be improper, and in all likelihood impossible. The way which would be ideal and also most practical would be to stop putting down other people and instead engage in the preparation of oneself for maximum improvement.[10]

φῇ ἐπιμελεῖσθαι, οὐκ εὐθὺς ἀφήσω αὐτὸν οὐδ' ἄπειμι, ἀλλ' ἐρήσομαι αὐτὸν καὶ ἐξετάσω καὶ ἐλέγξω...πείθων ὑμῶν καὶ νεωτέρους καὶ πρεσβυτέρους μήτε σωμάτων ἐπιμελεῖσθαι μήτε χρημάτων πρότερον μηδὲ οὕτω σφόδρα ὡς τῆς ψυχῆς ὅπως ὡς ἀρίστη ἔσται...

9. 36c 3 sqq. esp....ἐπιχειρῶν ἕκαστον ὑμῶν πείθειν μὴ πρότερον μήτε τῶν ἑαυτοῦ μηδενὸς ἐπιμελεῖσθαι πρὶν ἑαυτοῦ ἐπιμεληθείη ὅπως ὡς βέλτιστος καὶ φρονιμώτατος ἔσοιτο...

10. 39d 3 sqq. esp....μὴ τοὺς ἄλλους κολούειν ἀλλ' ἑαυτὸν παρασκευάζειν ὅπως ἔσται ὡς βέλτιστος.

The call to care for your soul has been recognized by many scholars as distinctively Socratic.[11] But what precisely did the Greek mean? Surely not an anticipation of the Protestant ethic.[12] The formula is used twice in our first quotation, each time with the addition that the *psyche* must be 'improved'. A conservative translation, bearing in mind the usage of classical Greek before Plato, would retain for *psyche* some equivalent for the Homeric 'ghost' and would interpret the adjective *beltistos* as indicating superior performance. The care required would connote the superintendence of a skilled operation, demanding close attention.[13] In short, the emphasis of the phraseology is not moral but functional: the object is to bring the ghost to the completion of its proper excellence. The question remains: what is the ghost's proper excellence? The formulas supply a clue. In the first quotation both *epimeleisthai* and *psyche* are respectively supplied with equivalents: 'to concentrate upon' is coupled with 'to think about'; and the *psyche*, the ghost which becomes the object of thought, is coupled with *phronesis*, 'the process of thinking'. In the second quotation the improvement of oneself which is the object of concentration is equated with 'maximum capacity for thinking'.

These are translations of the verb *phrontizein*, the noun *phronesis*, and the adjective *phronimos*. In authors of the fourth century and later, noun and adjective came to be colored by the notion of prudence, sagacity, or wisdom in a practical sense. The usage of the fifth century linked them more closely with the process of active thought, as the -*sis* ending of the noun might indicate,[14] and this was also true of the verb.[15] In the present instance we have to ask ourselves whether the Platonic Socrates' call to con-

11. Taylor, *Varia Socratica*, pp. 170–5; Burnet, 'The Socratic Doctrine of the Soul', *Proc. Brit. Acad.* 7 (1916), reprinted in *Essays and Addresses*, p. 140; Cornford, *Before and After Socrates* (Cambridge 1932), pp. 35–7; see also Guthrie, III, pp. 467–73, and J. Stenzel, 'Sokrates (Philosoph)', *RE*, 2. Reihe, v. Halbb. (1927), 811–90.

12. It sounds very much like this in Maier.

13. See the citations in LSJ s.v. ἐπιμέλεια, ἐπιμελοῦμαι, ἐπιμελής. The sense 'anxious' (LSJ) is inappropriate to the adjective: at Hdt. 1. 89 (loc. cit.) ἐπιμελὲς ἐγίνετο means 'attracted his attention'.

14. See Havelock, *Preface to Plato* (Cambridge, Mass., 1963), pp. 212–13 and J. Holt, *Les Noms d'action en -σις (-τις)* (Aarhus 1940).

15. Once more (cf. n. 13) the sense of 'to be anxious about' (LSJ s.v. φροντίζω II 2) does not seem justified by the citations.

centrate on the soul was an invitation to achieve prudence and
practical wisdom. The more likely intention was a summons to
exercise the mind. To equate one's ghost with the activity of
thinking would make some sense; to equate it with prudence or
wisdom would not. It remains true that phraseology like *phrontizein
phroneseos* (above, n. 8), to concentrate thought on thinking, is
curiously circular; which brings us to consider a point not hitherto
noticed, so far as I am aware. In the second and third of our
quotations the noun *psyche* has been displaced by the reflexive
pronoun. The two are alike treated as objects of concentration,
and are alike subject to maximum improvement. In terms of our
present everyday language, we may be tempted to exclaim: 'Well,
of course! A man's soul is also himself', and to dismiss the Greek
equation between the two as of no significance. But the everyday
language of today may be the unusual language of yesterday, and
the earlier history of the reflexive pronoun may warn us that such
a dismissal can be premature.[16]

16. G. M. Bolling, 'Personal Pronouns in Reflexive Situations in the *Iliad*',
Language 23 (1947), 23–33, concludes (p. 29): 'Reflexive constructions are very
rare' presumably in part due to 'the competition offered by the middle voice'.
Of his two classifications of these, only the first concerns this article, *viz.* 'constructions containing an oblique case of a personal pronoun identical in
meaning with the subject of the verb (not necessarily finite) of the clause or
phrase in which the pronoun stands' (p. 23). Of these, in the first and second
persons the *Iliad* exhibits six (pp. 23–4) and in the third, thirty-four (pp. 25–6).
Of this total of forty only eleven add an oblique case of *autos* to the pronoun, and
eight of these occur in the eight instances where the third personal pronoun
stands as a direct object of the verb. The 'canonical' forms of our Greek gram-
mars, *emauton, seauton, heauton,* do not occur at all. From his overall survey
Bolling concludes (p. 29), 'there is no difference observable in the selection of
the pronoun between reflexive and other constructions', but notes (p. 30) of
those where *autos* is added that 'phrases with distinctive reflexive meaning
appear, but have not yet become obligatory'. His own citations might tempt the
inferences (i) that they are on the way to becoming obligatory when expressing
the direct object of the verb, (ii) that since the obligation shows up in the third
person, the *autos* was an iteration – 'him yes him' – subsequently added
analogically to the other persons. At any rate, Bolling initiates his article with a
warning against the assumption that 'meanings expressed differently in English
(him:himself) Latin (eum:se) and *later* [italics mine] Greek (αὐτόν:ἑαυτόν)
were distinctively conceived by the poet of the *Iliad*'. The 'canonical three' do
not appear in the extant odes of Pindar (though two occur in fragments), and
emerge rather cautiously in drama (Aeschylus: 22, of which 16 are from the
Prometheus; Sophocles: 55; Euripides: 147). In Aristophanes there are 215, of
which 108 occur in *Knights, Clouds, Wasps,* and *Peace,* produced between 424
and 421. They multiply in the historians (Herodotus: 563, Thucydides: 374;

What we observe here is that the suggestion of circularity, already perceptible in such a tautology as *phrontizein phroneseos*, is reinforced when the reflexive pronoun is substituted for the noun *psyche* as the object of the subject's intellectual effort. This proposes a self-contained procedure: oneself acting upon oneself. But how precisely did this work? By what actual method was one to concentrate upon and to think about oneself, and at the same time to concentrate thought on thinking? A working model, it is suggested, is furnished if we track down the usage of the reflexive pronoun in an earlier passage of the same speech. This is the famous account of the Socratic response to the Delphic oracle which has announced: No one is more intelligent than Socrates. The pattern of the response is complex, not necessarily ironic, but designed so as to furnish a definition of what the *sophia*, the skilled intelligence (again we reject the usual but misleading translation 'wisdom') of Socrates may be. It is in fact a skill, but (as will appear) distinct from all other professional types.

Socrates on receiving the report engages in reflection, which produces a question: What does the god mean? The question is provoked by a contradiction between the statement of the oracle and another, formed within himself: 'I personally am not aware, within myself, of being intelligent.'[17] Yet the god's statement cannot be dismissed. Somehow the two propositions must be reconciled. But can they be? The collision produces a dilemma. So the respondent resorts to an investigation of the god's statement, though this costs effort.[18] He tests it by a form of Socratic induction: he goes to the so-called intelligent people and ascertains the degree of their intelligence. He finds, by inquiry, that they, like himself, have a strong self-conviction, but this time the content is the opposite of his own. They are convinced of their own intelligence. He is convinced of his non-intelligence. The result is a fresh

a high proportion of which are 'grammatical reflexives'). These statistics, for what they are worth, need interpretation for which space is lacking. But the contrasting rate of incidence in *Apology* (41 in 25 Stephanus pages) is notable. See below, nn. 26–31, 35, 36, 38, 40.

17. 21b 2 sqq. ταῦτα γὰρ ἐγὼ ἀκούσας ἐνεθυμούμην οὑτωσί · 'τί ποτε λέγει ὁ θεός, καὶ τί ποτε αἰνίττεται; ἐγὼ γὰρ δὴ οὔτε μέγα οὔτε σμικρὸν σύνοιδα ἐμαυτῷ σοφὸς ὤν...'

18. 21b 7 sqq. καὶ πολὺν μὲν χρόνον ἠπόρουν τί ποτε λέγει · ἔπειτα μόγις πάνυ ἐπὶ ζήτησιν αὐτοῦ τοιαύτην τινὰ ἐτραπόμην.

step in his own self-calculation, producing the conclusion: 'I am more intelligent in my conviction of ignorance.'[19] The craftsmen provide the supreme test of the oracle, for he knows that they do command skills, whereas he has only the self-conviction of a non-skilled man. But even they discredited their claim to intelligence by inflating its pretensions. Socrates returns to self-dialogue, posing, himself to his own self, a question framed as a choice of alternative situations available to him. When the two are opposed, he is in a position to respond to himself and to make personal choice of one of them: 'It pays me better to be in the situation I am in.'[20]

To be noted in this account are some verbal habits easily overlooked as savoring of ordinary speech: the reflexive pronoun occurs as object of the verb seven times, six of them in the first person; twice the subject is reinforced by the addition of the first personal pronoun where this is not grammatically necessary.[21] The verbs which connect subject with reflexive object connote operations which are mental or psychic: awareness (twice), self-conviction (twice), calculation, asking, answering. The procedure therefore is not only essentially circular but also introspective: the source of correct conviction lies within one's self. To be sure, there is evidence to be sought outside one's own self, but it lies within the convictions of other selves, and is then brought back as it were into one's own consciousness, and matched there against statements made by one's self. This matching procedure is not automatic, nor even easy. It requires effort, in response to a previous condition of mental dilemma, which sets in motion the process of investigation. Thereafter the syllogism which produces the correct conclusion is generated by a process of self-dialectic, as 'I' converses with 'me'. All the mental processes which are described in this passage are self-contained and ultimately autonomous. Reports from the external world outside oneself, when given by an oracle or by other

19. 21c 5 sqq. ἔδοξέ μοι οὗτος ὁ ἀνὴρ δοκεῖν μὲν εἶναι σοφὸς... μάλιστα ἑαυτῷ ...πρὸς ἐμαυτὸν δ’ οὖν ἀπιὼν ἐλογιζόμην ὅτι τούτου μὲν τοῦ ἀνθρώπου ἐγὼ σοφώτερός εἰμι...οὗτος μὲν οἴεταί τι εἰδέναι οὐκ εἰδώς, ἐγὼ δέ, ὥσπερ οὖν οὐκ οἶδα, οὐδὲ οἴομαι κτλ.

20. 22d 1 sqq. ἐμαυτῷ γὰρ συνῄδη οὐδὲν ἐπισταμένῳ ὡς ἔπος εἰπεῖν, τούτους δέ γ’ ᾔδη ὅτι εὑρήσοιμι πολλὰ καὶ καλὰ ἐπισταμένους...ὥστε με ἐμαυτὸν ἀνερωτᾶν ὑπὲρ τοῦ χρησμοῦ πότερα δεξαίμην ἂν οὕτως ὥσπερ ἔχω ἔχειν...ἢ ἀμφότερα ἃ ἐκεῖνοι ἔχουσιν ἔχειν. ἀπεκρινάμην οὖν ἐμαυτῷ καὶ τῷ χρησμῷ ὅτι μοι λυσιτελοῖ ὥσπερ ἔχω ἔχειν.   21. See above, nn. 17–20.

persons, are only stimulants, on the face of it misleading, which generate first dilemma and then introspective self-dialogue in order to produce a final and correct statement.

The parable reveals that the clue to the meaning of *psyche*, as used in the *Apology*, is found in its equivalence to the reflexive pronoun. Greek had at this time no word for the 'self' considered as a concept: it had only the personal pronoun with the addition of the intensive (*eme-auton*), in all three persons.[22] But the introspective procedure thus recommended insensibly called for a term to describe the area or frame of reference within which this introspective autonomous process could be conceived as operating. To identify this area, the traditional 'ghost' of Homer was appropriated, a surprising and even slightly shocking choice, one would think, but carrying one great advantage: *psyche*, in its related meanings of ghost, spirit, courage, life-blood, was always very much the source of life in the animate being. To conceive of self-dialectic as an operation of primary importance to a person's welfare and then to imagine it as proceeding within the ghost was to assert implicitly that the essence of life was introspective thought, and that the more you introspected the more alive you became. Thus was prepared a new content for the term *psyche*, of which the nearest equivalent in our tongue would be 'consciousness', rather than the more commonly accepted 'soul'.[23]

A comparison is now in order with the testimony of the *Clouds*, first produced when Socrates was in his middle forties, and the author of the *Apology* was perhaps six years old. The statistics of the incidence in this play of 'think'-words are formidable, more especially of *phronein*, *phrontizein* and their derivatives and compounds.[24] My present scrutiny will limit itself to the usage of the reflexive pronoun.

22. Above, n. 16. To translate *eme-auton* as 'my-self' rather than 'me-self' is essentially to assume a conception not expressed in the Greek.

23. The Socratic self-dialogue, already anticipated in such expressions as φροντίσας πρὸς ἑωυτόν, Hdt. VIII. 100, is the lineal descendant of such Homeric expressions as κραδίην ἠνίπαπε and θυμὸς ἄνωγέ με, with the important difference that the 'subject' and 'object' in the expression have been identified with each other, by an act of integration, the conceptual result of which is most conveniently expressed by extending the significance of the term *psyche*.

24. A total of 42. Of these 6 are by context non-technical (*phrontizein* 2, *phronein* 2, *paraphronein* 2, used in exchanges between father and son). But possibly the playwright had the words on his mind throughout? *Phren* occurs

An elderly citizen has to satisfy his creditors.[25] His son has run up the bills, and the plot is set in motion by his father's request: 'Please convert the habits of yourself and lose no time about it.'[26] The means of this self-conversion lie ready to hand in an institution presided over by Socrates, which, however, the son refuses to enter. The father takes his place and is enrolled as a pupil. But he can do so only by submitting to the same self-oriented discipline that he had demanded of his son. Requesting admission, he is confronted by the initial Socratic question: 'How comes it that you, unaware of yourself, fell into debt?'[27] This might have led on to a first lesson in self-awareness, but nearly 200 lines of anapaests

3 times (in the sense of intelligence), *phrontis* 7 'and *phrontisma* 1 (Socrates, disciples, chorus, and Strepsiades in mimicry), *phrontizein* 5 (Socrates, chorus, and Strepsiades in mimicry), *ekphrontizein* 2 (Socrates, and Strepsiades echoing), *metaphrontizein* 1 and *kataphrontizein* 1 (coinages put into the mouth of Strepsiades), *periphronein* 3 (Socrates and Strepsiades in mimicry), *hyperphronein* 1 (if Dover's reading of l. 226 is accepted: Strepsiades in mimicry), *phrontistes* 5, *phrontisterion* 7 (a coinage). A few comments are in order: first, this does not exhaust the list of 'think-words'; second, the number of comic coinages (3) and of instances of mimicry and echo (5) suggests that this group of terms was recognizable by the audience as current jargon, and as a fair target for verbal humour: a whole school of terminology is being parodied; third, the concentration of *phrontizein*, *ekphrontizein*, *periphronein* and *phrontis* in the utterances of Socrates and his chorus (cf. nn. 30–2 and 35 below) suggests that the terminology was recognizable as Socratic. If so, it was replaced in Platonism, with such exceptions as those illustrated in our previous quotations from the *Apology*. (Xenophon may here supply independent testimony, despite Dover's note on 94.) *Phronesis*, however, does not occur. Dover's note on φροντιστήριον l. 94, 'φροντίς and φροντίζειν were already common words. φροντιστής and φροντιστήριον first appear in this play', scarcely covers the case.

25. The same problem (minus the comic element) sets in motion the argument of Plato's *Republic* i 331b sqq.

26. Line 88, ἔκστρεψον ὡς τάχιστα τοὺς σαυτοῦ τρόπους. Dover, *ad loc.*, prefers to read ἔκτρεψον with some MSS, objecting that ἔκστρεψον (as also at 554) means 'to turn inside out'. But this is exactly the meaning required. Cf. 1455 (n. 40), a reference given by Dover in his Addenda p. 269. There the father is admonished that he has 'converted' in the wrong direction. I suspect that a Socratic doctrine of conversion is implicit in much of the 'soul-searching' which is to be the subject of parody, and that 'Strepsiades' represents a play upon this idea which is comically contaminated with the more familiar aspect of 'shiftiness'. Cf. Plato, *Republic* vii 518c 5 τὸ ὄργανον ᾧ καταμανθάνει ἕκαστος...οἶον εἰ ὄμμα...στρέφειν...οὕτω...περιακτέον εἶναι...d 3 τέχνη...τῆς περιαγωγῆς, τίνα τρόπον ὡς ῥᾷστά τε καὶ ἀνυσιμώτατα μεταστραφήσεται...: this ὄργανον is then identified (518e 2) with ἡ τοῦ φρονῆσαι (ἀρετή), which ὑπὸ...τῆς περιαγωγῆς χρήσιμον...γίγνεται.

27. 242, πόθεν δ' ὑπόχρεως σαυτὸν ἔλαθες γενόμενος;

intervene, which with mock solemnity introduce the Chorus and are made the vehicle of a dialectical exchange all the more ridiculous when conducted in a meter so inappropriate to the style of the elenchus. A lesson in atheism which disposes of Zeus raises the problem of the thunder and lightning, but, the sage argues, these are caused by collisions between clouds. The disciple is puzzled and asks himself: 'What is the evidence for this?', and receives the Socratic reply: 'I will give you instruction from yourself', and a suitably vulgar illustration follows. The self, in this case the digestive system, is the source which can supply true statements.[28] The pupil is now ready for the screening test preliminary to admission. The Chorus exhort him: 'Hand over yourself to our ministers and don't be afraid.' The test, applied by Socrates, is framed as a request for self-examination: 'Come, declare to me the habit of yourself. I have to know its quality before applying new devices to you.' Strepsiades passes the test, and is admitted, the Chorus exclaiming as he enters, 'Despite his age he is adding a tincture to the nature of himself by novel precedures: an exercise for him in intelligence'.[29]

The parabasis now intervening gives him time to take the introductory course (unspecified) from which he emerges into the view of the spectators at line 634. He has proved to be a very unpromising pupil with a poor memory, but his bare pass now entitles him, apparently, to attempt a fresh step in the curriculum, a lesson in metrics and a lesson in grammar, both of which he appears to flunk. These, however, turn out to be preliminary to the main exercise.

At line 694 he is 'couched' with the admonition: 'Think through one of the procedures of yourself.' The reply is 'For god's sake, not on this mattress [which is infested]! Let me do my thinking through on the ground.' Permission being refused, the blanket is pulled over him, while the Chorus intone with mock ceremony above him: 'Think, yes, think, and scrutinize. By all means condense your (own) self and make it spin. When you fall

28. 385, φέρε, τουτὶ τῷ χρὴ πιστεύειν; ἀπὸ σαυτοῦ 'γώ σε διδάξω. 392, σκέψαι τοίνυν ἀπὸ γαστριδίου κτλ.

29. 436, ἀλλὰ σεαυτὸν παράδος θαρρῶν τοῖς ἡμετέροις προπόλοισιν. 478–80, ἄγε δή, κάτειπέ μοι σὺ τὸν σαυτοῦ τρόπον, / ἵν' αὐτὸν εἰδὼς ὅστις ἐστὶ μηχανὰς / ἤδη 'πὶ τούτοις πρὸς σὲ καινὰς προσφέρω. 513–17, νεωτέροις τὴν φύσιν αὐ- / τοῦ πράγμασιν χρωτίζεται / καὶ σοφίαν ἐπασκεῖ.

into a dilemma, promptly take a jump into another thought.' The pupil, true to his role, continues his purely physical responses to the Socratic treatment: the ghost which should be undergoing Socratic improvement is reacting instead to the thirsty attentions of the bed-bugs. But the master persists: 'Keep thinking!' 'I am!' says Strepsiades. 'All right, what have you thought?' The reply, following the Socratic rule, takes the form of a further question. But the question is not of the Socratic type: 'Shall I ever survive these bed-bugs?'[30]

Socrates, however, has not yet given up: the introspective discipline proposed is difficult. 'But we must not weaken. Cover up again. Discovery must be made of the abstractive mind.' A pause intervenes. Has the disciple gone to sleep? Far from it. 'Cover up!' repeats the master, 'and start thinking', which prompts the disciple to put what, from the point of view of the non-Socratic, is the essential question: 'What do I think about?' He is at once given the Socratic answer: 'Begin with yourself; discover what you want and then express it.'[31]

The master then tries to help him apply the method: 'Cover up, make a small slit in your thought, and think through the procedures piece by piece, dividing and inspecting with correctness.'[32] 'Keep

---

30. 695, ἐκφρόντισόν τι τῶν σεαυτοῦ πραγμάτων (cf. below, n. 32). 697, χαμαί μ' ἔασον αὐτὰ ταῦτ' ἐκφροντίσαι. 700–5, φρόντιζε δὴ καὶ διάθρει / πάντα τρόπον τε σαυτὸν / στρόβει πυκνώσας. ταχὺς δ', ὅταν εἰς ἄπορον / πέσῃς, ἐπ' ἄλλο πήδα / νόημα φρενός. 723–4, οὗτος τί ποιεῖς; οὐχὶ φροντίζεις; ἐγώ, / νὴ τὸν Ποσειδῶ. καὶ τί δῆτ' ἐφρόντισας; A.-J. Festugière, *Contemplation et vie contemplative selon Platon* (Paris 1936), p. 70, describes the scene on the couch as 'une parodie de l'incubation religieuse'. I do not think religion has much to do with it.

31. 727–8, οὐ μαλθακιστέ' ἀλλὰ περικαλυπτέα. / ἐξευρετέος γὰρ νοῦς ἀποστερητικός. 735–7, οὐκ ἐγκαλυψάμενος ταχέως τι φροντιεῖς; / περὶ τοῦ; σὺ γάρ μοι τοῦτο φράσον, ὦ Σώκρατες. / αὐτὸς ὅτι βούλει πρῶτος ἐξευρὼν λέγε.

32. 740–2, ...σχάσας τὴν φροντίδα / λεπτὴν κατὰ μικρὸν περιφρόνει τὰ πράγματα / ὀρθῶς διαιρῶν καὶ σκοπῶν.
λεπτήν points to the medical meaning of σχάζω (cf. 409) 'slit a vein' etc. The self (or *psyche*) is swollen with *phrontis* (thus again equated with air, as at 762, and above, 230), but too generous a release would presumably leave the subject deflated. LSJ translates 'let go' (was this interpretation prompted by ἀποχάλα l. 762? see below, n. 35) but no parallels are cited earlier than Lycophron. The prefix in περιφρόνει was, I suggest, here intended to be intensive (as read in Plato, *Axiochus* 365b). Hence περιφρονῶ τὸν ἥλιον (225, mimicked 1503) means 'excogitate', not 'think about'. This sense accords with the self-circular procedure of intellection so far indicated as Socratic: the sun becomes

still!' he repeats; obviously the bugs are giving trouble. 'If one of your notions produces dilemma in you, let it go and stand off, and then use your thought to prod it into action again and lock it up.'[33]

A vocabulary of mental process in which dilemma plays its role here suffers purely comic contamination, and in the same vein the 'discoveries' announced by the pupil in response to this discipline (ll. 746–83) are pure burlesque. At first they seem to be on their way to winning Socratic approval – master and pupil alike are targets of the parody – and it is probably significant that while indulging these absurdities, Socrates not only prompts his pupil in a very non-Socratic manner[34] but also offers advice which reverses the previous methodological emphasis: 'Don't keep squeezing your thought round yourself. Treat the idea like a cockchafer; tie a thread to its foot and let it buzz a bit.'[35] The disciple's response is prompt: 'Hurrah, I've made a discovery...a most intelligent one. You yourself will have to join me in agree-

an object in (as well as of) one's own thought; φροντίζω and ἐκφροντίζω are variants with the same expressive intention. Then ὀρθῶς διαιρῶν καὶ σκοπῶν is not 'advice of a different kind' (Dover *ad loc.*) but represents in detail the operation generally described in περιφρόνει τὰ πράγματα; an external object is converted into an object of thought (hence styled *pragma*, a process) by reducing it to a logical classification. Dover's refusal (as against Schmid) to accept the phraseology as a Socratic echo seems perverse, even admitting that *diaeresis* was practiced also by the sophists.

33. 743–5 κἄν ἀπορῇς τι τῶν νοημάτων, / ἀφεὶς ἄπελθε, κᾆτα τῇ γνώμῃ πάλιν / κίνησον αὖθις αὐτὸ καὶ ζυγώθρισον (on the reading τῇ γνώμῃ see Dover *ad loc.*). The nouns *phrontis* (above, n. 24), *noema* and *noesis* (both recurrent in this play) can variously symbolize both the 'intellect' which does the 'thinking' and the 'idea' which is 'thought', depending on context. The language of conceptualization is still in its infancy. Here an appropriate 'idea' (*noema*) which temporarily eludes the 'intellect' (*gnome*) is described as a small animal which is being chased or tempted into the trap of the intelligence (or the self): if temporarily ignored it will relax; then a poke may get it into the trap. To interpret ζυγώθρισον as 'weigh up' (so Dover, against the preponderant testimony) is to take the epistemology of the passage too seriously: see also n. 35.

34. (Soc. loq.) 748, ἐπίδειξον αὐτήν. 757, εὖγ'· ἀλλ' ἕτερον αὖ σοι προβαλῶ τι δεξιόν. 773, σοφῶς γε νὴ τὰς Χάριτας. 775, ἄγε δὴ ταχέως τουτὶ ξυνάρπασον. This last recalls 489–90, ὅταν τι προβάλωμαι σοφόν / ...εὐθέως ὑφαρπάσει, an instance which Dover (xliii) perceives to be non-Socratic, and so uses to discredit the play generally as a Socratic document.

35. 761–3 μή νυν περὶ σαυτὸν εἶλλε τὴν γνώμην ἀεί, / ἀλλ' ἀποχάλα τὴν φροντίδ' εἰς τὸν ἀέρα / λινόδετον ὥσπερ μηλολόνθην τοῦ ποδός. The advice is a variant of 743–45: the elusive mouse has now become a sluggish beetle; *gnome* is still the 'intellect' but *phrontis* now replaces *noema* as symbol of an 'idea'.

ment.'³⁶ The discovery, addressed to the evasion of Strepsiades'
debts, that problem which had originated his Socratic education,
now hurries that same education to its swift and foredoomed conclusion. Two bright answers have won his teacher's approval. This
encourages him to seek a third compliment. The effect is 'fatal' in
more senses than one. Strepsiades flunks out.³⁷

Nevertheless he has learned a Socratic lesson. Making a fresh
approach to his son to enroll in the Socratic school, he tells him
what he will get: 'The intelligence proper to man; you will
recognize yourself, your lack of instruction, and your thickheaded-
ness.'³⁸ This brutal directness succeeds, rather surprisingly, where
previous paternal persuasion had failed. But Strepsiades now has an
advantage. He has recognized the basis of the master's method.

From this point on the Socratic flavor of Aristophanes' burlesque becomes less apparent. The role assigned to the son, the
doctrines addressed to him, those put into his own mouth, are
(with some exceptions) more recognizably sophistic.³⁹ But as the
old man, towards the end of the play, repents and reproaches the
Chorus for leading him on, they administer to him a last Socratic
lesson: 'Yourself to yourself – yes, you – are the cause of what has
happened, by converting yourself towards procedures which are
evil.'⁴⁰

36. 764–5, ηὕρηκ' ἀφάνισιν τῆς δίκης σοφωτάτην, / ὥστ' αὐτὸν ὁμολογεῖν
σέ μοι. The 'discovery' is technical, not intuitive: hence σοφωτάτην: cf. the
similar exclamation reported of Archimedes; the 'object' discovered is an
abstract procedure identified by another -σις noun (above, n. 14; this one
first in Herodotus); the result is a concurrence of two selves in joint agreement
(which in the Platonic writings is dialectical).

37. 778–9 and 783.

38. 841–2, ὁσαπέρ ἐστιν ἀνθρώποις σοφά. / γνώσει δὲ σαυτὸν ὡς ἀμαθὴς εἶ
καὶ παχύς. Cf. Apology 20d 8. Was the anonymous gnome, visible somewhere at
Delphi (not an 'official' inscription: see Plato, Charmides 164d 3 sqq.), known and
popularized by this date?

39. I assume that the contest of the two logoi is a parody of a sophistic
epideixis (cf. the exhortation at 889, combining sophistic and Socratic terminology, and above, n. 34) held not only for the benefit of the spectators (890) but
for the instruction of Pheidippides as mathetes (886; cf. a parallel situation in
Plato's Protagoras 316b 1sqq. and 317c 3sqq.). This form of instruction replaces
the Socratic method which is requested at 877 and refused at 887. The thesis that
the arguments and idioms of the play from 888 onwards exploit sophistic rather
than Socratic material needs more extended defense than is possible here.

40. 1454–5, αὐτὸς μὲν οὖν σαυτῷ σὺ τούτων αἴτιος / στρέψας σεαυτὸν εἰς
πονηρὰ πράγματα. On στρέψας see above, n. 26.

It is now possible to see how sophisticated is the play we have been reading. So much of the humor relies on the device of parodying a verbal syntax which, if contemporary and post-humous record are compared, can be identified as in all probability Socratic.[41] The same roles are assigned to the reflexive pronoun, the same verbs of intellection recur connecting the subject with itself as object. The same suggestion of an autonomous and isolated exercise within the self, which produces correct thoughts, which are also correct statements, but at the cost of difficulty and dilemma,[42] seems common to both documents. In the comedy this self-isolation is given physical parody, as the pupil is 'couched' and covered up.

Finally, does the play show any indication that the Socratics, in order to identify the self which is the seat of this procedure, had chosen the symbol of the Homeric ghost? We return to the famous line in which the Socratic institution, a small structure at the back of the orchestra, is first identified for the benefit of the audience. 'Here you see the think-tank, inhabited by intelligent ghosts.'[43] This translation of *psyche*, which I have retained throughout this paper, is fully justified by the present context: the traditional ghosts of Homer are here identified in the persons of the Socratics, who, in the succeeding scene, are indeed perceived to be ghost-like, i.e. pale and underfed. This is Aristophanic humor at its more obvious. But the father is also using the word in its Socratic sense: he is in the course of persuading his son to join the Socratic circle, and cannot step out of character.[44] So we learn that this circle had begun to use the traditional word 'ghost' in a new sense, as equivalent to the thinking and intelligent self, here attested by its collocation with the adjective *sophos* and with the noun

41. Dover takes the contrary view (xliv); that though 'Socrates' tutorial method as portrayed in *Nu.* could pass as a base caricature of the dialectical skill with which, in Plato, he secures the cooperation of others in a quest for metaphysical proofs', there is nothing uniquely Socratic in these passages of the play. The method is 'characteristic of any active intellect', a judgement which presupposes that the ordinary language of today is also that of yesterday.

42. A scholiast on 703 'acutely observes that the advice...to drop a line of enquiry which has led to an impasse...is Socratic' – Dover, p. xliv.

43. 94, ψυχῶν σοφῶν τοῦτ' ἐστὶ φροντιστήριον.

44. I borrow this observation from D. Claus, *Psyche* (Doct. Diss. Yale 1970), p. 257.

'think-tank'. Both combinations would sound absurd to the less sophisticated members of the audience. 'Ghost' in classical Greek, up to Socrates' day, had many properties to be sure, but the capacity to use intelligence and to think was not among them.[45] The cognoscenti on the other hand would get the point and at this level of allusion would savor the subtlety of the Aristophanic jest.[46]

The Socratic problem, though it will always yield uncertainties, is not entirely beyond solution. Skepticism need not be excessive if we are prepared to inspect with some meticulousness the vocabulary used by characters labelled 'Socrates', 'Strepsiades', and 'Chorus' in a document of the last third of the fifth century B.C. and match it against that employed by a character labelled 'Socrates', and by his interlocutors, in documents composed in the fourth century.[47] The present investigation has focused on the usage surrounding the reflexive pronoun. This does not exhaust the possible correspondences.[48] If the procedure yields results, this says a good deal for the sophistication of Aristophanes, and indeed it is difficult to see why a dramatist whose informed skill and taste in composing 'paratragic' passages, to use a term currently fashionable, is readily admitted by scholars should be excluded from the

45. See Guthrie, p. 468. For the exceptions see Havelock, *Preface to Plato*, pp. 197–8 and 211, n. 3. David Claus, *Psyche*, exhaustively reviews the history of the usage of the term from Homer to Euripides.

46. There are seven occurrences of *psyche* in *Clouds* (94, 319, 415, 420, 712, 719, 1049) as against four in *Wasps*, four in *Peace*, three in *Acharnians*, two in *Knights*, and three in *Birds* (if ψυχαγωγεῖ 1555 be included). Usage in the *Clouds* seems to hover between the Homeric and the Socratic, exploiting the humorous possibilities at both levels. A Socratic level of meaning is discounted by Handley, 'Words for "soul" "heart" and "mind" in Aristophanes' (above, n. 6), pp. 205–25, and also by Dover (note *ad loc.*) but at the cost of isolating ψυχή from its comic involvement with σοφῶν and φροντιστήριον. It is this which moves it over from the Homeric to the Socratic sense.

47. The economy of this paper has required restriction to a 'match' between *Apology* and *Clouds*. But the supporting documentation could be extended into Plato's earlier dialogues and other pertinent notices in Old Comedy. For other notices in Aristophanes see R. Philippson, 'Sokratische Dialektik in Aristophanes' Wolken' (above, n. 6), pp. 30–8, and R. Stark, 'Sokratisches in den Vögeln des Aristophanes' (above, n. 6), pp. 77–89.

48. Tautologous pronominal expressions for 'per se', so common in Plato, may be parodied at 194, 697. (Festugière, *Hippocrate, l'ancienne médecine* (Paris 1948), pp. 49–50 excludes the technical sense of αὐτὸ καθ' αὐτό from pre-Platonic authors, without considering *Clouds*). Expressions in the *Republic* covering educational theory show surprising correspondences with the *Clouds*, as already noted in the case of 'conversion' (n. 26).

composition, with equal skill, of 'paraphilosophical' passages. Athens was a fairly small place, and Aristophanes a cultivated artist. His mere presence at Plato's *Symposium* does not guarantee membership in the Socratic circle, but it does place him in the intellectual company of the wits of the time.

It is these same wits to whom, as he claims in the second parabasis, the original version of his play was addressed. To flatter the intelligence of the audience in advance of the vote, as he did in what was presumably the 'first' parabasis,[49] was normal. But in the 'second' he complains with reiteration that a witty and sophisticated play had failed to win the reception it had every right to expect from like-minded sophisticates.[50] At one point it is even implied that these composed a special group whom the author was determined not to 'let down'.[51] The contrast drawn between other comedies and this one is between slap-stick comic business and rowdiness on the one hand, and intrinsic verbal effects on the other. His art is one which 'introduces a series of novel (verbal) figures all unique, all witty, all sophisticated'.[52] The political courage which he also proceeds to claim for himself[53] is a merit of different order, and one which in a comic poet would have more political appeal. Doubtless this is his reason for recalling the fact that he could compose a *Knights* as well as a *Clouds*. But the ingenuities which are his hallmark are designed to appeal to a civilized sense of humor rather than provoke a guffaw, and his audience is expected to live up to the standard of 'thinking' required.[54]

---

49. 575.   50. 520–2; 526–33; 546–8.

51. 527: whether ὑμῶν (Dover) or ὑμᾶς is read makes little difference in the context. Ar. argues that he had a right to expect a favorable reception for the *Clouds* after the success of the *Banqueters*. This play also had contained comic treatment of education: see Dover *ad loc.*, and Havelock, 'Why was Socrates Tried?', *Phoenix* Suppl. 1 (1952), 95–108.

52. 544, αὐτῇ καὶ τοῖς ἔπεσιν πιστεύουσ' ἐλήλυθεν. 547–8, ἀλλ' αἰεὶ καινὰς ἰδέας εἰσφέρων σοφίζομαι / οὐδὲν ἀλλήλαισιν ὁμοίας καὶ πάσας δεξιάς. 'Forms of comedy' (the meaning assigned here by LSJ to ἰδέας) would not proliferate on the scale implied.   53. 549.

54. 560–2, ὅστις οὖν τούτοισι γελᾷ, τοῖς ἐμοῖς μὴ χαιρέτω· / ἢν δ' ἐμοὶ καὶ τοῖσιν ἐμοῖς εὐφραίνησθ' εὑρήμασιν, / εἰς τὰς ὥρας τὰς ἑτέρας εὖ φρονεῖν δοκήσετε. On φρονεῖν see above, n. 24. The tone of 561–2 would accord well with Dover's interesting suggestion (p. xcviii) that the 'second edition' was designed for a growing public of readers.

In short, the language in which he defends his own product is itself colored by intellectualism, and seems deliberately aimed at a corresponding element in his public. That this element existed and that Aristophanes was its poet is indicated by Cratinus' line which describes the 'cultivated spectator' as 'a rather subtle verbalist, a pretty-idea-chaser, a Euripidean–Aristophanic buff'.[55] It is a description which closely fits the 'paraphilosophic' humor of the *Clouds*.

We must conclude, however, that the applause of the wits in 423 B.C. was not loud enough to drown the groans or compensate for the silence of those who found that a comedy of manneristic idiom with very little politics and a minimum of slap-stick was too much for them – or not enough. The vulgar, at least at this date, had found Socraticism less interesting than did Aristophanes.[56]

55. Cratinus fr. 307, ὑπολεπτολόγος γνωμιδιώκτης εὐριπιδαριστοφανίϡων. Cf. *Clouds* 320, (ψυχή) λεπτολογεῖν...ϡητεῖ and 321, γνωμιδίῳ γνώμην νύξασ' ἑτέρῳ λόγῳ ἀντιλογῆσαι. Hence the quarry of a γνωμιδιώκτης would not be 'sententious maxims' (LSJ Addenda, where this spelling of the emendation is adopted) but 'fine points to score with'.

56. A Yale seminar on 'The Socratic Problem' (1969) greatly assisted the completion of this paper. I gratefully acknowledge the contributions and criticisms of C. Gill, J. Goranflo, G. Parassoglou, and J. Svenbro.

The relativism of Protagoras

A. THOMAS COLE

THE HISTORY of Greek thought might be less problematical were it possible to assume that the figure we know as Protagoras was in reality two persons of that name, who lived separate existences in the fifth century B.C., but managed somehow to become hopelessly confused in the mind of later antiquity. One of them was the pattern and prototype of that disreputable breed the sophist, the other a serious political thinker of considerable insight and originality. It is the former, not the latter, who, on this assumption, should be credited with the relativist doctrine that man is the measure of all things and that things are always just what each person imagines them to be, as well as with the destructive corollaries of this doctrine: that no act is wrong if the doer does not think it so and that false statement and false opinion are impossible. He is also the man who taught his students how to make the worse cause appear the better, and how to argue both for and against the same proposition, alleging in justification of the latter practice that the contrary of every statement is just as true as the statement itself. His professed agnosticism led to the burning of his books at Athens and to his own expulsion from the city. And the story of how he perished at sea shortly thereafter must have carried for many of its hearers a salutary moral: such is the fate which heaven always holds in store for those who doubt the power of the gods. Since this is the person to whom, with one conspicuous exception, all ancient writers seem to refer when defining or describing Protagoreanism as a philosophical position, I shall call him for convenience the doxographers' Protagoras.

The other man would be, in a sense, the biographers' Protagoras, for to him alone applies most of what we know about the life of a fifth-century personage of that name. I prefer, however, to speak of him as the Platonic Protagoras, inasmuch as what we know of his doctrines derives almost entirely from two dialogues in the Platonic corpus. This Protagoras was the respected confidant and advisor of the great Pericles, the lawgiver for the pan-Hellenic colony of Thurii, and a teacher much sought after and highly valued by numbers of people all over the Greek world. According to Plato's testimony he exhibited the highest regard for righteousness, reverence, moderation, courage and all the other moral qualities the Greeks esteemed most, and never taught his students anything but what he believed would make them better citizens. He is also the man whose forty years of phenomenal and uninterrupted success as a teacher are noted and commented upon by Socrates in the *Meno* (91e).

Simple and convenient as it is, this analysis of the tradition regarding Protagoras breaks down at several points. The differences of character and doctrine to which it calls attention are sharp, but they are offset by certain similarities that cannot be overlooked. In particular, the Platonic Protagoras expresses the same complete skepticism with regard to the gods as does his doxographical counterpart, proclaims in similar fashion that man is the measure of all things, and understands the latter doctrine in precisely the same way – as equivalent to the assertion that things are to each observer exactly as they seem to be. Such parallels are sufficient to show that our two Protagorases must have been one and the same person. Yet the problem of how this person managed to contain within himself such contradictory elements remains. It is, in fact, central to Protagorean scholarship.

It has been customary hitherto to seek a solution along one of three lines. For some scholars, Protagoras is simply a hypocrite; a second group of interpreters makes him the victim of a kind of philosophical schizophrenia; a third assumes that his doctrine was distorted and misunderstood by the vast majority of later commentators. According to the first theory, Protagoras was shrewd enough to realize that a frank avowal of his subjectivism would be unpopular, that he must always accommodate the character of his discourses to the prejudices and moral sensibilities of his audience.[1]

1. This view (deriving ultimately from the general definition of sophistic given in *Republic* 493a–d) was the standard one until challenged by Grote. Among more recent exponents are A. E. Taylor (*Plato* (London 1926), 247, n. 1) and G. Vlastos (see his introduction to the Jowett–Ostwald translation of the *Protagoras* (New York 1956), xx–xxiv). The former suggests that Protagoras himself would have regarded his own ability to improve his pupils as merely 'a special aptitude for appreciating the tone of the current tradition of a place

The Platonic Protagoras is, therefore, simply part of the public image which the doxographers' Protagoras sought to create for himself. The second theory regards the doxographers' Protagoras as an epistemologist unconcerned with drawing any practical conclusions from his theoretical investigations into the character of knowledge, thought, and discourse, and the Platonic Protagoras as a moralist and politician equally unconcerned with finding a theoretical justification for the practical programs he adopted or advised. The two halves of the tradition concerning him are therefore a reflection of two unconnected aspects of his thinking.[2] The third theory requires us to believe that the doxographers misunderstood the man-measure principle – that the measure to which Protagoras referred was not man the individual but some norm of human nature by which individual peculiarities and aberrations as well as the entire content of man's experience might be measured and judged. It follows that the real Protagoras was the Platonic Protagoras – the Western world's first humanist rather than its first relativist; and if he taught his students to argue on both sides of the same question and make the inferior argument victorious he was merely seeking to give them training in rhetoric and dialectic.[3]

One of these theories may be right. But none of them, I think, is so solidly supported that there is not room for another – which I propose to offer in this essay.[4] The substance of my argument is

and impressing it on his hearers'. The latter views the sophist as a skillful propagandist with the greatest contempt for the 'thoughtless, suggestible, manipulable' majority, yet ready to offer himself as an apologist for democratic practice lest he offend that same majority and those men among its leaders who were his patrons.

2. So, most strikingly, H. Gomperz, *Sophistik und Rhetorik* (Leipzig 1912), pp. 196–200 and 272–3: 'Die beiden Erscheinungen sind eben zwei Aüsserungen eines Geistes...in dem eine fast priesterliche Einseitigkeit und eine fast schauspielerische Vielseitigkeit um den Sieg rangen, wie vielleicht nie wieder in einem Menschen.' For similar views, see the survey in A. Capizzi, 'Protagora', *Pubblicazioni dell'istituto di filosofia dell'università di Roma*, 4 (Florence 1955), 256–7.

3. For the various forms which this 'generic' interpretation has taken in modern times, see Capizzi (above, n. 2), pp. 112–13.

4. The general view of Protagoras to be developed here has not, so far as I know, been proposed before, though it is indebted to earlier discussions for several details (see below, nn. 8, 9, and 11). Two indebtednesses of a more pervasive character should be mentioned here. The first is the essay of G.

quite simple – that the difference between the two Protagorases which theories one, two and three try to account for is largely imaginary; that there is nothing, either in the man-measure principle as understood by Plato and the doxographers or in the disreputable techniques of argumentation associated with his name, that Protagoras himself would have felt to be inconsistent with his role as a benefactor of society working in the best interests of all those whom he served as educator or advisor. I shall also attempt to show that my interpretation connects a number of otherwise isolated motifs in the tradition relating to Protagoras, and that Protagoreanism as I understand it is a phenomenon which, though not confined to fifth-century Athens, is perfectly understandable in that setting. I do not claim that this interpretation ought to be accepted simply because it makes Protagorean thought a coherent unity or because it removes the necessity of assuming that certain later writers fundamentally misunderstood Protagoras or mistook the public Protagoras for the real one. But where the evidence for reconstructing a man's thought is as limited as it is here, any interpretation which gives a consistent and straightforward reading of all the most important ancient testimony is worth serious consideration.

I

Modern scholars were not the first to be puzzled by the apparent contradictions between different aspects of Protagorean theory, or between Protagorean theory and Protagorean practice. The subject is raised by Plato in the *Theaetetus*, one of the two dialogues in which Protagoras and his views figure most prominently. The matter at issue there is the compatibility of the man-measure doctrine with Protagoras' claim to professional competence. How, Socrates asks (161c–e), is it possible for someone to believe that things are to each observer what they seem to be, and still main-

Vlastos cited above (n. 1), for its almost convincing restatement of the first of the three theories discussed in the text. The second is E. A. Havelock's *A Preface to Plato* (Cambridge, Mass., 1963), for the general conception of the development of Greek thought in the fifth century of which I make use in attempting to view Protagorean relativism in its historical context (see especially chapters 11–12, pp. 197–233).

tain that he, or anyone else for that matter, is capable of being a teacher? If he teaches, he imparts knowledge that his students do not already have. He therefore has a better idea or understanding of his subject than they, and so what appears to be correct to him will be more nearly correct than what appears so to his students.

An answer to this objection is put forward in the dialogue (166d–167c) – not by Protagoras himself, who was dead at the time the conversation it records is supposed to have taken place, but by Socrates, who offers to defend Protagoras as Protagoras himself might have done were he able to participate in the discussion. Plato makes it quite clear that the resulting speech, usually known as the Apology or Defense of Protagoras, does not reproduce anything he had read in a book of Protagoras or knew by hearsay to have been what Protagoras actually said.[5] If Protagoras ever offered an answer to the sort of objection Socrates raises, Plato has not preserved a record of it. There is nothing therefore to prevent us from assuming that the Apology is a purely Platonic invention. On the other hand, Plato may have read enough of Protagoras or talked enough with people who had heard his lectures to have a fairly good idea of how Protagoras would have conducted such a defense had occasion arisen, and so to produce an argument which Protagoras would not have disowned had he seen it. We must, therefore, reckon with the possibility that the speech contains what would have been the sophist's own answer to the question that has most vexed and divided his modern interpreters, and study its contents with corresponding care.

Protagoras begins by reaffirming his contention that things are always just what they seem to be. He insists, however, that this is not inconsistent with the belief that there are teachers or experts from whose instruction man can draw profit. For among the various things which seem and are true to a given person there are some which seem and are bad and some which seem and are good. The services of the teacher or expert are required when 'things appear and are bad for a person'. It is the task of the expert to intervene in such situations and 'cause things to appear and be good' (166d–e). This rather cryptic doctrine is restated in the

5. Cf., especially, 169d–e, where the Apology is said to be, not Protagoras' own argument (*logos*), but simply one which Socrates has advanced on the former's behalf.

form of a medical analogy (166e–167b): to the sick man the food
he eats tastes bitter and is bitter. The doctor must not try to persuade him that the food he eats is not bitter – a fruitless undertaking in any case – but rather to cure him, to change his physical
condition (*hexis*) in such a fashion that food will seem (and be)
pleasant instead of unpleasant. And the task of the expert or
sophist is the same: to change a man's condition or attitude in such
a way that things seem good to him instead of bad (167a). Only
whereas the physician uses drugs, the sophist uses discourse (*logoi*).
In either case the new condition is better than the old, but it does
not involve a more accurate perception of the way things are.

The argument is perfectly clear and perfectly compatible with
the individualist interpretation which all of antiquity gave to the
man-measure principle. Things are to each person as they appear,
and the evaluations which different persons put upon the same
things often differ so much that these persons must be regarded as
existing each at the center of his own independent world. On the
other hand, some people are like a healthy man in that they find
their world to be pervaded by their own sense of well-being, and
so perfectly satisfactory. Others, like the sick man, find life nothing
but a succession of aches and pains; and they derive small consola-
tion from knowing that they are correct in assuming their world
to be an unattractive place. The sophist helps such people to
exchange an unsatisfactory world for a more satisfactory one –
either by changing their attitude so that all the things which once
seemed bad now seem good (a process analogous to the cure by
drugs mentioned in 167a); or, if this is impossible, by having them
widen or narrow the range of their attentions and activities in such
a way as to exclude as much as possible of apparent bad and include
as much as possible of apparent good (a kind of cure by regimen –
cf. Protagoras' remarks later in the Apology about improvement
of pupils through having them avoid bad friends and associations:
168a).[6] In neither case is it necessary for the sophist to have any

6. The two methods are different, since one effects a change in the patient
himself, the other a change in his environment. But the presence in the Apology
of references to both methods, the persistent use of the formula 'to make good
appear in place of bad' – which could apply to either – and the importance of
both in contemporary Greek medicine would all suggest that Protagoras himself did not draw a sharp distinction. Indeed, there are many pedagogical
situations in which it is hard to see how anyone would be able to draw such a

special knowledge not available to the patient of what is going to prove satisfactory; he can run a very successful practice on nothing more than an empirical familiarity with the sort of remedy that has worked in the past, proceeding by trial and error from there.

This aspect of the theory is important and is perhaps best illustrated by another analogy. The activity of physician or sophist can be thought of as an improvement of a man's eyesight through experimentation with different lenses. The oculist's services are required once a patient becomes for some reason or another dissatisfied with the way things look to him, either because what he sees is less varied and detailed than what he once perceived or because the act of seeing causes him discomfort. Whatever the cause, he is someone for whom things as they appear are unsatisfactory. (*Satisfactory* and *unsatisfactory* are probably the translations which best bring out the purely subjectivist reference of the terms 'good' and 'bad' as they are used in the Greek text at this point.) While the oculist is experimenting with one lens after another, the patient continues to be the only person able to decide whether or not there has been any improvement, just as at the outset he was the only person able to decide that his situation *needed* improvement. The oculist himself may be much less satisfied with his own eyesight than the patient is with his, or he may for that matter be totally blind – so little does the ability to substitute more satisfactory for less satisfactory perceptions in someone else imply the possession of more satisfactory perceptions on the part of the doctor who effects the change.

The opinions and judgements to which Protagoras refers in his analysis of the sophist's function are of a special kind: those which proclaim an object or situation to possess sensible qualities like sweetness or bitterness, or else those other properties (goodness, badness or the like) which make it a thing to be sought after or avoided. The passage therefore throws no light on the doxographical notices which credit Protagoras with the extension of the

distinction. If, for example, a student abstains from certain practices as possibly harmful, it is because he has been persuaded to do so – i.e., has undergone a change in attitude analogous to that wrought in a patient's internal condition by drugs. And, on the other hand, prolonged attention to right associations – like a prolonged regimen – may produce a changed condition that is no longer adversely affected by what once was a source of discomfort or discontent.

man-measure principle to include all opinions, and so with a general denial of the possibility of false statement. We cannot know what Protagoras might have meant by such a doctrine, nor can we even be sure that he should be credited with it at all.[7] On the other hand, for the particular sort of opinion with which it deals the Apology does put the individualist interpretation, which both Plato and the doxographers give to the man-measure principle, into the context of Protagorean pedagogy in such a way that a comprehensible doctrine emerges. Making the way things appear good instead of bad is not the mere art of persuasion as taught and practiced by the doxographers' Protagoras; but neither is it the reforming of individual belief by reference to some social or collective standard such as the Platonic Protagoras might wish to apply. It is, rather, an intervention from outside to aid the individual in extricating himself from a difficulty of which he is already aware – a technique of helping all and sundry toward the particular good which they desire but lack the will or method to obtain. If this art is to be of universal applicability it must recognize not only an autonomy of individual judgement and preference, but also the fact that, in fifth-century Greece at any rate, most people saw the good in an exclusively social context and were unwilling and unable to see it in any other. The one consideration explains why the doxographers' Protagoras places the man-measure principle at the center of his system; the other why the Platonic Protagoras is so willing to think in terms of the accepted morality of his day – to approve all the things which seem just to the city.

The interpretation of the Apology on which this reconstruction of Protagorean thought rests is not universally or even generally accepted.[8] It is, however, the interpretation that seems to me most

---

7. The first author to attribute this view definitely to Protagoras is Diogenes Laertius (IX. 53). The earlier passages that associate it with his name (Isocrates, *Helen* 2; *Euthydemus* 286b–d; *Met.* Γ 4 1007b 18–23) do not necessarily imply any more than that it was the common property of eristics and sophists – something which Protagoras (or his followers) might have used on occasion but which was not an original or essential part of his thought.

8. Its first and, so far as I know, only supporter was H. Langerbeck, 'ΔΟΞΙΣ ΕΠΙΡΡΥΣΜΙΗ: Studien zu Demokrits Ethik und Erkenntnistheorie', *Neue Philologische Untersuchungen* 10 (1935), 22–6. For a further defense of Langerbeck's view, with a discussion of the additional problems for the interpretation of the Apology which it raises, see 'The Apology of Protagoras', *Yale Classical Studies* 19 (1965), 103–18.

probable on purely linguistic grounds; and its failure to obtain wide acceptance is largely owing to the fact that scholars have attempted to identify the conception of the sophist's role set forth in the portion of the speech analyzed here (166–167b) with a completely different one, which appears in the following passage (167c). The latter is utilitarian in character; the sophist is described as striving to revise prevailing ideas of right and wrong with a view to making them more useful. This conception obviously contradicts the man-measure principle whose compatibility with his position as a teacher Protagoras is supposed to be defending; and it is said by Socrates himself (172a–b) to correspond, not with the views of Protagoras, but with a modified or 'incomplete' version of those views.[9] If we interpret the whole Apology in the way most scholars do, we must take Socrates' statement in 172a–b as referring to the entire speech, and so as tantamount to the admission that, having promised (in 164e–165a and 165e–166a) to defend Protagoras as the latter himself would have done if alive, he launched immediately (166b–167c) into an argument which he knew Protagoras could not have accepted. I find it hard to believe that this is what Plato meant Socrates to be saying. Both the text of the first part of the Apology and the character of Plato's own reference to the second part point to the existence of two different conceptions of the role of the sophist, one of which has at least a good chance of being genuinely Protagorean.

II

It might be argued that, even granting the authentically Protagorean character of the above analysis of the sophist's role, it can hardly have been more than a *tour de force*, the work of someone determined at all costs to produce a pedagogical theory consistent with the man-measure principle and willing to abandon the theory in favor of something more practical when the need arose – as it surely would have. For the theory may seem more than a little peculiar by our standards. It represents the art of doctor and sophist as strikingly one-sided – directed solely toward making the patient feel better. The doctor will be unconcerned with

9. For this point, which is too often ignored in discussions of the Apology, see, most recently, Capizzi (above, n. 2), p. 45.

the man who because of illness finds harmful food enjoyable, and the sophist will be equally indifferent to the plight of the man who is proceeding contentedly toward his own destruction through adherence to a policy which he mistakenly believes to be beneficial.

The objection, particularly in so far as it pertains to the role of the doctor, is less serious than might seem at first sight. Medical care in the fifth century did not include periodic check-ups to search for illnesses of whose existence a patient was unaware. In most instances the latter's own feeling would be the only indication of disease, and making him feel better would be tantamount to effecting a cure. One early medical treatise says as much when it declares that the patient's feeling (*aisthêsis*) must be the measure (*metron*) by which the physician in every instance proceeds (*On Ancient Medicine* 9). The passage, with its reference to *metron*, is the closest parallel we have to Protagoras' own statement of the man-measure principle; and the author of this treatise sees the art of medicine as coming into being through a substitution of what seems good for what seems bad that is quite similar to the process described in the Apology. The existence of disease was first discovered when sick men found themselves unable to eat the same food as the healthy without experiencing discomfort; efforts to discover nourishment more suitable for them – to substitute, that is, something which would seem good for something which seemed bad – led to the scientific study of diet, on which the medical art is based (*Anc. Med.* 5).

The restriction which the doctrine of the Apology places on the activity of the sophist might seem to be more serious; but whatever we may think of such a notion of pedagogy, it is illustrated consistently by everything the Platonic Protagoras says or does. In the first half of the dialogue in which he has the title role he delivers a long discourse, usually known as the Great Speech. The starting point for the speech is an uncertainty which Socrates claims to feel at 319a–320b. He is curious about Protagoras' claim to be able to teach men how to be good citizens, which in the context of the dialogue is equivalent to teaching them to distinguish right behavior from wrong in their dealings with each other. Socrates says that he has always assumed the art of being a good citizen to be unteachable. If it could be taught, one would expect it to be passed down from generation to generation in certain families like any other trade. But obviously it is not passed down in this way, as is evident in the case of Pericles, certainly as good a citizen as Athens ever had, but one who was unable to transmit his skill to his sons. Moreover, when a matter involving a specialized technology like shipbuilding or architecture is brought before the assembly for debate the Athenians are in the habit of listening only to experts in those fields and laugh down any amateur who ventures to put in a word. Yet they think that any man has a right to a hearing when the matter being discussed involves right or wrong – which again would suggest that, since there are no specialists in it, the citizen's art cannot be taught.

Protagoras might have answered Socrates' objections more simply than he does – by saying, for instance, that there do exist men who, like himself, are teachers of civic excellence, and that the Athenians are foolish not to give them the same sort of attention they give other specialists; or that Pericles, unlike Protagoras, had no real knowledge of the subject and so could not have been expected to transmit it to his children. But both of these answers, however flattering they might be to Protagoras, would suggest to the audience of loyal Athenians gathered to hear the Great Speech that there was something seriously wrong with the way public business was conducted in Athens. Both answers would explain away one seeming evil (the fact that something so desirable as civic excellence cannot be taught) by calling attention to another (the fact that the Athenians pay no attention to the real experts in the subject and entrust their lives and fortunes to a man who is largely ignorant of it). And so the tack which Protagoras takes is quite different. The gist of his argument is that men learn good and bad in the same way they learn a language (cf. 328a) – by being told constantly from the time they are small that this is good and this is bad (325d), just as they are told that this object is a chair and this a table. There is therefore no one teacher of civic excellence, just as there is no one teacher of Greek: everyone learns it from everyone else (327b), and so every citizen can recognize right and wrong, just as he can recognize what is Greek and what is not. It is only proper, there- fore, that everyone have a right to be heard in the assembly, even though his view may not be the one that the majority ultimately accepts. Moreover, since civic excellence is not a specialized discipline passed down from father to son, one could obviously not expect children of parents who are especially accomplished in it to show the same accomplishment. It follows that excellence is neither unteachable nor, on the other hand, the special preserve of a group of experts whose claims the Athenians fail to recognize. Rather, there is a veritable glut of competent teachers, and Athenian policy is the one best calculated to make use of this great good fortune. The only trouble is that Socrates has not realized up to now just how well off he and his fellow-citizens are (327d–e).

A more striking example of how to turn bad into good in the way things appear to a student could hardly be asked for. And in this, the only report of Protagorean pedagogic technique which has survived, Plato may well be, consciously or unconsciously, reproducing a pattern which was detectable whenever the sophist taught or lectured.

Protagoras makes it clear in his speech that he is not the only teacher of civic excellence – merely a man generally recognized as slightly better at it than others. It is not surprising, then, that he seems to see in the whole process by which this excellence is learned a substitution of better for worse exactly analogous to that effected by the Great Speech. This aspect of his doctrine is illustrated most clearly in the famous *Protagoras* myth, which precedes the Great Speech (320d–322d). Here Protagoras explains how the civic excellence men teach each other first came into existence. Men originally lived, he says, in isolation, without cities and without the civic art. In this condition they were continually being devoured by wild beasts, whose physical equipment for survival was far superior to their own; and so they came together for protection into cities. Once this had occurred, however, they fell to quarreling and killing each other, as was only to be expected, given their ignorance of the civic art of telling right from wrong. To remedy the situation, Zeus bestowed on mankind the two components of this art – justice and reverence – so that all might learn them and there might be as a result 'the ordered existence of cities and uniting bonds of alliance' (322c).

The myth has been interpreted in various ways, and scholars have sometimes felt that a self-proclaimed agnostic like Protagoras could not possibly have said that Zeus gave men justice and reverence.[10] But the whole passage makes perfect sense in the light of the educational theory of the Apology. Life without the civic art is the initial unsatisfactory condition of which men become aware. The acquisition of civic excellence is that change in attitude which allows them to see good (concord, exchange of goods and services) in a situation where previously they had seen evil (anarchy, mutual wrongdoing).[11] And Zeus, since he brings about the change, is, most appropriately, the original and archetypal sophist. Note, however, that, like the good Protagorean he is, Zeus does not urge or force justice and reverence upon mankind. He merely offers them as a way out of a situation of whose disadvantages man himself has become perfectly aware.

The whole conception is exactly paralleled in the medical treatise mentioned earlier for its possibly Protagorean use of the term *metron*. The author of that work regards the skill of the doctor as closely allied to a much more widely diffused one which arose in primitive times in response to the discomfort men felt when they tried, as they did at first, to subsist on the same diet of berries and grasses which sufficed for other animals. To remedy this situation men learned to distinguish foods which were readily digestible from those that were not, just as in the Protagoras myth men remedy the disadvantages of trying to live, as animals do, without the civic art, by learning to distinguish right and honorable behavior from wrong and shameful behavior.[12] The civic art is one in which no one can be an amateur (*idiôteuein*) if there is to be a city at all (327a); and so is the art of replacing bad with good in

10. Cf. the remarks of E. A. Havelock in *The Liberal Temper in Greek Politics* (New Haven 1957), pp. 93–4, with the earlier discussions cited there (408–9).

11. For this interpretation of the Protagoras myth, I am indebted to M. Untersteiner, *The Sophists* (Engl. transl. Oxford 1954), pp. 61–2 – though my understanding of what Protagoras would have meant by 'good' and 'bad' is quite different from his.

12. Neither passage uses subjectivist terminology to describe the process of improvement, but this is not in itself enough to make the analyses incompatible with what appears in the Apology. The identity of being and seeming may be taken as assumed from the start; to insist upon the point at every stage in the exposition would merely lead to awkwardness and complication. The important thing to observe is that there is no place in either passage where good and bad *must* be anything other than what they appear to be – no place at which men's feeling for what is good and bad is represented as corrected or revised in the light of someone else's superior understanding.

what men eat. No one is an amateur (*idiôtês*) in it, but all experts to some degree – out of necessity (*Anc. Med.* 4).

By making the civic art universal among city dwellers Protagoras need not be suggesting, as has often been supposed, that a feeling for what is just and honorable is an essential component of man's nature, which would mean that any individual who fails to recognize such qualities is in some sense an incomplete or inadequate measure and so not fully human. All he implies is that the existence of a widespread reluctance ('reverence') to violate a certain pattern of social relationships, and of compensatory procedures ('justice') for restoring the *status quo* in situations where harm done to one individual disturbs the pattern,[13] are prerequisites for a mode of collective existence which most men find preferable to any other, collective or individual.[14] Moreover, as the success and durability of civic institutions shows, almost all men are capable of guiding their lives in accordance with right and reverence of some kind.[15] On the other hand, since a capacity for mastering the civic art is so widely prevalent, men who suffer from a deficiency in it will generally be able to trace the trouble to its source. They will realize that what is bad in their situation springs from an inability to see a right course of action or to follow such a course of action when they do perceive it.[16] They may then need the help of someone who, like the sophist, is generally recognized as superior to others in inculcating the civic art. But

13. This interpretation, besides giving to the word 'justice' (*dikê*) one of its oldest and most basic meanings (right return – an eye for an eye) is also that which best explains why justice and reverence can be regarded as equivalent to the sum total of civic skill. They are, respectively, the ordinary and extraordinary devices for the preservation of the social order, the deterrent and corrective of unlawful action.

14. The fact that men do find this preferable does not mean that Protagoras believed man to be a 'political' animal. An opinion – unless it is unsatisfactory to the person who holds it – is simply to be taken as it is; there is no point in seeking to discover how or why it came into being.

15. Protagoras never suggests that what is regarded as just or deserving of reverence cannot vary from city 'to city. Hence, even were city life universal among mankind, the fact that justice and reverence are necessary for a city to survive would not imply that 'just' and 'honorable' are moral universals.

16. That men do find deficiency in civic excellence an evil is evident from Protagoras' whole description of the way this excellence is passed from generation to generation; men recognize it as something beneficial and so are eager to help each other acquire as much of it as possible (327a–b); and they make a pretense of possessing it even when they do not possess it at all (323a–b).

the latter can merely suggest a way out of the difficulty; only the men themselves can know whether his advice is successful – and so they remain thoroughly competent judges of what is good and bad, right and wrong, for them during the whole time they are seeking improvement.[17] In similar fashion the man who suffers from an illness may need the suggestions of the doctor as to what food he ought to avoid in the future – although of course he is the sole judge of whether the proposed remedy is efficacious.

By making the civic art nearly universal Protagoras also suggests that most men are capable of accommodating themselves to the particular variety of justice and reverence current in the city in which they live – just as most men will be satisfied with the normal dietary customs of a given region. But just as there are sick men who cannot live on what suffices for most people, so there is the sort of person for whom the normal diet of justice and reverence that suffices for the majority will appear bad and in fact be bad. This person is the criminal, and in 322d he is expressly termed a 'disease of the city'. In some instances it may be possible to cure such a person by changing his condition or attitude to the point where this diet does seem satisfactory (cf. the process of correction and improvement described in 325a and 325d–326d); in other instances the only thing to do is to give him a change of diet by expelling him from the city (325a–b). For it is impractical to require the entire citizenry to accommodate its way of life to his.

Such in its general outlines is the art of making good appear in place of bad as practiced by the Platonic Protagoras and as detected by him in the activities of others. The doxographers' Protagoras may have been practicing the same technique when he taught his students how to 'make the worse *logos* better' (B 6 Diels). It was always assumed in antiquity that by the 'worse *logos*' Protagoras meant the morally reprehensible argument, and that to make this argument better was to make it victorious over the morally praiseworthy argument. Yet there is nothing in the phrase itself that demands such an interpretation, and the phrase itself was probably all that the doxographers had to go on. I suggest,

17. This subjectivistic conception of the sophist's meliorative role seems to follow from 328b, where Protagoras is careful to speak simply of a superior ability he *thinks* he possesses to produce in others what they *themselves* recognize as improvement.

therefore, that making the worse argument better was simply
another example of teaching men how to make the best of what
seemed to them a bad situation. It might seem at first glance that a
'bad situation' is something very different from a 'worse argument', but the two become practically identical in the three
passages from late fifth-century drama in which the Protagorean
notion of better and worse *logoi* seems to be most closely echoed.
In Euripides' *Suppliants* 486–93 the Theban messenger complains
that mankind knows peace as a better *logos* but prefers war instead;
in *Phoenissae* 559–60 Jocasta speaks of a patriotic and a tyrannical
course of action as the two *logoi* which confront Eteocles. And in
Clouds 883–1104 the better *logos* of traditional education is pitted
against the worse *logos* of its modern rival. The contrast in each
instance is between what are regarded as better and worse
arguments – but also between the external situations or courses of
action (peace *vs.* war, etc.) which are described by each pair of
logoi and between which a choice must be made.[18] One might
preserve the double reference of the Greek by translating *logos* as
'proposition': peace, patriotism and traditional education all
represent the better – i.e. more satisfactory or attractive – of two
propositions, and making the worse proposition better would
necessarily involve making a given situation or alternative seem
better.[19] In the *Clouds* each proposition is made to speak in defense
of itself. The resulting situation is analogous to what obtains in a
court of law when each of the contending parties seeks to make his
own case the better argument, and so to make the circumstances
of his case seem better – i.e. more favorable – to himself. It is easy
to see how one of the disputants might wish the aid of Protagoras
in improving his *logos*, and this may be the sophistic pedagogical
situation of which Aristophanes gives a distorted picture in the

18. The same holds true of another famous set of sophistic *logoi*, those delivered by Pleasure and Virtue in Prodicus' account of the Choice of Heracles
(Xenophon, *Memorabilia* II. I. 21–30). Heracles' choice is between two arguments, but also between the two ways of life to which these arguments are linked.

19. For similar correlations of *logoi* with an external circumstance or set of
circumstances, see *Euthydemus* 285e where (during the demonstration of a
purportedly Protagorean proposition) each of the things that is, is said to have
its own *logos*, consisting of the statement that it is; and Sextus, *PH* I. 218, on the
'*logoi* of what appears to be' referred to by Protagoras. The latter are seen as
inherent in things themselves – just as we might speak of various propositions
as inhering in the circumstances of a case or situation.

opening scenes of the *Clouds*. The play's hero, Strepsiades, finds himself at the start of the action in what could almost serve as a case-book example of the sort of position that appears and is bad. The circumstances of his case, so far as he can see, point to nothing but bankruptcy. Strepsiades is obviously someone who could profit greatly from that instruction in household economy which, according to Plato's testimony (*Protagoras* 318e), Protagoras offered; and Protagoras might have been able to do one of two things – either to show Strepsiades how aspects of his situation which looked hopeless need no longer seem so, how with the exercise of proper ingenuity and thrift he might turn his losses into assets; or else, in the event that the pupil proved totally inept in these techniques, to show him how to bear poverty with more equanimity. In the former event, the case which Strepsiades could present for himself might be sufficiently improved so that he could make it prevail over the case of his creditors the next time they hauled him into court. In the latter, his case would at least be strong enough to win him some respite from the criticism of family and friends. In cither event Protagoras' advice would have been more practical than what Strepsiades actually gets from Socrates, and probably more honest as well. For Strepsiades, being an average Athenian with conventional ideas, would not want to benefit himself by transgressing the laws of his city. In teaching students how to defend the contrary of every proposition Protagoras may simply have been recognizing the fact that the situations which men like Strepsiades will have to face or help others to face are very varied, and that learning to make opposite *logoi* appear better is a simple and feasible means of training them for as many eventualities as possible.

III

The amount of evidence that can be adduced to support the view that the Apology does give a genuinely Protagorean view of the sophist's role is not large, simply because what we know of Protagoras is so limited. Such as it is, however, the evidence is remarkably consistent. My case can be supported by one further argument, of more dubious validity, but still significant enough to be worth mentioning. The figure of Protagoras constructed here is simply too familiar from the twentieth-century scene for me to believe that he is nothing more than the result of Plato's fancy or my own attempt to read some sort of consistency into an inconsistent tradition. He must be, rather, someone who really existed in the fifth century and enjoyed enormous success for somewhat the same reasons as do his modern counterparts.

At the turn of the century it was common in some circles to speak of Protagoras as if he were the first pragmatist[20] – on the assumption that in rejecting, as the pragmatists did, the traditional distinction between true and false belief, he was substituting a pragmatic one in its place. There is nothing in the ancient accounts of the man's teaching to support this interpretation; and I think, therefore, that it must be rejected. But while the characteristically American philosophy of pragmatism was fumbling for the sophist's meaning and not quite, as it seems to me, getting it, an authentically Protagorean point of view came to prominence in a very different area of American life. If the above interpretation of him is correct, Protagoras is nothing less than the patron saint of advertising, progressive education, publicity and personnel work, guidance counseling and a host of related disciplines. In some instances it is even possible to point to chapter and verse in the Protagorean gospel as the ultimate source of a modern disciple's text. If an advertiser addresses his appeal to the tired, the run-down, the generally out of sorts, promising them quick relief through the use of his product, he is offering to make things appear good instead of bad in exactly the Protagorean manner; and if he provides a money-back guarantee for those who remain unsatisfied, he is in effect echoing what the sophist says in *Protagoras* 328b–c:

> When a student finishes my course he pays the stipulated fee if he wants, and if he doesn't want to he goes to a temple and, swearing an oath as to how much he thinks my instruction has been worth to him, pays me so much and no more.

The notion, so widespread in modern America, that education is not the transmission of a set body of disciplines but a combination of psychotherapy and vocational guidance designed to help the individual student meet the problems that confront him recalls the famous indictment of the liberal arts in *Protagoras* 318d–e:

20. See, especially, F. C. S. Schiller, *Plato or Protagoras* (Oxford 1908).

Other teachers do their students harm, for they take people who have just effected their escape from classroom disciplines (*technai*) and lead them back to the same old thing, setting them to learning mathematics and music and geometry and astronomy. The student who comes to my school will learn nothing but what he came for: the art of arriving at sound decisions (*euboulia*) on matters both public and private – how to make a financial success of himself and occupy a position of leadership in the community.

Our tendency to consider a whole range of problems once analyzed and dealt with in a very different way as arising from unhappiness, maladjustment, illness of one sort or another is precisely the Protagorean insistence on making the sophist a doctor, combined with the equally Protagorean assumption that evil does not lie irrevocably in either the person or his situation but simply in his relation to the situation – so that a proper change in attitude will remove the difficulty. And we are just as Protagorean in our complete confidence in the technique of improving appearances – in our feeling that no matter what the problem is there must be some sort of expert who can be called in to solve it in a fairly painless way. William H. Whyte, in his well-known indictment of the organization man, cites[21] as typical of what he dislikes the attitude revealed by one item in a standardized questionnaire put to executive trainees. The question is as follows: what does an employer say to workman A who wishes to know why workman B got the promotion which A had expected? Should he say: (1) you were better qualified, but B has seniority; (2) B got the job because his uncle owns the plant; (3) you must work harder; or (4) let us see how you can improve your work? The correct answer is, of course, number 4, which, as Whyte points out, is the mealy-mouthed answer. But it is also the Protagorean answer. For (1) and (2) call attention to additional evils in the man's situation of which he might not have been aware before – as does (3), if the man is either lazy or working as hard as he can. (4), on the other hand, removes initial discouragement, holds up the prospect of improvement, and suggests that the latter will not be difficult. It is simply a matter of a heart-to-heart talk and a little constructive

21. *The Organization Man* (New York 1956), pp. 409–10.

thought. (4) is thus the only answer which effects the substitution of good appearances for bad in the way Protagorean pedagogy requires. Whyte further points out that to answer the question properly one would have to know which, if any, of the three facts mentioned in answers (1) to (3) was correct. But for the Protagorean who made up the questionnaire the facts of the matter are of negligible importance. Since the workman's situation will be bad, good, or indifferent according to the view he takes of it, the impression the employer should strive to create is simply the one which will be the most encouraging. With Whyte's example one should compare *Theaetetus* 167e–168a, where Protagoras explains to Socrates that the successful teacher must never make things any more difficult for his pupils than is absolutely necessary: he should not trip them into self-contradictory statements, but simply try to help them out of the confusions and perplexities they are already in by pointing out the past mistakes which led to them. 'If you do so,' he says, 'pupils will like you and court your society and be disgusted with themselves and turn to philosophy, hoping to escape what they were before and become different persons.' The fear of unpopularity, of suggesting that improvement involves anything so disagreeable as hard work, is one shared by Protagoras and the framer of our questionnaire, and could be documented at greater length with additional modern examples. But enough has been said to show that there is nothing unique or peculiar in the technique of improving appearances which I have ascribed to Protagoras and that, in certain situations at least, no success is so immediate or so sure as that which awaits the man who can perfect it.

IV

Our survey of the sophist's modern disciples has placed him in some rather dubious company, but it should not lead us to the conclusion that Protagoras himself was either a fool or a charlatan. Modern Protagoreanism is a complex phenomenon and so, I suspect, was its ancient counterpart. On occasion it may involve nothing more than the creation of individual and mass euphoria – instruction in the power of positive thinking, or, in other situations, one-upmanship (for, corresponding to Socrates and his Thoughtery as portrayed by the satirist Aristophanes, we have Mr Stephen

Potter and his Academy of Lifemanship at Yeovil). On the other hand, it may be a perfectly legitimate form of social or individual psychotherapy, one whose desirability is not lessened by the fact that it is rooted in the world of appearances. The variety exhibited by modern Protagoreanism should serve to remind us of this, as well as to suggest a further point of some importance for our understanding of Protagoras himself. Among practitioners of the method it is possible to find at one extreme the complete charlatan, the man whose claim to substitute better appearances for worse is simply a euphemistic way of saying that he is not concerned with real improvement at all, only with producing sufficient temporary or apparent relief to enable him to collect his fee. At the other extreme there is the convinced subjectivist relativist who believes that things are to each person as they seem, and that however destructive a course of action may look to others it is in fact good for a man if he thinks it so. Between these two poles there will be many who adopt Protagoras' approach for purely practical reasons. As the success enjoyed both by the sophist and by his modern disciples indicates, the approach offers an effective way of dealing with some of the problems which arise in any society that brings large numbers of people together and establishes a free market for the exchange of ideas and skills among them. A person may sincerely believe that his way of doing or looking at things is superior to someone else's, and yet there are often good reasons for not saying directly, 'Your way is no good; try mine'. No one likes to be told he is a fool, or that he does not know what he is doing. He will be more likely to try a new method and profit from it if he is approached only when dissatisfied with his own procedures and then has the alternative suggested to him in such a fashion that he thinks it is for all practical purposes his own idea, or one in whose devising he has had an important share. Other practical considerations as well might weigh heavily with Protagoreans both ancient and modern. It is obvious that in a society as heterogeneous as even fifth-century Athens was there will be many occasions in which the way things seem to be *is* far more important than the way they really are. Such a society can offer at best a very partial satisfaction for the needs of all its citizens; the average man is better off if he focuses his attention only on those goods which the city does provide and accepts this partial view of the political and social reality as a whole one. And no regime, however well-meaning, can dispense entirely with propaganda: directing one's attention exclusively to the appearance which a matter is likely to present may offer the only possible way of coping, at least temporarily, with a problem which would otherwise prove far too complex.

Were we, then, better informed about fifth-century thought, we should probably have to distinguish between hypocritical Protagoreans, practical Protagoreans, Protagoreans by conviction, and perhaps other varieties as well. That Protagoras himself did not belong to the first class seems fairly certain. Plato is not, on the whole, sympathetic to the Protagorean position, but he never casts doubt on the sincerity of the man's motives. Concerning the relative importance of the theoretical and practical considerations that underlie the Protagorean method we can be much less sure. In its fully developed form it probably rested on both, though one or the other may have been the starting point for its creation. Protagoras himself would surely have regarded his practical success as a striking confirmation of the theoretic assumption on which he worked; or, to put it in more Protagorean terms, he would have been convinced that he owed his own eminence in the practical world of his day to going on the assumption that things are as they appear – convinced that things in general seemed better to him on this assumption than they would have on any other.

V

Whatever the exact relationship of Protagoras' epistemology and ontology to the rest of his philosophy, they are remarkable for the extreme frankness with which they admit the identification of seeming and being. Herein lies the most striking difference between the sophist and his modern counterparts, a difference which is probably best explained by reference to the different historical situations in which the two systems arose. The modern relativism with which we have been concerned has had to be maintained in the face of a philosophical and ethical tradition that tends to recognize the just and the good as absolutes, valid at all times and all places, irrespective of what people think them to be. Hence its tendency to confine itself to the practical world in response to whose demands it has often arisen, and to conceal even from itself, perhaps, the character of its basic assumptions. The situation was quite different in Protagoras' day. Early Greek ethics made no sharp distinction between real and apparent good; and like Greek theology, it was polycentric. If certain actions were considered worthy of imitation, or certain conditions desirable, and called good for that reason, it was not because other possibilities had been passed in review and found wanting, but simply because they had not been considered. Nor was it felt to be odd that different and even opposite things should be regarded as good. Socrates was puzzled that men as unlike as Achilles and Odysseus should both be taken for exemplars, and felt that one must have been better than the other (cf. *Hipp. Min.* 363a–364b); Greeks of an earlier period would not have given the matter a second thought. When the Greeks first came into close contact with their eastern and western neighbors the phenomenon of other nations paying allegiance to completely different sets of values did not produce anything like the shock caused by the voyage literature of the seventeenth and eighteenth centuries. A work like Diderot's *Supplément au voyage de Bougainville* would have been ineffective, simply because the point it makes would have been felt to be obvious. Herodotus draws from the variety of customs he describes in his history the relativist conclusion – that what is valid for one group of people is not necessarily valid for anyone else. But he never suggests that any practice is less right because everyone does not believe it to be right, or that it is possible for one thing to be right while other things merely seem right. Quite the contrary: the very diversity of the practices which different nations recognize as right is advanced as a proof of the validity of those practices.[22] It almost seems that had he found a custom which everyone in the world considered good he would have dismissed it as something on a par with walking upright or eating and sleeping – an inevitable outgrowth of man's physical nature, to which no particular ethical significance could be attached. In extending such reasoning

22. Herodotus' relativism does operate within certain limits, but the area which they exclude is not a large one. Only the cannibalistic Androphagoi are said to be utterly unacquainted with law and right (IV. 106); Herodotus' complaint is not that they practise a bad νόμος, but that they practise none at all; and though Herodotus himself disapproves of the custom of copulating in temples (II. 64–5), he makes it clear that he does not expect everyone to share his squeamishness.

to all differences of opinion on right and wrong, Protagoras was
not so much setting himself up in opposition to earlier views, as
recognizing, with an explicitness not found before, the sovereign
power which different opinions and customs, each within its own
limited sphere, had always enjoyed in Greek life and thought.

This attitude was probably fairly widespread in his generation
(a generation which included Herodotus, Pindar, and Pericles);
yet the fact that Protagoras finds it necessary to affirm rather than
merely assume the identity of seeming and being indicates that
even in his own lifetime the possibility of a separation was beginning
to be envisioned. In the next generation, the separation was widely
proclaimed and accepted – by Euripides, Socrates, Thucydides,
and Democritus, among others. These men are all unwilling,
either in analyzing social and political phenomena or in seeking
some practical standard for social and political behavior, to take
as a point of departure the shifting world of seeming good and evil
in which Protagoras had so contentedly moved. The change is
strikingly illustrated in the way two motifs, one Protagorean and
one Herodotean, are used by later writers. 'What action is
shameful', remarks a character in Euripides, 'if it does not seem
so to the person who commits it?' (fr. 19 Nauck). The observation
is perfectly harmless in a Protagorean context and would not have
been intended to shock anyone. Yet in Euripides it *is* shocking –
not simply because it is adduced as an argument in favor of incest,
but also because it is so phrased as to suggest another remark,
'what (in general, for anybody, anywhere) is shameful if someone
can be found who thinks it isn't?' If the distinction between
honorable and shameful is to apply at all it must be recognized as
universally valid.[23] Herodotus says in III. 38 that if all the nations
of the world were to pick from among all the customs practiced
anywhere those which seemed to them the best, each nation would

---

23. A somewhat similar modification of what may be a Protagorean motif
appears in a doctrine attributed to another member of the next generation,
Prodicus of Ceus. In the *Eryxias* (397e) Socrates credits him with the view that
the same thing may be good to one person and bad to another – but only to the
extent that one person may know how to make proper use of it and another not.
Here good and bad become properties which reside, not in the unstable realm
of men's attitudes toward things, but only in the ends which these things are
made to serve; and the latter are presumably to be regarded as fixed per-
manently by their very nature as either good or bad.

choose its own. The late fifth-century author of the work on *Contrary Statements* (*Dissoi Logoi*) is probably thinking of this passage when he says (II. 18) that if every man were to bring the customs he thinks shameful to a common pile, and if all were then allowed to inspect the pile and remove from it any customs which they thought honorable, there would be, after all had been given the chance of making such a selection, nothing left in the pile at all. For Herodotus the tenacity with which each sticks to his own customs is all that matters; for the later writer it is the incredible divergence of customs. And he draws from this divergence the conclusion that, since everything anyone thinks shameful is thought honorable by someone else, the honorable and the shameful must be the same thing. To be separate qualities with a real rather than an apparent existence the honorable and the shameful must appear the same to everybody.

This sort of contrast appears time and again when one compares the works of the late fifth century with those of the two preceding generations. It is evident, for example, in Euripides' assumption that there is a fixed standard of what is shameful, so that gods may be deemed gods no longer if they fail to adhere to it (fr. 294. 6 Nauck) – contrasted with, say, Pindar's assertion, in a famous fragment (169 Snell), that justice may be determined by a god's whim; that the ordinance of Zeus can make what is on other occasions most outrageous most just. It is evident in Thucydides' preoccupation with something which he calls 'human nature' and which is constant at all times and in all places – as against Herodotus' willingness to let men's natures be as varied as their customs. It is evident in Democritus' assertion – perhaps made in direct polemic with Protagoras – that the sweet and bitter exist merely by opinion and convention, whereas in reality there are only atoms and the void (B 125 Diels); that though one man may think one thing pleasant and another another, the good is the same for all (B 69). And it is evident in Socrates' never-ending attempt to bring consistency and unity into the chaos of earlier ethical ideas, an attempt which appears as clearly as anywhere in the discussion he has with Protagoras following the latter's Great Speech. Anxious to arrive at a more accurate definition of the good which Protagoras teaches men to acquire, Socrates suggests that it ought perhaps to be identified with pleasure; and he is at the outset

(351b–e) stoutly resisted by Protagoras, who insists that both the good and the bad are sometimes pleasurable and sometimes not. His answer is the natural and expected one, for it would be impossible for him to accept the identification Socrates proposes. The good and the pleasant are always, in Protagoras' view, as varied as men think them to be.

To suggest reasons why this intellectual revolution should have occurred just when it did would require too long a digression into the history of the fifth century. I will only point out here that the number of texts in which the contrast between the two generations appears provides further support for my contention that Protagorean relativism is a characteristic development for the mid fifth century, not an atypical one; and that it is by reference to this revolution and its effects that we can best explain why the two Protagorases described at the outset of our discussion seemed so different. The doxographers, taking as their starting point a bare statement of the basic tenets of Protagorean relativism, assumed that, since it rejected the idea of a permanent, immutable good independent of what appears good in a given place at a given time, it must have required, rather than merely allowed, men to live at random or seek out some non-moral standard by which to bring order to their lives. The facts which they record about Protagoras' views are, therefore, accurate. But the facts are selected facts, and so the general picture which emerges from them is misleading.

Had he as little to go on as the doxographers, Plato would probably have produced a very similar account of Protagoras. But he wrote in the early fourth century, when there still remained a vivid enough memory of the man for him to realize that he could not have been the sort of person one would expect the author of the man-measure principle to be. Hence Plato's portrait is neither lopsided nor misleading. But it achieves balance at the expense of consistency. The doctrine found in the Apology, by which Protagorean epistemology and rhetoric are linked into a single system with Protagorean ethics and pedagogy, is only briefly introduced in a single dialogue, and in such a way as to suggest that Plato did not fully understand its implications. Elsewhere Protagoras the educator and Protagoras the author of the man-measure principle are treated as if they were different persons.

The completeness with which the intellectual revolution of the late fifth century was carried through explains one other thing as well – namely, why Protagoreanism had to wait twenty-four centuries to be revived with anything like the thoroughness its originator envisioned. Whether Protagoras would applaud or condemn the achievements of his modern disciples, we do not know; and even the services of a necromancer, were they at our disposal, would be of little use here. The ghost of Homer, when questioned on the matter by the narrator in Lucian's *True History*, freely admits to having composed all the athetized lines in the *Iliad* and the *Odyssey*. One would not expect our sophistic ghost to be so candid. He would probably do no more than address his attention, as was his custom, to the skeptical or downright discontented among us and say, 'Yes, of course; the state of things produced by the popularity of my method *is* deplorable – if that is the way you look at the matter. But I don't think the situation is likely to change – you might as well try to accommodate yourselves to it.' And then, if we would only allow him, he might go further and try to help us out a bit – by offering a demonstration of that art of improving appearances in which he was the unequalled and unapproached master. Whether we agreed with what he said or not, the speech would be, I think, well worth hearing.[24]

24. The substance of this paper was delivered before the Yale Classical Club in the fall of 1964. For criticisms received then, as well as for subsequent suggestions from Messrs Adam Parry and S. Dale Harris, and my wife, Katherine, I am most grateful.

Thucydides' historical perspective

ADAM PARRY

THUCYDIDES' *History of the Peloponnesian War* is an intensely personal and a tragic work. A careful reader feels this from the very first sentence: '...I began writing the History from the moment the War broke out; I expected it to be a great war and more worth a λόγος than any war that had preceded it.' This tone is maintained throughout the work. Even if we leave aside the dozens of personal judgements in the *History*,[1] its intensity of feeling everywhere reminds us of Thucydides' personal involvement.

We learn from ancient criticism that Thucydides was admired as the historian of πάθος, as opposed to Herodotus, the historian of ἦθος. The sense of the tragic, which exists as a fine suffusion in parts of Herodotus' work, dominates the whole *History* of Thucydides. This sense of the tragic is something quite different from the clinical objectivity which has been so often, and often so thought-

---

1. A number of these are well-known to everyone at all acquainted with Thucydides; e.g., the comment on war as βίαιος διδάσκαλος in the account of Corcyraean revolution, III. 82. 2. More personal, and less well-known, is the comment he makes later in the same passage on the moral degeneration which revolutionary activity brought upon all of Greece, III. 83. 1: οὕτω πᾶσα ἰδέα κατέστη κακοτροπίας διὰ τὰς στάσεις τῷ Ἑλληνικῷ, καὶ τὸ εὔηθες, οὗ τὸ γενναῖον πλεῖστον μετέχει, καταγελασθὲν ἠφανίσθη. No less personal, in a different way, is the unexampled rhetorical question in VII. 44. 1, where the historian, with all the impatience of an intensely orderly mind, comments on the essentially confused nature of all military actions, even those that take place in broad daylight, where even the individual participant, like Tolstoi's Captain Tushin, hardly (μόλις) knows what is going on around himself, and then asks how anyone can have any clear knowledge (πῶς ἄν τις σαφῶς τι ἤδει;) of a battle by night, such as Demosthenes' attempt to storm Epipolae. A valuable close study could be made of the revelations of personal attitude in the *History*. Such a study would comment on the author's tendency to use distancing, 'scientific' language at points where emotion is strongest, as in οὕτω πᾶσα ἰδέα etc., above; and on the reasons for the many evident exaggerations in the text; e.g. v. 26. 3: the prophecy that the war would last thrice seven years was the only one in the whole course of it that came true; or the estimate (III. 98. 4) of the 120 hoplites who fell in the battle against the Aetolians in 426.

lessly, ascribed to him.[2] His very reluctance to speak of himself, his way of stating all as an ultimate truth, is, if we must use the word, one of his most *subjective* aspects. When you can say, 'so-and-so gave me this account of what happened, and it seems a likely version', you are objective about your relation to history. But when, without discussing sources, you present everything as αὐτὰ τὰ ἔργα (I. 21. 2), the way it really happened, you are forcing the reader to look through your eyes, imposing your own assumptions and interpretations of events. To say all this is of course not to cast doubts on Thucydides' veracity or on the validity of his methods of inquiry, little as we know of them.

The reasons for Thucydides' personal involvement are evident enough. He was a passionate admirer of Periclean Athens. 'The devout disciple', Wade-Gery calls him.[3] When he has Pericles say (II. 43. 1), 'You must each day actually contemplate the power of the city – τὴν τῆς πόλεως δύναμιν καθ᾽ ἡμέραν ἔργῳ θεωμένους – and fall in love with her – καὶ ἐραστὰς γιγνομένους αὐτῆς, and when you grasp the vision of her greatness – καὶ ὅταν ὑμῖν μεγάλη δόξῃ εἶναι' and so on; when he has Pericles speak in this vein, can we doubt that he was, and as he writes is in retrospect, one of those who heard Pericles' words with willing ears? Now compare this passage with a famous one from the *Archaeology*. This is I. 10. 2, where Thucydides interrupts his account to speculate on the

2. The notion of Thucydides as the passionless scientific gatherer of facts goes back to the positivistic interpreters of the nineteenth century (e.g. Gomperz, *Griechische Denker*[2], 1, 401f.), and despite protests like those of F. M. Cornford (Preface to *Thucydides Mythistoricus*, vii: 'Xenophon, I suppose, is honest; but his honesty makes it none the easier to read him'), has become the standard handbook view, much enforced by the double and doubly dubious equation Thucydides = ancient medical writers minus modern medical research methods. See A. Parry, 'The Language of Thucydides' Description of the Plague', *University of London Institute of Classical Studies Bulletin* 16 (1969), 106–17. Wade-Gery in the *Oxford Classical Dictionary* shows an ambiguous attitude characteristic of much modern judgement. On p. 904, he says finely: '[Thucydides] uses a language largely moulded by poets: its precision is a poet's precision, a union of passion and candour'; but shortly thereafter falls into a slightly sentimental version of the old cliché: 'Thucydides would no doubt prefer to substitute, for those great names [W.-G. has compared him to Shakespeare and Marlowe], the practice of any honest doctor.' The conception of the self-effacing doctor is as alien to Thucydides' aims as to his practice. One need only consider the sense of rivalry which informs his attitude to Homer as well as Herodotus.

3. In *Proceedings of the Cambridge Philological Society* (1953).

possibility of utter destruction of Athens and Sparta. Later generations would not guess, from her meager foundations, how powerful
Sparta had once been; and if the same thing were to happen to
Athens – 'Αθηναίων δὲ τὸ αὐτὸ τοῦτο παθόντων – her power
would be judged to be twice what it is, from the evident appearance
of the city. Once again we have a vision of Athens – *circumspice*! –
but in how very different a perspective. If Thucydides, as I
believe, wrote I. 10. 2 along with the rest of the *Archaeology*, after
404, or if he wrote it earlier but let it stand in his final version,[4] he
is not only making a good logical point: he is also indicating the
perspective from which he is writing the *History*. Although not in
the literal sense envisaged in I. 10. 2, Athens has been destroyed,
her greatness has vanished. The transition from the first passage,
Pericles' words in II. 43. 1, to the vision of destruction in I. 10. 2
marks Thucydides' experience of the Peloponnesian War. For him
it was the end of the world, after the world had reached its high
point. This experience must be seen as the basis both of his dramatic presentation and of his theory of history as he had worked these
out in the text we have.

Thucydides' final theory of history is one which he can only
have evolved after the defeat of Athens. This is evident enough if
we read I. 23. 1–3, where he sums up the conclusions of the
Archaeology.

> Of former actions, the greatest was the Persian – τῶν δὲ
> προτέρων ἔργων μέγιστον ἐπράχθη τὸ Μηδικόν – and yet this
> in two battles by land and two by sea had a swift conclusion.
> But of this war the duration was great, and disasters to
> Greece took place in it – παθήματά τε ξυνηνέχθη γενέσθαι ἐν
> αὐτῷ τῇ 'Ελλάδι – such as no others in an equal space of
> time. Never were so many cities captured and made empty
> of their inhabitants, some by the barbarians, some by the
> Greeks themselves as they fought against each other; and
> there were those that changed their populations on being
> captured. Never were there so many exiles and so much
> slaughter, slaughter in battle, slaughter in civil war. Things
> which formerly had been known by story only, but had been

4. The two alternatives come, practically speaking, to the same thing. The
'analytic' view becomes of interest only if it can be argued that the text was
put together without the author's intent.

rarely attested in fact, now ceased to be incredible, earth-
quakes, which were at once the most extensive and the most
violent of all history, and eclipses of the sun, which came with
a frequency beyond any recorded in earlier times, and in some
places droughts, and from them famine, and that not least
worker of harm and in part utter destroyer, the death-dealing
Plague. And all these things were the accompaniments of this
War.

Thucydides' vision of history is of greatness measured by war,
and greatness of war measured by destruction, or πάθος.[5] This
vision is a product of Thucydides' own experience. Unlike all the
other great historians of the ancient world, he writes of the events
of his own lifetime. He is so strongly concerned with this experience,
that he has by modern scholars been accused of having no understanding of the past, or of regarding it with contempt.[6] To some
degree, that is so; but we can conjecture from the *History* itself that
he did not begin with this perspective.

It is likely, on the contrary, that Thucydides, as a young man,
began with a genuine interest in the past, and did researches in the
Herodotean manner. Witness the vestiges of these researches in the
Cylon, Themistocles and Pausanias episodes and in the excursus
on Harmodius and Aristogeiton.[7] When the War breaks out, he
decides to devote the time he can spare from the affairs of the City
either largely or wholly to recording its progress. He does so
because he sees that it will be a great war or the greatest of wars,

5. The end of book VII illustrates this principle again. 'The Sicilian ἔργον
[87. 5] was the greatest of this war, and of Greek history, most glorious to the
victors, most unfortunate to the defeated.' The two poles of glory and suffering
seem balanced, for a moment, and we might have a Herodotean view. But
Syracusan triumph has throughout book VII been pale next to Athenian grief;
and here in the splendid final sentence that follows the one quoted, he talks
only of the extent of the disaster for the vanquished.

6. Cf. Collingwood, *The Idea of History* (Oxford 1946), e.g., p. 30.

7. A. Momigliano (*Memoria d. R. Accad. d. Scienze di Torino* LXVIII, 1930)
seems to have been the first to make the suggestion that there are early essays
incorporated into the text. In the work we have, all four 'digressions' play an
important part in the structure of the whole. See recently, on Harmodius and
Aristogeiton in book VI, Stahl, *Thukydides* (München 1966), ch. 1. Stahl, however, sees in this episode only a general point. The obvious relevance of the
story in the *History*, *pace* Dover, *Historical Commentary on Thucydides*, vol. II (Oxford
1970), p. 329, is to enforce the historian's point that the Athenian δῆμος was
characteristically fatuous and self-destructive in rejecting Alcibiades.

but he does not yet see it in terms purely of destruction. On the contrary, he must have been hopeful of its outcome – or at least that is the mood of 431 as he dramatizes it in the *History*. We may even go so far as to suppose that he includes himself in the wry comment in II. 8. 1 about the many young men both in the Peloponnese and in Athens who because they had no experience of it were not reluctant to make themselves part of the War. He was young, he believed Pericles, and he was a keen professional soldier. The long course of the War changes his mind. By its end he has become convinced that this war is so final a version of the historical process as to supersede all preceding events, and that the greatness of historical events is measured by their power to destroy. He might have said of it, as he does of the Plague, εἰ δέ τις καὶ προύκαμνέ τι, ἐς τοῦτο πάντα ἀπεκρίθη – 'all earlier disasters ended in, were subsumed by, this one'. He therefore can see its structure only when it is past, when all there is to lose is already lost. Then he can write of the loss and of what was lost for the benefit not of his contemporaries, but of men of some later civilization who will thereby be better enabled to understand the destruction of their own (I. 22. 4). So he does write about the past, but his own, the experienced past; and he has no great interest in earlier events, because they after all only led up to this one.

The purpose of the *Archaeology*, that is, of chs. 1–22 and their summary in ch. 23 of book I,[8] is to state and develop his theory of history and thereby to justify his exclusive concern with the Peloponnesian War. For all his famous obscurity, Thucydides' style is such as to make the patterns of his thought very evident. Taking over the devices of the Sophists and turning them to an individual use, he writes an exposition in which ideas and events are strongly marked by key terms. These key terms are semi-abstract nouns and verbs designed to distill the elements of experience into an articulate pattern. He establishes the relation between judgement and fact in the first sentence, a first example of that pervasive contrast of λόγος and ἔργον which dominates

8. The *Archaeology* is of course not Thucydides' term. As modern critics have used it, it refers strictly to chs. 2–19 of book I. But 23 in fact refers back to I. 3, elaborates 18. 2 in the Persian Wars, and makes in final form the point of the whole beginning of the work, so that 1–23 is an obvious unit.

his work and is what we might call its central metaphor.⁹ The great
fact is the War, τὸν πόλεμον. It is the supreme ἔργον; as in 1. 23. 1,
Thucydides often uses the word ἔργον as a synonym of war or
battle.¹⁰ The other side is the judging intellect, the intellect that
can give a conceptual shape to events, and that is expressed in the
word ἀξιόλογον: I expected this war to be ἀξιολογώτατον τῶν
προγεγενημένων. This contrast is maintained throughout the
Archaeology. ἐκ δὲ τεκμηρίων ὧν ἐπὶ μακρότατον σκοποῦντί μοι
πιστεῦσαι ξυμβαίνει (1. 1. 3). The facts are now the evidence and
the intellectual judgement is expressed by σκοποῦντι, σκοπεῖν
being one of Thucydides' favorite terms. Analogous terms of
intellectual discernment occur 23 times through the end of ch. 21.
The historical facts which make up the object of intellection appear primarily as words meaning *power*. History in fact is movements of power. Thus forms of the word δύναμις occur 10 times to
the end of ch. 21 and if we include synonymous expressions, e.g.
δυνατός, δύνασθαι, ἰσχύς, βιαζόμενοι, ἐκράτησαν, κρεισσόνων,
etc., we have a count of 35. Two other terms which by repetition
assume a special function are first, compounds of ἵστημι, usually
in the middle voice, which are regularly used to mark significant
qualitative changes in the historical situation, and second, the adjective μέγας, which, in contrast to Herodotus' glorifying use of it –
ἔργα μεγάλα τε καὶ θωμαστά – means size of power as measured by
size of war.

He argues that the earlier Greeks – meaning by this I believe
all earlier generations down to the Peloponnesian War – did not
have comparable greatness, 'either in wars or in other matters'
(1. 3). Note that in this sentence greatness in every other sphere of
life is made subordinate to greatness in war. There was no greatness because there was no power, and it soon becomes apparent
that power means order, because he at once begins a description
of earliest times, 2. 2, where with disconcertingly inconsistent
syntax he describes the disorganization of that period. He dramatizes this state‚ by his style, moving rapidly from genitive absolute
to a series of nominative plural participles, to a nominative
absolute to another genitive absolute, with subordinate clauses of

9. Cf. my Harvard doctoral dissertation (1957), Λόγος *and* Ἔργον *in*
Thucydides.
10. E.g., 1. 23. 1: Τῶν... προτέρων ἔργων... τούτου δὲ τοῦ πολέμου; 1. 49. 7.

varying kinds in between, before he finally comes to the main verb ἀπανίσταντο, the imperfect of ἵστασθαι to mark the frequency of change of historical situation which prevented any order from being established. The sentence contains several key terms. There was no *communication*, no *capital*, 'so men *shifted* their dwellings easily, and so had *strength* neither in the size of their cities nor in other *material means*'.[11]

This is the beginning of history; one might almost say, man in a state of nature. Thucydides describes it in negative fashion, listing those appurtenances of civilization which were lacking, things deriving from, and adding up to, power. The effect of power and resource (παρασκευή) is first to create order. Minos was first to *get a navy* (4. 1) (ναυτικὸν ἐκτήσατο), and thereby he *got power* in the Aegean Sea (τῆς νῦν Ἑλληνικῆς θαλάσσης ἐκράτησε); he *established* his sons (ἐγκαταστήσας) as rulers in the islands, and set about clearing piracy off the seas (τό τε ληστικὸν...καθῄρει) so that he could get *revenue* (τοῦ τὰς προσόδους μᾶλλον ἰέναι αὐτῷ). This establishment of order by removing piracy made possible the accumulation of *capital*: 'The establishment of Minos' navy made it possible for those living close to the sea to *amass money* and achieve security, and some began to surround themselves by *walls*.'

The missing elements of civilization begin to be filled in. And so on through the *Archaeology* a series of civilizations, as power, are established, each with its elements of ships, capital, walled cities – the features, obviously, of Athens in 431 – and, the final transformation, war. Thus Agamemnon (9. 1) is superior in power (δυνάμει προύχων), and this, not the legendary oath to Tyndareus, enabled him to gather the expedition against Troy.[12] The way in which the Mycenaean rule came to be inherited by Agamemnon is then described in 9. 2. The foundations of that rule were laid by Pelops, who by having a *supply of money* (πλήθει χρημάτων) *built up power for himself* (δύναμιν περιποιησάμενον). In 9. 3 we read that

11. Παρασκευή is often translated by specific words like 'equipment'; in Thucydides' system it assumes a much larger meaning.

12. This famous interpretation of Homer is often cited to illustrate the historian's critical powers. It shows the boldness of his thought, but also how limited a reader of Homer he was. Homer does not mention the Oath to Tyndareus; and the *Iliad* makes it clear that the Greek warrior-princes fought primarily for booty and to maintain their position in society.

Agamemnon took over this rule (ἅ...Ἀγαμέμνων παραλαβών), acquired more *naval power* than anyone else (ναυτικῷ...ἐπὶ πλέον τῶν ἄλλων ἰσχύσας), and so was able to make the attack on Troy.

And the Tyrants (13. 1): 'As Greece became more powerful (δυνατωτέρας) and more and more engaged in the acquisition of money (τῶν χρημάτων τὴν κτῆσιν), tyrannies began to be established (καθίσταντο) in the Cities; revenues (τῶν προσόδων) increased; and Greece began to provide herself with navies (ναυτικὰ...ἐξηρτύετο).'

And finally, Sparta and Athens (18. 1–2): 'The Spartans, having power (δυνάμενοι, used absolutely), established (καθίστασαν) governments in other cities; while the Athenians equipped themselves (ἀνασκευασάμενοι; cf. παρασκευή), took to their ships and became a sea power (ἐς τὰς ναῦς ἐσβάντες[13] ναυτικοὶ ἐγένοντο).' Then after the Persian Wars (18. 2) all of Greece ranges itself on one side and the other (διεκρίθησαν). 'For these were greatest in power; the might of the one was on land, the other in ships.'

Thucydides sees these establishments of order and power as admirable, and his style communicates this admiration to his readers. The severe impetus of that style, where words for *power* and *force* continually spring up to dominate the order of the sentence, enforces the sense that the creation of this sort of dynamic sovereignty is the most serious pursuit of man. I say *creation*, because each of these civilizations, these complexes of power, is seen as an order imposed by human intelligence. The notion that civilization is a product of the human mind, rather than of institutions and laws vouchsafed to man by the gods, is a characteristic Sophistic concept, and no one expresses it more clearly than Thucydides. Sea-power in particular, as we shall see, is an aspect of the intelligence, and the growth of this, culminating in the Athenians' becoming entirely nautical (ναυτικοί), parallels the development of civilization in general.

But there is so far one essential point missing in Thucydides' account of history. That is, destruction, πάθος. The reason lies in the importance he attributes to Athens and to the Peloponnesian

---

13. The phrase ἐς τὰς ναῦς ἐσβάντες looks like a standing slogan in Athenian imperial apology, the kind of thing Pericles says he will not indulge in in the Funeral Speech, 11. 36. 4. Cf. the Athenians at Sparta, 1. 74. 2. From such pat Athenian self-advertisement Thucydides constructed his historical system.

War. He presents us, in the *Archaeology* as a whole – that is, including ch. 23 – with two historical curves, two lines of historical development. One is the rise and fall of a series of civilizations. The Empire of Minos had to dissolve before the Empire of Agamemnon could be established, and Agamemnon's had ceased to exist by the time of the Tyrannies, while these in turn were variously undone to make way for fifth-century Athens and Sparta. In terms of this historical curve, which could be represented as a periodic curve on the graph of history, the Empire of Athens (let us for the moment forget, as Thucydides often does, about Sparta) is but one term in an endless series, perhaps the largest term so far, but still not a unique point, not the convergence of all history. The second historical curve is a line of continuous development, ignoring minor ups and downs, from earliest times – I. 2. 2 – to Athens in 431 B.C., when, with what has been blamed as exaggeration,[14] Thucydides says that her individual power exceeded that of Athens and Sparta together when their alliance at the time of the Persian Wars was at its height. It is this second curve which makes Athens and the fall of Athens into what I have called the final version of the historical process. The rise and fall of earlier empires must accordingly be seen as steps upward, and so he stresses their rise only, casually alluding to such matters as the confusion and faction attendant on the return of the Greeks from Troy, which could have been presented as the calamitous dissolution of Agamemnon's realm. Rather than this he stresses the creativeness of the early empires, presenting all history as a single trajectory, reaching a height in Periclean Athens, and coming to an end with the close of the 27-years War. The ruin of all empires is subsumed under that of Athens.

I. 23. 1–3 is the inevitable and fitting summary of the scheme of history which Thucydides has developed throughout the *Archaeology*. Civilization is the creation of power and is splendid and admirable, but it inevitably ends in its own destruction, so much so that this destruction is virtually the measure of its greatness. And all this is a pattern which Thucydides finally worked out *after* the defeat of Athens in 404, and it expresses his personal experience.

But some questions remain. Is the process absolutely inevitable? And if so, how are we to regard the historian's presentation of

14. Cf. Gomme, *Historical Commentary on Thucydides*, I (Oxford 1945), p. 134.

Pericles and Pericles' policy? And how does Sparta fit into the scheme?

The answer to the first question seems to be *yes*. For one thing, Thucydides has Pericles himself say so in a beautiful passage from his last speech, II. 64. 3:

> Know that Athens has the greatest name among all men because she does not yield to disasters, because she has expended most labor and lost most lives in war, because she has acquired the greatest power in all history; and the memory of that power will be left eternally to succeeding generations, even if we should now sometime give way; it is the nature of all things to decline. They will remember that as Greeks we ruled over most Greeks, that we fought against others singly and all together in the greatest wars, and that we had the city richest in all things, and the greatest.

Δύναμις – μεγίστη – πόλεμος – μέγιστος – ἐλασσοῦσθαι – μνήμη (a memory only) – μεγίστη: here we have all the essential elements of the Thucydidean scheme, and expressed by the statesman who, Thucydides tells us in the next chapter, had such justified confidence in victory.

Other considerations too enforce this sense of inevitability. First the comparison with the Plague. Strong verbal echoes confirm our sense that the Plague is presented as a kind of concentrated image of the War.

The word ἐπιπεσεῖν, *to fall upon violently*, which is used of the Plague (II. 48. 3), is used again of the inevitable effects of war in the description of the revolution in Corcyra: 'things many and terrible befell the cities of Greece in the course of revolutions, things which happen and always will happen as long as the nature of man remains what it is' (III. 82. 2). And he uses in his description of the Plague the same word σκοπεῖν, *to discern*, that he had used in I. 22. 4 of his description of the whole War, where he expresses the hope that his work will be judged useful 'by those who shall want *to see clearly* what happened in the past and will by human necessity (κατὰ τὸ ἀνθρώπινον) happen in the same or in similar fashion in the future'. Of the Plague he says, in II. 84. 3, 'I shall confine myself to describing what it was like [instead of offering either explanation or cure], and to putting down such things as a man may use, if it should strike again, to *see it clearly*, and to recognize it for what it is.'

Finally, the connotations of Thucydides' basic terms imply the inevitability of the process his *History* describes. I have spoken already of his use of λόγος and ἔργον and of equivalent terms as a kind of fundamental metaphor in his historical presentation. I use the word *metaphor* advisedly, if we recall Aristotle's statement that the use of metaphor involves the perception of similarity in apparently dissimilar things. Following out his notion that the course of civilization and thereby of all history is man's imposing an intellectual order on the world outside him, Thucydides continually makes a division in his presentation of history between words meaning judgement or speech or intention, etc., and others meaning fact, thing, resource, power, etc.

On one side of the constantly repeated and endlessly varied opposition, we find e.g. λόγος, γνώμη, διάνοια, ἀκοή, ὄνομα, ἐλπίς, διδαχή, μέλλοντα; on the other, ἔργον, παρασκευή, μελέτη, δύναμις, βία, ἔρως, φύσις, ὄντα, παρόντα. The point of this whole terminological system is to present history as man's constant attempt to order the world about him by his intelligence. Each actor within the historical drama attempts to formulate, present and enforce his own interpretation of external events and situations. This is done in speeches, and accordingly Thucydides, in I. 22. 1–2, divides his whole work into 'what [the participants in the War] said *in speech*' (ὅσα λόγῳ εἶπον: λόγῳ dative singular of category) and 'the reality of what was done' (τὰ ἔργα τῶν πραχθέντων). But both of these as seen from Thucydides' own point of view are past actions and hence both fall under the heading of αὐτὰ τὰ ἔργα of the War at the end of the preceding chapter. And the λόγος that matches αὐτὰ τὰ ἔργα, in its widest sense of all actions and speeches in the War, is, of course, Thucydides' own *History*.

Of all the words on the fact–external reality side of the opposition, ἔργον is by far the most common and has the widest range of meaning. It is a fundamental Greek word and means anything *wrought* or *done*, *work* being its obvious cognate. Thus it can mean *deeds of war* (the Homeric πολεμήια ἔργα), or, very commonly in Thucydides, a *battle*, or the whole business of a war, as in I. 23. 1, where he begins τῶν δὲ προτέρων ἔργων, and then continues τούτου δὲ τοῦ πολέμου; or 1. 80. 1, where Archidamus, urging the Spartans to caution, says that he and his contemporaries have too much experience of wars for anyone to long to be in one: ὥστε ἐπιθυμῆσαί τινα τοῦ ἔργου.

But then there is a slightly different direction in the meaning of ἔργον, whereby it stands for *fact, reality*, the thing that was *actually done*. This is the nuance of meaning that makes it appropriate for the common fifth-century idiom wherein λόγος and ἔργον are distinguished: 'He *says* such and such, but *actually*...' Some of this stretch of meaning is in the English word *deed*. We can speak of 'deeds of war' and at the same time have an adverb *indeed*; and the sinister nursery rhyme 'A Man of Words and not of Deeds' joins the two meanings. The man does not perform deeds and in some way he lacks reality.

So Thucydides, by using the word ἔργον in a great variety of contexts, and in associating with it, by a series of antitheses, other words such as δύναμις and πόλεμος, is indicating, building the notion into the structure of his language, that power and war are simply aspects of reality. War is the final reality. There can be no civilization, no complex of power without war, because the one word implies the other.

If it be objected that I am playing a word-game here, the answer is that it is Thucydides' own word-game, and that he uses it to express an interpretation of history that he makes explicit in other ways as well.

The other unanswered questions are the role of Pericles and that of Sparta. They can be answered together. Throughout the *History*, Thucydides presents the Athenian character as dominated by λόγος and the Spartan character as dominated by ἔργον. In two Spartan speeches, those of Archidamus and Sthenelaidas in book 1 (80–5 and 86) and in one Corinthian speech, that at the Second Congress in Lacedaemon, also in book 1 (120–4), the Spartans and their allies are characterized as distrusting the intellect and putting their faith in fact. 'We are trained to believe', Archidamus says in 84. 3, 'that the chances of war are not accessible to, cannot be predicted by, human reason' (οὐ λόγῳ διαιρετάς: the last word has interesting philosophic associations).[15] 'And so', he goes on, 'we put our faith in strict

15. Cf. Diels, *Fragmente der Vorsokratiker*, III, s.v.

discipline' (μελέτας 85. 1). Sthenelaidas is more brutal: τοὺς μὲν λόγους τοὺς πολλοὺς τῶν 'Αθηναίων οὐ γιγνώσκω, he begins in 86. 1. He means (a) 'I choose to ignore the protracted speech of the Athenians in defence of their Empire', and (b) 'As a Spartan I reject the use of speech and reason and urge immediate recourse to fact; that is, to war.'

By contrast the Athenians and Pericles in particular urge that reason is the indispensable preliminary to action. 'We differ from other men', Pericles says in II. 40. 2, in the Funeral Speech, 'by not believing words harmful to action, but rather that harm lies in not working out beforehand in words what must actually be carried out.' As everywhere in his great speech, Pericles worries the distinction for all it is worth. The Athenians' τέχνη and ἐπιστήμη, intellectual words, are several times contrasted with the Spartans' μελέτη and ἀλκή, words of institution or instinct. The contrasted speeches of the Peloponnesian generals and of Phormio in II. 87ff. are another good example of such contrast.

The implications of this much-elaborated opposition between the two national characters are something like this. Inasmuch as civilization is the successful imposition of intelligence on the brute matter of the outside world, Athens, not Sparta, represents civilization. The Athenians in fact are the moving force throughout the *History*. They, from the moment they followed Themistocles at the time of the Persian Wars and took to their ships – this itself an act of the creative intelligence: I. 18. 2 διανοηθέντες ἐκλιπεῖν τὴν πόλιν καὶ...ἐς τὰς ναῦς ἐσβάντες – from that moment on it is they who have created an Empire far greater than those of Minos and Agamemnon. It is they who have changed the map and the character of Greece. They, in the formation of history, are a sort of second cause alongside of intelligence, as Plato, in the *Timaeus* (47e 2f.), added Necessity or the Wandering Cause to the Demiurgic Mind. They are that incommensurate, irrational factor in reality which makes it sure that ultimately you can never win; what corresponds in the large scheme of history to what Thucydides calls παράλογος, that which the keenest intelligence cannot foresee.

In Thucydides' scheme therefore, there is only one civilization in 431 B.C., that of Athens. Its power, created by intelligence, inevitably becomes war: 'As the Athenians became great, the Spartans were compelled to war' (I. 23. 6), and eventually this war destroys the civilization that brought it about. The Spartans are merely the external agents of this destruction. Pericles is the essence of Athenian intelligence. The word constantly attached to him is γνώμη. He is that aspect of intelligence which will not yield to the pressures of external reality. The reason the Athenians could have won the war if they had followed his judgement throughout is that this judgement is presented as transcending the vicissitudes of actual events. 'I continue to hold to the same conception (γνώμη),[16] citizens of Athens, not to yield to the Peloponnesians...' So begins his first speech, the first words he speaks in the *History*.

The same assertion of unwavering judgement in the face of the παράλογοι of reality dominates Pericles' last speech after the Plague. In general, men's conceptions, and the words they use to express them, vary with events, and alter with every alteration they find. Pericles alone is above this, and hence Thucydides attributes to him an almost superhuman judgement, which he asserts could have carried the Empire through to victory if the Athenians, who to Pericles are part of the recalcitrant matter of history, had been able to follow it.

It may fairly be objected that Thucydides has no right to insist on the inevitability of the fall of empire on the one hand and on the invincibility of Periclean policy on the other. It is the great paradox of his work and a point where his system seems to break down. Two considerations should modify this criticism. One is the peculiar nature of the Athenian Empire as Thucydides has Pericles conceive it. The Athenians do not merely use sea-power to build their realm: they become almost entirely identified with sea-power: they 'became nautical'. Inasmuch as sea-power is especially the creation of the intelligence, we have here a vision of the Athenian Empire as pure product of the mind, and consequently inaccessible to those elements in the world which the mind cannot control. 'Consider', Pericles tells his countrymen in his First Speech (i. 143. 5), 'if we were islanders, who could be more safe from the enemy?... You must *approach this conception* as close as possible, and let your homes and lands go'.[17] This vision of Athens

16. E.g., i. 140. 1; ii. 12. 2; ii. 34. 6; ii. 43. 3; ii. 59. 2 (comments on Periclean γνώμη by implication); ii. 62. 5 (possibly the most revealing instance); ii. 65. 8.
17. ὅτι ἐγγύτατα τούτου διανοηθέντας. Cf. i. 18. 2, οἱ Ἀθηναῖοι διανοηθέντες ἐκλιπεῖν τὴν πόλιν καὶ...ἐς τὰς ναῦς ἐσβάντες and cf. n. 13 above.

as a power so completely created by the intellect as to be proof against the waywardness of reality is almost fantastic; and yet perhaps true to the historical Pericles' own imagination.

The second consideration is deeper. It is the foreknowledge of Athens' defeat which Thucydides attributes to Pericles in his Last Speech. There the historian suggests that there is a valid sense in which it does not matter whether Athens falls or not, because the quality of her memory will remain; and that Pericles was clearly aware of this sense.[18] As conception in the present becomes fact in the past, so fact in the past, in this case the uniqueness of Athenian power at one moment of history, stays alive in the present as concept. In this way, Periclean Athens does escape the grim system which Thucydides develops as the intellectual foundation of his narrative. Because Athens under Pericles remains an ineffaceable image in the mind, the city is truly invincible, and to fix this image is precisely the purpose of Thucydides' account.

18. Esp. II. 64. 3, the great expression of imperial heroism. The same note is struck in II. 43. 3, where some of the language, especially ἀνδρῶν γὰρ ἐπιφανῶν πᾶσα γῆ τάφος is rhythmical, metaphorical and lapidary to a degree that, historically or not, distinguishes Pericles from other speakers in the *History*, and sounds almost like a quotation. The prophetic element in these and other passages of Pericles' last two speeches has been judged obviously anachronistic by scholars like Kakridis (*Der thukydideische Epitaphios* (München 1961), pp. 5f., etc.). We shall never know what Pericles really said on such occasions. But it does not seem to me impossible that he said something like what Thucydides has attributed to him. Shall we confidently deny Pericles both foresight and a tragic sense of life? If Kakridis and others are right, they must not only reject the historicity of these statements in the text as a document; they must also find no verisimilitude in the text as a dramatic work.

The psychoanalysis of Pentheus in the *Bacchae* of Euripides*

WILLIAM SALE

I. INTRODUCTION

MY PURPOSE here is to analyze Pentheus, not to discuss the *Bacchae* as a whole. But the psychoanalytic critic suffers from a questionable reputation, and should welcome the chance to show that his credentials as a man of taste, if not as a scholar, are reasonably well in order. Necessity offers that chance, for a few preliminary remarks on the nature of Dionysus are vital to any analysis of Pentheus, psychoanalytic or otherwise; perhaps while making them I shall be able to give some reassurance as to my own literary sanity. After that I want to go through each of the Pentheus scenes as if it were a session on the couch; then a look at one of the case-histories in the psychoanalytical journals may enable us to reconstruct a life-history of Pentheus' illness. I am not threatening to present a completely unfamiliar play: the reader will have to decide whether I have used the facts of another man's life and another man's illness to illuminate or to strait-jacket the life and illness of Pentheus. But the hard evidence I use will all be taken from the play. If there is disagreement – and I have yet to encounter the psychological interpretation that won much initial favor – it will be over how to interpret what is in the play, not over my dragging in hypotheses from outside that have the approval of famous names in psychiatry. To take an example from elsewhere – I do not think it rash to say that Hippolytus despises sex because an illicit sexual act made him into a social anomaly, a bastard; and I think I can therefore understand better why he withdraws from normal society. But though his bastardy and withdrawal are in the play, to put them together requires our hypo-

---

* This article was originally given as a lecture to the Yale Classical Club on 6 November 1969, and has been only slightly altered. Protracted discussion of sources and the opinions of others has therefore been eschewed, and the style remains somewhat informal. My best thanks for the criticisms of Adam Parry.

thesizing scenes in Hippolytus' formative life to which we are not privy. In Pentheus' case such formative events can be extracted from what we see, if only we may take certain natural interpretative liberties. After I have finished taking those liberties, I shall say a few words to urge again that there is more to the play than Pentheus' neurosis and madness, that he is but one instance of how not to come to terms with Dionysus.

For there is no doubt that Dionysus is a living reality. As Otto puts it: 'The elemental depths gape open, and out of them a monstrous creature raises its head...the god himself. All earthly powers are united in him: the generating, nourishing, intoxicating rapture; and the searing pain, the deathly pallor, the speechless night of having been.'[1] That seems to me a pretty good description, except that Otto adds that when we see the monster we necessarily go mad; I don't believe this of the Euripidean Dionysus. The latter is no *mainomenos*, no mad god, nor are his true worshipers, the Lydian chorus, *mainomenai*. Madness does not arise from *seeing* Dionysus, but from rejecting that vision: from saying, I do not want to die, I do not want to live. Sanity results from confrontation: from saying, I see that life and death are a single terrible joyous thing, and I am willing to live. A little less metaphysically: we need to know that we are animals who belong to the animal world, and we need to know this, not as a biological and abstract fact but as an experiential and emotional fact. We must meet our animality face-to-face, as a kind of Thou, and talk to it and give it a name – Dionysus. Of course there are many people in the world who never do this, and yet survive. They are the Cadmuses, who admit that they are animals but who do not know it; they go through the motions of life, but when they gaze at the wilderness or talk to each other or make love, they are never wholly *there*. Cadmus in our play was fortunate – Dionysus made him learn his animality in the most violent way, by turning him into a serpent. Most Cadmuses, like most Jasons, go on as they are, getting away with their puny lives, never falling, never feeling, waiting for something or striving for it, not knowing that the ultimate something is death, never opening their eyes to life – never seeing in the depths of the bestiality we all share the sole possibility of being alive.

1. W. F. Otto, *Dionysus* (Bloomington 1965), pp. 140–1.

But the *Bacchae* is not mainly about Cadmus, about the drifters and equivocators. Rather it is about a man who fights Dionysus with all his being, conscious and unconscious – except that portion of his being which is Dionysus. It is Pentheus whom we must come to understand. First, one precaution: if we are to believe in Pentheus and his fate, we must of course discount the possibility that anything that happens to him is miraculous, just as we discount the miraculous in the *Hippolytus*. We see or hear of bulls that arise from the sea, palaces that collapse and giant fir-trees that bend; I don't think these happenings command literal belief, nor does our incredulity ruin the plays. Dionysus is the Thou of life and death – he *is* the natural, not the supernatural. Pentheus is a real man, real in all his parts; if we believe in the play, we must believe that what happens to him is natural. The central fact about Pentheus is illness and madness. He is sick from the moment we first see him: as Tiresias says: ἡ δὲ δόξα νοσῇ, 'your thoughts are sick' (311). And again: μαίνῃ γὰρ ὡς ἄλγιστα νοσεῖς, 'you are desperately sick, sick unto madness' (326–7). This makes him a logical candidate for psychoanalysis.

II. PENTHEUS ON THE COUCH

When Pentheus comes to his first session he immediately offers us a fantasy to explore; speaking of the Bacchae on the mountains, he says:

> And in the midst of their reveling bands, bowls stand
> Filled with wine, and one after another they
> Creep to lonely places, serve the lusts of men...
> Aphrodite they put ahead of the Bacchic god (221–5).

We are right to call this fantasy, since we know that it is not merely untrue, but groundless. We have just been assured by Dionysus and Tiresias that the women are alone on Cithaeron; Pentheus himself has just stressed that the women, specifically, have gone away; what men are available to satisfy those female lusts, at least in the abundance which Pentheus' morbidity imagines? The fantasy reflects unconscious desire, as Wilamowitz, Zieliński and Dodds all agree;[2] but while these gentlemen suggest that the wish is libidinal, I prefer greater caution and perhaps greater subtlety.

2. See E. R. Dodds, ed., *Bacchae*, 2 ed. (Oxford 1960), pp. 97–8.

By asserting that the women put Aphrodite ahead of Dionysus, Pentheus is saying, in a confused way, that they are up to no good. I use the word 'confused' because, according to the strict logic of his anti-Bacchic stance, he ought perhaps to be applauding them for putting the familiar Greek goddess Aphrodite ahead of this dirty foreigner. But it is just such confusions that psychiatrists legitimately pounce upon. If Aphrodite is the real culprit, then what upsets Pentheus about Dionysus is Dionysus' sexual side.

Similarly in lines 260–2:

> When the gleam of the grape appears at the feasts of *women*,
> I say there's nothing healthy any longer in their *orgia*.

Why? Pentheus is no temperance crusader; he takes no stand against wine as such. Clearly it is what wine will do to this disgusting female sex that troubles him: it will encourage their nastiness, and off they will slink, the readier to serve the lusts of men.

But Pentheus is not a man to deplore passively whatever he finds disgusting and nasty; if the *orgia* are unhealthy, Pentheus will heal them. The cure, of course, is violence, arms, imprisonment:

> All the ones I caught, my servants bound their hands
> And keep them inside common prison walls.
> Those that escaped, I'll hunt them on the mountains (226–8).

Now he can't indulge his taste for violence, clearly, unless he can persuade himself that the women are misbehaving: his prurient fantasy, therefore, is framed as an excuse, an excuse for hunting and catching and binding. He is not saying: 'Let those women be making love up there so that I can join them and make love too' – not even unconsciously. He does say later, 'Let them be making love so that I can *watch*', but right now the motive is, 'so that I can punish'. He wants to attack women. It follows that he is angry with women as well as disturbed by sex, and seeks this justification for assaulting them because they are engaged in it. But – it may be objected – but perhaps all he wants to do is punish an improper indulgence; to which the reply is, 'Who, besides Pentheus, thinks that anyone is improperly indulging?'

These vigorous and inappropriately savage feelings, though chiefly directed towards sex and women, are not confined to them. Pentheus has heard that a Lydian stranger has come to town and is enticing young women with his promises of Bacchic joys. Perhaps we should not attempt to weigh this charge; Pentheus says that this is what he heard, and he may have. But the charge is false, at least in its sexual implications; and it is false in precisely the same way as the charge he has neurotically hurled at the Theban women on Cithaeron. The only way to deal with such a sexual criminal, says Pentheus, is to behead him – or rather, to cut his neck away from his body (241). 'Neck' is an odd word to use – *trachelos*, used also of neck-like objects – and I think the psychiatrist may be forgiven for analyzing Pentheus' accusation as, 'He has committed sexual crimes – castrate him!' This Lydian stranger, whether a candidate for castration or for decapitation, must now face other charges: he has been going about calling Dionysus a god and saying that he was stitched into Zeus' thigh. 'Don't', asks Pentheus, 'don't these things deserve hanging?' Do they? Are all religious fanatics to be hanged? I doubt whether anyone will be eager to defend Pentheus with the analogy of the accusers of Socrates. Then, shocked at seeing Cadmus and Tiresias dressed as Bacchants, he storms at and threatens the seer and strikes the thyrsus from his grandfather's hand. We shall see this sort of ir-rational brutality again; it has run through Pentheus' life since early boyhood, when he would stroke his grandfather's beard and say:

> Who has done you wrong, who dishonored you?
> Tell me – I'll punish the criminal (1320–2).

Pentheus' first session has been rich in information, information from which the natural psychiatric inferences would be that he hates sex because he fears it, that he hates women because he fears them, that the rage which searches for opportunity to explode is closely associated with a deep-seated fear of sex within himself. But these are hypotheses only; we don't know enough yet.

Pentheus' second session – his first dialogue with Dionysus – gives us material we have seen before: the tendency to see the Stranger as a sexual being exclusively, and to derogate him for it (455–9); the indulgence in various forms of violence (493–514); the search for excuse for punishment (489). He says that Dionysus' hair is a token of lewdness, and therefore he cuts it off; he strikes the thyrsus from his hand, just as he had struck it from Cadmus'; he sends him off to prison: 'Dance there, in the shadows of the dark!' New is Dionysus' charge:

> You do not yet know what you are saying, nor what you
> are doing, nor who you are (506, as emended by Dodds).

To which Pentheus replies with external credentials: I am Pentheus (that is my label), child of Agave and Echion. Of course a Greek would find it quite natural to identify himself by his family, but not in response to such a charge as Dionysus has just leveled. I take the god's words in their simplest meaning: you don't know what your own inner nature is, nor what your words and actions mean. When Pentheus replies, 'My name is Pentheus', he only makes Dionysus seem all the more justified. I don't mean merely that there are certain deeply hidden desires that Pentheus is not conscious of; I mean that he has no sense of his identity, of the meaning of his actions, of the purport of his words.

When next we see Pentheus, much has happened, and since he himself does not describe it for us we must take it as Dionysus presents it. There is lightning, there is earthquake; part of the palace falls; Pentheus tries to tie up a bull and slash to death a phantom Dionysus; and yet when he comes back on stage, the only thing he says is that his prisoner has escaped. 'How do you come to be outside,' he asks, 'having broken my fetters' – as if he had made no attempt to stab Dionysus *after* he had broken away and *before* he emerged from the house. I do not infer with Verrall[3] and the young Norwood[4] that none of these things actually happened: they are as realistic, and as unrealistic, as anything else in the play. They are not imitations of the probable; they are not the mirror held up to nature. They are thus to be understood symbolically. The question is, Symbolic of what? And the answer to that question is likely to arouse antagonism, no matter what the answer is – no two people can be counted on to agree on the meaning of any symbol save the most simple and trivial. I would not expect to outrage anyone if I were to suggest timidly that the earthquake and the lightning symbolize the very real power of unleashed animal nature. Nor is it likely to be alarming to hear that such power is all the greater after it has been repressed: if we co-operate with Dionysus, he will be kindly and gentle, or at least not savage; if we try to subdue him, he will recoil vehemently. But to assert that these remarks about Dionysus correspond to *psycho-*

3. A. W. Verrall, *The Bacchants of Euripides* (Cambridge 1910), pp. 64–81.
4. Gilbert Norwood, *The Riddle of the Bacchae* (Manchester 1908), pp. 37–48.

logical reality may awaken some discomfort. And to go on to say that in this scene 'Pentheus is performing the futile task of constraining the animal Dionysus within himself' invites the accusation that I have found words to suit my own psychoanalytic theories – unless, of course, the words are recognized as belonging not to myself but to Winnington-Ingram.[5] I know that these words do not command instant acceptance, because Dodds has dismissed them as 'oversubtle';[6] but I still think them persuasive. When Pentheus tells Dionysus to dance in the shadowy darkness of his stable-prison, I interpret this as a relegation of the Dionysian within Pentheus to Pentheus' own unconscious. When Dionysus says that Pentheus 'fed upon his hopes' (617) I take that to mean that what he hopes to do is bind and assault his own animality. When Dionysus bursts forth, and the palace is cracked, I take this to mean that the prison of Pentheus' mind is torn asunder by this impossible attempt. And when Pentheus shows no awareness of what has happened, I take this to mean that all has occurred in the dark regions of the unconscious, in those deeper elements of the self that emerge, as Plato says, chiefly in dreams.[7]

Such an interpretation should not appear very startling. No one would deny that Pentheus wants to curb animality in other people – that has been his chief activity on stage so far. Would such a man not also want to curb it in himself? Perhaps not, if he were a sexual megalomaniac, who wants to reserve all sex for himself, to hoard it. But whatever else may be wrong with him, Pentheus seems to have not the slightest trace of *this* symptom. At one point Dodds himself refers to the palace as a fantasy-castle.[8] And where do fantasies occur, if not in one's own mind?

We can all agree, I think, that the bull that Pentheus tries to tie up is a symbol for masculinity – *somebody's* masculinity. Does this mean that it stands for aggression, force, power? A bull would certainly work as such a symbol. But it has not been characteristic of Pentheus to try to curb anyone's aggressiveness – it is sexuality and the folly of old men that he hopes to restrain. If Winnington-Ingram is right, and this bull is Pentheus' own animality, then it is his own sexuality; certainly not his aggressiveness, which has

5. R. P. Winnington-Ingram, *Euripides and Dionysus* (Cambridge 1935), p. 84.
6. Dodds, p. 154.
7. Plato, *Republic* IX 571C.   8. Dodds, p. 156, lines 638–9.

been allowed to run rampant from the start. Similarly, when Pentheus slashes away at the phantom Dionysus, I see this as an effort to kill his own libido, to castrate himself psychically. Both here and earlier, he is so vehement, so bull-like, in what he undertakes; he seems to want to say, 'I am a man'. Yet in choosing his sexuality as his target, he seems to want to say, 'I am not a man'. Surely this is why Dionysus tells him that he doesn't know who he is: can you know who you are, if you don't know what sex you belong to?

No good psychoanalyst will allow his symbolic interpretations to go unverified, just as no polite literary critic ought to force them down his audience's throat. Is there any other evidence that Pentheus wants to repudiate his own masculinity? We may note that at the end of the first session we conjectured that Pentheus was deeply afraid of sex within himself. His morbid anxiety over what he imagines women to do when they let themselves go suggests that he is really anxious over what he himself might do, if he were to let himself go. But that was a conjecture, and we shall not use one conjecture to verify another. We shall wait, and if we see Pentheus vigorously asserting his maleness in a healthy way, we shall revise our views.

Pentheus begins what we might somewhat arbitrarily call his fourth session – the prison scene was the third – by listening to a long account of how arms cannot prevail against the Bacchae and immediately issuing a call to arms. Women are powerful: armies must be mustered. Now women *are* powerful – that is an objective fact which our play goes to some lengths to emphasize. But it also emphasizes that physical force is no way to meet that power, and that proposition too, I think, is entirely reasonable. But Pentheus is not reasonable. His infantile fantasies propose savagery, soldiers, swords. In such a spirit he rejects all of Dionysus' pleas. 'Bring me my arms, and *you* stop talking.' Suddenly Dionysus offers the challenge: would you like to *see* them? And against the surge of this temptation Pentheus yields at once – nothing would please him better. All critics of the play agree that Dionysus is now beginning to take over Pentheus' soul. But some seem to regard the god as imposing from outside a madness that has nothing to do with what Pentheus has been all along. This, I submit, is altogether un-Greek and impossible. Dodds himself says that 'the poet shows us the supernatural...working upon and through nature...the persecutor is betrayed by what he would persecute – the Dionysiac longing *in himself*'.[9] I would put it a little differently; I would say that the Dionysiac longing is sexual, and that it is bursting forth in the form of *voyeurism*. Dionysus is not to be resisted forever. He will emerge. But Pentheus cannot let him emerge as normal sex. We are watching a phenomenon that has all the signs of *dementia praecox*: the crumbling away of the personality and its defenses through a violent assault of libidinal feeling in the face of a situation, a temptation with which the individual simply cannot cope. The madness, the breakdown, has already begun when Pentheus cried out, bring me my armor! This is an impossible solution, and is immediately relinquished in favor of the voyeuristic wish, which is a compromise. It allows him to join the company of the Bacchae, not as a friendly fellow reveler, but as a hostile spy. At the same time it gives some scope, not dangerous, to his sexuality. Those lewd acts in which the women are engaged – he cannot participate, that would be too threatening. But he can watch it happen, and get his satisfaction vicariously.

But to look, he must first dress as a woman. This he resists at first: *aidos* restrains me (828). A most suggestive remark! Only *aidos* is holding him back; otherwise... He wavers – 'I cannot' – but the alternative is bloodshed, and his resistance gives way at once. Either fight with women, then, or dress like one. He cannot fight – women are too powerful for that; so he becomes a transvestite, a compromise female. The obvious alternative is not available to him – behave towards them as a grown man behaves towards women, with strength and tenderness.

After Pentheus has left the fourth session, Dionysus tells the chorus that if he were sane, he would not be willing to put on women's clothes (851–2). This remark has, I think, been more responsible than any other in the play for throwing readers off the track. It is almost invariably taken to mean that Pentheus' transvestism can be discounted as a manifestation of his character – it is the imposition of an external Dionysus, who wants him to be the laughing-stock of Thebes. But although Dionysus says that this is what he wants, I quite agree with Dodds in feeling that as a motive it is very weak.[10] Certainly if Dionysus hoped that this

9. Dodds, p. 172.   10. Dodds, p. 181.

would happen, he was disappointed; we hear not a word of any laughter, any mockery, any shame. Nor can the true motive be disguise – Pentheus is willing to go openly, which would fit Dionysus' destructive designs perfectly well. It is not as if Pentheus were planning to join the Bacchants.

In fact Dionysus warns us away from looking on the female clothing as disguise by *saying* that it is part of Pentheus' madness. In his former state, which was sick but not psychotic, Pentheus would never have done this. Transvestism, therefore, is not pragmatism, but pathology. And we have no right to say that it has nothing to do with Pentheus' previous character. You might as well say that Ajax' slaughtering of the sheep had nothing to do with Ajax – *he*, at least, didn't think that. No, madness may be excited from outside, but it is the expression of ourselves – and let us remember that Dionysus is inside as well as outside, that he is the totality of animal nature wherever it is found. Let us also remember that Euripides knew transvestites, that the phenomenon was no doubt far more familiar to him that to editors of the *Bacchae*. We need only think of the *Thesmophoriazusae*. All this is borne out in the next, the fifth session. Pentheus has entered his role with enthusiasm: he asks coyly whether he looks like Ino or Agave; he worries about his dress as any lady might – 'Is my blouse buttoned? Is my slip showing?' (934–8). Now we were seeking, a few moments ago, to see whether there would be any more signs of Pentheus' repudiating his masculinity. Surely he has done this, and in a most spectacular fashion.

But having seen our hypotheses confirmed, we must now tread warily; for Pentheus has not entirely assimilated himself to the female. He has not actually castrated himself. He continues to use the masculine form of the participles (e.g. 930–1): in his fancy he is both male and female. In fact he walks on stage seeing double: there are two suns in the sky, two cities of Thebes, and he himself is double (918–21). He says, 'I am not a man', but does not go all the way – or as far as he might – towards becoming a woman; he says, 'I am a woman', but keeps his grammar masculine. He sees a bull – the male is projected safely outside himself, an external being (922); but of course there is no real bull there, and the male is still really inside. He has joined the hated, powerful sex in order to neutralize it, but he keeps his penis. There is a special pathos in line 962:

I am the only *man* of them who dares to do this.

We can conclude that Pentheus has powerful urges towards castration, that such urges must lie near the root of his constantly expressed hostility towards sex; but in the very depths of his being he still keeps his penis, and still hopes to use it.

At the end of the session he yearns to come home from the mountains carried in his mother's arms – in a half-line dialogue with Dionysus, the god half-supplying his thoughts, he comes closer and closer to his heart's desire, to be a little boy again in his mother's arms – to be one with the mother, not a separate thing, and therefore female; but to be still a little boy, and therefore male (966–70).

The sixth session takes place on the mountain, and we are invited to play once more the uncomfortable game of symbolic analysis. As in the prison scene, here too we are confronted with the miraculous, the unrealistic: the fir-tree bends down, Pentheus climbs aboard, and the tree grows erect again without displacing its passenger. Surely we have a right to ask a few questions:

1. Why does the poet set Pentheus on top of a fir-tree, only to have him come tumbling down again? There are any number of more straightforward ways of putting Pentheus into the harsh clutches of the Bacchae.

2. If he must be on a fir-tree, why not have him climb it? He himself has complained that he cannot see. Why not tell him to go climb a tree? Why have Dionysus bend it down? Why have him re-erect it? For the sake of the supernatural? But that is precisely what we neither expect nor want: Dionysus is animal nature; is not, fundamentally, and in everyday reality, a supernatural being. Wilamowitz, in despair, says that all this happens to give Dionysus something to do.[11] Dodds says, No, it is a traditional element of the story, very likely a reflex of primitive ritual.[12] I would like to have been present at that ritual, in which great untouched fir-trees were made to bend down and rise up gently, without shaking off their riders, and then were torn up by the roots.

3. Why are the women unsuccessful in pelting Pentheus, or in

11. Wilamowitz, *Textgeschichte der griechischen Bukoliker* (Berlin 1906), p. 214.
12. Dodds, p. 209, on 1058–75.

prising up the tree with makeshift crowbars? Why must they pluck up the tree – at Agave's instigation?

It is my guess that the supernatural aspects of this scene are symbolic, and I am sure the reader has already guessed at what I think they symbolize. The rising fir-tree is an erection, a display of the penis that Pentheus would not relinquish; the uprooting is his mother's emblematic castration of that penis. We see in this scene very much what we have been seeing all through the play: a man who in the deepest recesses of his soul wants to be a male – that is the erecting fir-tree – but who is constantly repressing, constantly suffering castration – that is the tree uprooted. But we are also seeing something else: it is not Pentheus who is ultimately responsible for his emasculation – it is his mother. She is a castrating woman; Pentheus' self-emasculation, indeed his whole anti-sexual stance, can all be understood in the light of this one fact. Pentheus displays himself sexually, Agave turns on him savagely. Naturally he will be terrified of sex; naturally he will be terrified of women. Mother has taught him that sex is dirty; mother has taught him to reject his penis, to be like her. Yet at the same time he will be bitterly angry with her for turning on him, for castrating him, and angry with all women, since they threaten to cause him to expose himself and be humiliated.

This means that our psychoanalytic approach does nothing to alter the emotions everyone has always felt during the course of the play: we begin by disliking Pentheus and end with powerful sympathy. His last words are:

> Look, mother, I am your child,
> Pentheus; you gave me birth in Echion's house.
> Pity me, mother; don't kill your child
> Just because of the bad things I did (1118–21).

The cry of a frightened little boy. Think of those earlier, fatuous threats to take arms against women, women who are so powerful; then think of these very words I have just quoted, shouted out to the huge, terrifying mother: pathos and horror are what we feel now, horror over the savagery of Agave, pathos over the helplessness of the little boy caught in her grip. The dramatic breakdown of Pentheus' psyche has brought us back close to the beginning of Pentheus' life – and to the very beginning of the illness which in this scene is costing him his life.

III. PENTHEUS AND MR P.

We have failed as doctors – we have allowed our patient to die. But perhaps we can make partial restitution by reconstructing the course of his disease. To do that, it is sensible to go to the psycho-analytic literature, not in the hopes of finding another Pentheus, because each patient is unique, but in the hopes of finding analogies. If a number of Pentheus' symptoms occur in conjunction elsewhere, we shall feel happier about claiming that they cohere naturally in his personality. If some of these symptoms seem to develop one from another – if as a whole they can be traced back to certain crucial events – then perhaps we can reconstruct the life history of Pentheus' disease along parallel lines. I don't know how close we could get were we to scour the journals from beginning to end, but a quite cursory search gives us the useful Mr P.[13] I have no idea whether that initial is indeed his; I have chosen it in such a way as to forestall any psychoanalytic guesswork on the reader's part – Mr P. gets his initial from Pentheus.

Mr P. had spent his childhood in a world of women, an elder sister and a powerful mother. His father, a truckdriver, was peripheral, either shouting ineffectually, or simply not there at all. His mother and sister he felt to be masculine, and in his fantasies he supplied them both with penises. They in turn were overtly hostile, or at least threatening, to his own masculinity: he has one vivid memory from the age of 4 of their dressing him in one of his sister's slips; his mother shared her bath with him until he was 12; his sister and he slept in the same bed and played with each other, but if he got an erection she would slap him and say, 'You're a girl, you're a girl.' Like almost every boy he had castration anxieties: these come naturally when the boy discovers that women don't have penises, and he wonders if he must give up his own; such anxieties are strengthened when he finds in his father a rival for his mother's love. In the course of normal development these feelings are overcome through the reassurance that both his parents love him, and through the boy's gradually developing capacity to be like his father, to identify with him and thus come to feel that he

13. Murray Lewis, 'A Case of Transvestism', *International Journal of Psychoanalysis* (1964), 345–51.

too may keep his penis. But Mr P.'s father wasn't there, and his mother and sister seemed to be saying, 'Don't be like father, be like us.' Hence he had to cope with his castration anxieties in less healthy ways.

In the face of all this, one side of Mr P. developed a powerful yearning for maternal symbiosis – to be *with* mother and sister, to be like mother, and even, it appears, to be his mother's missing penis. As the years went by, he turned increasingly to secret transvestism, a symptom which allowed him to handle no fewer than three different problems:

First, it pleased his mother, at least in his fantasy, because she seemed to want him to be like her. In fact she would no doubt have been overtly disturbed had she seen Mr P., as an adolescent or an adult, actually dressed as a woman; but if she could have been honest with herself, she would have had to admit that this was precisely the sort of behavior that she had been encouraging in her son all along.

Second, it alleviated castration anxiety. Just how this worked is not entirely clear from the article, because the doctor wants to juggle two theories, and his patient apparently didn't turn up enough material to permit him to make a decisive choice between them.

The first theory is that transvestism anticipates castration. Mr P. had seemingly wanted to shout – either to mother or to father – 'Don't castrate me, I'm only a girl.' Dressed as a girl, he could, in imagination, protest that he had already castrated himself, that there was no need for anyone else to bother.

The second theory starts from Mr P.'s fantasies, shared with many transvestites, which endowed his mother with a phallus. Such daydreams deny the possibility of castration, by a simple enough process of reasoning: 'If women have no phalluses, then they have been castrated. But that's too frightening for me, I won't have it that way. Therefore, women have phalluses.' Having worked this out, Mr P. was able to say, 'I can do what mother and sister want, and become a woman, without giving up my penis.'

Whichever of these theories is right, transvestism is a way of coping with castration feelings.

Finally, as a woman with a penis, he was now permitted to use it. Had he merely tried to display it as a part of a male body, even to himself, he would have been inviting castration, but if he dresses as a woman, he has either already castrated himself – on one of our theories – or has denied the possibility of castration – on the other – and can go ahead and masturbate. Thus through his transvestism he has rejected his masculinity but allowed himself sexuality.

Mr P. learned further, during the course of his treatment, that his own identity was very much involved with his penis, so that a threat to one was a threat to the other. This caused him to proceed to an entirely different symptom, to what for him were extravagant assertions of masculinity. He wore a crewcut and a leather jacket, bought a motorcycle, told the doctor, 'I am taller than you and my car is bigger'. He was aware that the crew cut, the jacket and the motorcycle were exceedingly irritating to his mother – no doubt they ran exactly counter to her covert wishes that he be feminine – and he came to see just how angry he was with his mother for forcing him to be a girl. He would go out with women, but only so long as he could regard them as objects, wherewith to flaunt his masculinity. As soon as they revealed personalities, he would abandon them.

Now let's see if this material can help us trace the psychological history of Pentheus. First off we notice that his childhood, like Mr P.'s, was spent in a world of women. At least we see no trace whatever of his father Echion – I defy any reader of the play to say a word about Echion except that he spawned Pentheus and then, so far as we know, vanished. The throne of Thebes was never his portion, but passed directly from Cadmus to Pentheus. Granted that Cadmus was around during Pentheus' childhood, it is never asserted that he functioned *in loco patris*.

Next, we note that Agave is masculine. In her madness she conceives of herself as a great hunter; she wants to please father – Cadmus – not through her femininity, but by being *like father*.

> Father, you can make the greatest boast: you sowed
> The most heroic daughters of them all (1233–4).

She makes it perfectly clear that her exploits as a hunter stand in contrast to her feminine pursuits:

> I left my shuttles by the looms, and came
> To greater things – the hunt of beast with hand (1236–7).

She must surely have been fiercely jealous of boys, for they could go off and hunt and do great exploits, and thereby please their fathers. Let us recall too why she is among the Bacchae on the mountains – she had repudiated Dionysus, animal nature (26–7), and with it doubtless her female being.

If she was jealous of men, and if she was hostile to sex, her feelings about her son's penis can be easily imagined: off with it! And if we have interpreted the death scene of Pentheus aright, that is just what she does: she goes through a symbolic castration of her son's erect penis. And now I must make a leap, and assume that what happened on the mountain had happened before, that Pentheus had once – shall we say – displayed his erect penis to his mother, as most little boys, after all, do do, and that she reacted to this gesture in anger and disgust. This would have left the boy Pentheus just as it leaves the man Pentheus in the moment before his death: terrified, desperately trying to shout his identity, faced with psychic death, the death of his willingness to be an animal, the death that he in fact suffers. Just so Mr P. was encouraged by his sister and mother to think that his penis made them angry or disgusted them; just so Mr P. cannot hold on to his sense of who he is in the face of the pressure applied by these powerful, frightening women.

One reaction, perhaps the most basic, to his terror, is to say, 'If only I were a baby again, safe in mother's arms!' This, of course, is what psychoanalysis calls regression: if there is trauma at one stage of development, it is obviously natural to try to go back to an earlier and safer stage. Mr P. wanted to be with his mother, to be part of her, as he confusedly imagines he was once. Similarly Pentheus hopes to be carried back to Thebes in his mother's arms, as if he were a little baby. I am aware that these hopes are expressed *before* the castration scene in our play; immediately before it, in fact. But just as I have taken the liberty of assuming that the castration scene, last in Pentheus' life, was the first in his illness, so now I take the liberty of assuming that the penultimate scene in Pentheus' life was the second in his illness, 'Mommy is angry with me now; I wish I were a little child in her arms again.'

But the boy Pentheus soon came to see that such hopes were not to be, and was driven to find other solutions. If we move one step further backwards in the play, we encounter transvestism; can we

assume that transvestism was the next step forward in Pentheus'
illness? It was that in the case of Mr P., though for Mr P. it remained the primary symptom, while in Pentheus' case we have to
assume that his transvestism, if it was ever acted out, was so no
longer as he grew up. That is no real drawback – it was waiting
there, so to speak, lurking in a corner of his psyche, to be acted out
when Dionysus called it forth. When it *is* acted out, it reveals itself
as the solution to three childhood problems – the same three that
poor Mr P. also confronted:

First, Pentheus can please his angry mother by being like
mother; let us recall lines 925–6:

> How then do I look? Don't I have the carriage
> Of Ino, or Agave, of my mother (μητρός γ' ἐμῆς)?

Second, Pentheus can alleviate the terrors of castration by
anticipating it, by looking like a woman, by pretending to be a
woman, as in 937–8:

> My pleats do seem askew, by the right foot, anyway.
> But on the other side the robe is straight along the ankle.

In doing this he attempts to thrust the masculine outside himself,
remember: καὶ ταῦρος ἡμῖν πρόσθεν: and you are a bull in front
of me (920).

Finally, Pentheus can allow some scope to the masculine, para-
doxically. He can go to the mountains and indulge his voyeurism –
compromise intercourse – and have his symbolic erection; he can
continue to use the masculine participles while acting like a
female; he can be μόνος ἀνὴρ τολμῶν, the only man who dares
(962).

It therefore makes sense to argue that the antepenultimate stage
in Pentheus' life is the third stage in the growth of his illness, that
transvestism is for him the natural efflorescence of the seeds of
disease which we have already assumed to have been sown. The
next step backwards in the play is unfortunately not echoed in
Mr P.'s life; we have no knowledge that he was a voyeur. Well, we
can't have everything. But what is important is that voyeurism
fits *Pentheus*. It gives him sexual gratification – that is to say, some
scope for the irresistible Dionysus – without compelling him to
expose his penis. And it gains him entry into the coveted world of
women, from which he has felt excluded ever since his mother

expressed horror at his exposed phallus. Just before experiencing that surge of voyeuristic feeling, Pentheus had been threatening to take arms against the Bacchae. His underlying reason for wanting to strike out at the women is his savage anger with Agave; but the fact that he should choose to use weapons expresses his neurotic fear of his mother's terrible strength.

The next scene in the play, moving backwards, is the prison scene. This corresponds to no particular stage of Pentheus' life. It expresses rather the condition Pentheus is in at any time after his initial crisis. He is always restraining the bull within himself, always slashing at his Dionysus image – constantly denying his masculinity, constantly trying to kill his animality. The same is true of Pentheus' uncertainty over his identity; it is not a stage, but a permanent resulting state. We should recall that Mr P. also repressed his masculinity, and that this also left him confused as to who he was.

We are now back at the beginning of the play, where Pentheus' behavior, like so much of Mr P.'s, is superficially hypermasculine. Pentheus does not wear a leather jacket nor sport a crewcut. Rather he blusters, pushes people around, and especially wants to make war on women. Obviously he does this because he is angry with them, just as Mr P. rode his motorcycle and cut his hair in order to irritate his mother. No sort of normal male attitude towards women exists for either man: if they are not trying to be like women, they are trying to behave in inappropriately masculine ways.

Let us be fair, and note another difference between our two patients. Mr P. is not reported to have thought sex a bad, a dirty thing, though he certainly never found it a satisfying one. Nor did Mr P. fantasize pruriently in order to act out his hatred of women. But that does not create difficulties for our understanding of Pentheus. We do not expect two people to be exactly alike; and where Pentheus differs the difference is easy to explain. Pentheus was naturally angry at his mother for her turning on him; he was probably also angry because he envied her her sex. But he wanted, deeply and passionately, to please mother and be like her. Anger with parents is generative of guilt in the best of us. Therefore if he is to let himself be angry, he must have an excuse, and this he gives himself by imagining that she is up to no good, that she is doing dirty things on the mountains. The beginning of the play gives us the last stage in the development of Pentheus' illness.

That is the history of our patient. When we first saw him, he was the finished, or at least the end, product of a pathological progression. As we go forward through the course of the play, three things happen:

First – Pentheus' defenses break down, in an orderly fashion, as he regresses further and further towards the initial traumatic scene with Agave. The range of symptoms displayed can all be traced back to that one scene, the last of his life, the first in his sickness. Surely such a pattern is dramatic enough, the climax being a fusion of the end and the beginning. Just so the climax of *King Oedipus* brings on stage precisely those three people who were present at the great crisis of Oedipus' babyhood, when he was handed over by one shepherd from Thebes to another shepherd from Corinth: in the end is the beginning. Similarly, but along more psychological lines, in *Ghosts* the hero's last outcry is his first, the plaintive demand for joy that his mother had dedicated herself to denying him: 'Mother, give me the sun!'

Next as Pentheus' defenses break down, he reveals more and more of himself to us; we get to know him better, in a real and intimate way.

Finally – as so often happens, when we get to know someone better – not in the sense of getting more familiar with his masks, but going into the deepest layers of his character – we get to like him better. We started out, I think, by detesting the *man*; we pass to pity for a grotesque invalid; we end by weeping for a little boy.

IV. CONCLUSION

All of this makes us want to get mad at someone, and most people want to get mad at Dionysus. That, of course, is silly – you might as well get mad at the stars in their courses. It is much more sophisticated to get mad at Agave, although I defy anyone to do that after the scene in which she is brought back to her senses and stands before us with her son's bloody head in her hands (1282). And anyway her father Cadmus takes responsibility upon himself – he was faking when he worshiped Dionysus, he was just as culpable as anyone (1344). And then maybe we should stop and wonder whether this anger, this blaming of ours, makes any sense. The culprit, if there is one, is humanity's urge to transcend the bestial, an unfortunate urge that is forever with us. 'Torpedo the Ark', as Ibsen said referring to Noah's misguided providence. Or, since that is no longer possible for you and me (though it seems increasingly possible for our leaders) perhaps what we must do is listen to the chorus' advice. I can't rehearse it all here, but I can call attention to two symbols. One is the dance itself: on the one hand orderly, controlled, expressing the side of humanity that is aware, that knows what it is and that it is; on the other hand body in wild motion, animal. The other symbol is confrontation, occurring most poignantly at the beginning of the second episode. The chorus is cowering with fear over the imprisonment of their leader. Suddenly the divine voice descends, overwhelming, yet regular and orderly, not merely in its quantitative rhythm, but even in its pitch: *ió – klúet' emâs, klúet' audâs – iò Bácchai, iò Bácchai.* The chorus does not quite know at first who this is; but notice the same regularity of meter and pitch in their answer:

τίς ὅδε, τίς ὅδε, πόθεν ὁ κέλαδος
ἀνά μ' ἐκάλεσεν Εὐίου;

How utterly wild; how totally controlled! The god calls again:

ἰὼ ἰώ, πάλιν αὐδῶ
ὁ Σεμέλας, ὁ Διὸς παῖς.

And now the chorus knows whom it is answering. But such knowledge, though conveying the wildest excitement, still shows that supreme orderliness and precision. This is the cry of aware recognition of the god of the beast, their master, the thunderer; this is the voice of sanity:

ἰὼ ἰώ, δέσποτα, δέσποτα,
μόλε νῦν ἡμέτερον ἐς
θίασον ὦ Βρόμιε, Βρόμιε.

Aetiology, ritual, charter: three equivocal terms in the study of myths

GEOFFREY S. KIRK

THE SUBJECT of this paper (originally written as a lecture and given at Harvard and Yale in March 1970) may seem a far cry from the main theme of the present volume. Yet it is beyond dispute that the culture of the fifth century B.C. in Greece was still heavily affected by myth, whether as a traditional framework for poetry and drama or as an intellectual force to be combated by Sophists or as a firmly established store of *exempla* for practical and moral life. In fact it is doubtful whether any other western society is known in which traditional mythology played so great a role. Perhaps the predominant function of the old myths in an age of increasing rationalism was as a categorial structure that provided a set of familiar points of reference against which other ideas and interpretations could be measured. So far, so good; but how far is the accurate discrimination of the *primary* functions of myths, the main subject of the pages that follow, relevant to the developed uses and schematized forms of myths in the Classical era? It would be misleading to claim more than an indirect connection; yet two brief generalizations may be to the point. First, fifth-century attitudes to the truth of myths varied from incredulity to uncritical belief; but what we need to perceive more clearly, if possible, is the *emotional tone or aura* evoked by the myths for educated Greeks – something that does not clearly emerge from the literature, and that makes the reactions of Euripides, in particular, very hard to assess. In this respect a fuller understanding of mythical pre-history (or, more accurately, of the functions of the myths before their decadence) is bound to be germane to the later situation. Second, although the literary evidence presents the myths in a sophisticated and deracinated form, there were still regional myths, associated often enough with local cults and customs in many parts of fifth-century Greece, which continued to have some

6-2

kind of life of their own, which coloured the attitudes to literary myths, and which may have retained some connection with the complex primary functions of all myths in pre-literate societies.

The study of these primary functions has been permeated by the assumptions that myths explain things, that they are an aspect of religion, and that they arise primarily out of tribal legend and collective needs. These assumptions find a loose and unsatisfactory expression in the three terms that appear in the title. In examining these terms and the different functions and aspects that they conceal I hope also to indicate the limitations of the idea that all myths serve one function and one only, that there can be a single 'theory of myths', or that operating in one form or aspect precludes simultaneous operation in another.

The first of the offending expressions is 'aetiology'. From the time of Andrew Lang, the destroyer of solar mythology, and the growth of the idea that all myths are trying to explain something rather than being simple allegories of natural events, scholars have been avid to apply the label 'aetiological' either to complete myths or to important aspects of them. Martin Nilsson, regarded by many as the ultimate resort on questions of Greek religion and myths, persisted in maintaining that the main division of non-religious and non-historical myths is into folktales on the one hand and aetiological tales on the other – that is, that most 'serious' myths are aetiological in essence.[1] I am certainly not disposed to deny that many myths in many societies do serve an important explicatory or at least problematic purpose (although there are of course other possible functions, including those brought under the heading of 'charter'); but the term 'aetiological' is applied equally to superficial *aitia* of the just-so kind – to the origin of proper names or natural features, for instance – and to abstract encounters with problems at the very root of human existence, like that of the relation of the individual to society or of life to death. Between these poles lie still other modes of mythical explanation, like those involved in cosmogonical myths. The difficulty is that all these explanatory modes tend to be functionally distinct, so that the application of the one generic label of 'aetiology' – and most critics are content with that – is inadequate and misleading.

1. M. P. Nilsson, *Geschichte der griechischen Religion* I (2nd ed., Munich 1955), pp. 16ff., 35.

Even within the most concrete kind of aetiological myth (the kind represented by tales that account in some sense for names like 'hyacinth' or 'Perseus' or striking natural features like the Pillars of Heracles or the Clashing Rocks) there are specific differences that deserve careful categorizing. In other cultures such explanatory tales can be seen working differently and often more seriously than they do in the sophisticated forms in which Greek mythology has survived. For the Aboriginal Australian virtually every stone is important for its shape and its relation to water and small animals and insects like witchetty grubs that can be caught and eaten; and this literally vital information is recorded and somehow explained in myths, in traditional tales – for example a particular tree is there because an ancestor needed to rest in the shade at that point in his journey. A fantastic landmark like the huge monolith of Ayers Rock in the south-central Australian desert becomes, for the Pitjandjara, a focal point for myths.[2] Every nook and cranny in it is equated with some mythical creature or person or some aspect of the life of animals and culture-heroes in the Dreamtime. More important, the rock serves not only as an encyclopaedia of mythical persons, animals and events, but also, by its physical configurations, as an actual determinant of their mutual relations.

In other landscapes the aetiological relation will often be different. For the Amazonian forest-dweller the prominent natural features are rivers, swamps, and clearings; but he resembles the Australian in his interest in the heavens and the constellations – which tend to be less important, however, for other inlanders whose landscape itself is more dramatically varied. It is curious, until we think about it in this context, that we know of no substantial myths explaining some of the most striking natural features of Greece: the peak of Lycabettus in Athens, the Meteora pinnacles in Thessaly, or remarkable seaways like the passage between Peparethos and Ikos (modern Skopelos and Alonisos), which lies on a major sailing route to the Thermaic gulf and also to the Euxine and provides an awe-inspiring experience in all but the most serene weather. Much of the traditional lore of Greece seems to have been lost in the long process of heroic and divine schematizing, and in the destructive economy of literacy; but it seems probable that, even apart from this, it was mainly beyond the

2. C. P. Mountford, *Ayers Rock* (Sydney 1965), *passim.*

borders of the familiar world, on the edge of the exotic, that landscape became truly mythical, that Scylla and Charybdis dwelt.

An analogous phenomenon is the absence of plausibly archaic
Greek myths to motivate some of the most remarkable celestial
events. The diurnal passage of the sun is accounted for by the idea
of Helios and his chariot, his return to the east by the bowl in which
he sails round the river Okeanos; but such impressive occurrences
as eclipses seem to have attracted no early myths (since Xeno-
phanes' joke about the sun missing its footing is certainly no such
thing).[3] It was this lack of an elaborate celestial mythology that
permitted the fantastic and improbable allegorizings of the
nineteenth-century nature-myth school, and that still allows Karl
Kerényi to write of Prometheus as lunar as opposed to the
violently solar Titans.[4] Moreover the existence of a vacuum in this
respect is confirmed by the unconfined explosion of star-myths in
the Hellenistic age, as well as by the free theorizing of the Pre-
socratic thinkers themselves. Yet the avoidance of certain kinds of
trivial *aition* before the Alexandrians at least spares us a difficulty
known from the study of other cultures; for it is all too easy to be
misled over the primary role of a traditional tale by an apparently
casual and almost automatic accretion of aetiological motifs. In a
Tsimshian myth made particularly familiar by Lévi-Strauss in his
article 'La geste d'Asdiwal' there are specific explanatory details,
for example of the origin of flint in a certain valley, that are
probably quite secondary and bear no organic relation to the
underlying structure of the tale in all its variants – a structure that
seems to be related to quite different kinds of problem, like that of
marriage with different grades of cousin and the evaluation of
activities like hunting and food-gathering.[5]

Quite different in operation from the whole class of concrete
aetiologies of names and places are those that profess to give an
origin for national, tribal or family institutions and possessions.
Greece is not exceptional in its myths of the foundations of cities,
as of Thebes by Cadmus, or of festivals, as of the Olympic games
by Heracles; or in its anecdotal and quasi-historical claims to

3. Aetius II. 24. 9 (=DK 21 A 41a).
4. K. Kerényi, *Prometheus* (New York 1963), p. 61.
5. *The Structural Study of Myth and Totemism*, ed. E. R. Leach (London 1967),
pp. 1ff.

certain territories, as Athens claimed control of Eleusis through the person of Theseus, or in obviously fictitious tribal ancestors like Ion and Aeolus. There have always been those who see all myths as interpreting or reflecting historical events of the dim past, so that Heracles' conquest of monsters becomes a symbol of Argive power extending across and beyond the Peloponnese. In its universalist form such a theory is certainly an aberration, to which the majority of traditional tales cannot be accommodated without the most violent distortion of probability and the surviving evidence. Yet some myths are, nevertheless, obviously connected with historical events, in terms not only of eponymous tribal ancestors and the like but also, more realistically, of what is better termed 'legend', as with many of the myths of the Trojan War in Homer. There is often an explanatory element in such myths, but it is not identical in kind with that contained in the various kinds of concrete aetiology (moreover it overlaps the third equivocal category, of myths as 'charters' or validations of social institutions and beliefs).

More serious, both these types of aetiology are distinct, not only in their aims but also in their basic procedures, from the speculative or problematic kind. Pretty stories about the origin of the lyre or flute, migration tales to account for the similarities between Aeginetan Aphaia and Cretan Dictynna or Britomartis, myths that embody the political relations between Argos and Tiryns – all these are distinctly different from those that purport to account in some way for men's loss of immortality or a golden age, or for the simultaneous instincts to revere the old and to throw them on the trash-heap. The first group typically operates by the assignment of a mythical or quasi-legendary inventor, founder or conqueror, sometimes in a distorted echo of historical events. The second typically involves the formulation of an abstract and often intractable problem in terms that are not merely narrative and traditional but also in some sense analytic and symbolic – often in such a way that the symbols themselves seem to imbue the actual situation with a special emotional tone. The one process tends to involve looking around, as it were, in the tribal store of reminiscence and tradition and selecting an appropriate precedent or paradigm; the other surely entails a distinctively intuitive and indeed imaginative expression of individual and collective preoccupations through the language of traditional tales, tales that are now used symbolically and even 'structurally'. In both cases fictitious or largely fictitious people and events are deployed to provide a causation of actual phenomena in the present; but in the first and simpler instance it is a question of merely applying a familiar narrative situation to a real situation, whereas the second process is deeper and more complex. The fresh expression of a serious preoccupation in mythical language often requires the adaptation of elaborate situational models quite distinct from the simple personifications and combinations of folktale motifs that satisfied the more concrete kind of aetiological need. Explaining the name of the Hellespont merely involves dropping off Helle *en route* from Thessaly (where Athamas was king) to Colchis (where her brother Phrixus was associated with the Golden Fleece). The mother's name, Nephele or 'Cloud', suggests a suitable device, paralleled for instance in the earlier Mesopotamian tale of Etana:[6] let the children ride on the back of an aerial monster, and let Helle plunge into the channel that seems to bear her name. That at least is one possibility. At all events the minor complexities of the process are likely to resemble those encountered by an oral singer shuffling and elaborating a traditional repertory of themes and tale-types rather than those exemplified by a poet or philosopher *intuiting* (subconsciously eliciting from his experience) a fresh and suggestive association of ideas and things. And many kinds of myth, as most of us would probably agree, have more in common with the activities of the instinctive and yet speculative poet than with those of the more mechanical kind of oral singer.

The range of aetiology is not yet exhausted; so far I have considered only its most obvious extremes. Myths can suggest causes of phenomena and events in more ways than these. The important observation is that they are not often *merely* allegorical. Admittedly E. B. Tylor thought that the main function of anthropomorphizing myths was to make natural phenomena acceptable by personalizing them, and more recently Thorkild Jacobsen has had conspicuous success in interpreting certain Mesopotamian myths in that way.[7]

6. J. B. Pritchard, ed., *Ancient Near Eastern Texts*[2] (Princeton 1955), pp. 114ff.
7. *Before Philosophy* (Penguin Books, 1946–), e.g. p. 157; *Journal of Near Eastern Studies* 12 (1953), 166–9; cf. my *Myth: its Meaning and Functions in Ancient and other Cultures* (Berkeley and Cambridge 1970), pp. 88ff.

But personifying or anthropomorphizing tends to reveal plausible new relationships that are not necessarily evident in the natural phenomena when viewed more directly. To envisage Ouranos, sky, as the husband of Gaia, earth; to say that he rests upon her, that he touches her, that he fertilizes her by dropping rain from which she conceives vegetation and life in her inner recesses – all this is not merely to dramatize the relation between the two, it also elicits fresh implications about this relation, not so much in cosmographical terms (for those were the starting-point of the allegorical transposition) as in the implication of vital changes from fire to moisture to earth to fertile life. As cosmology extends to cosmogony the range of intuition is increased, and the pattern of human birth and multiplication, of genetic differentiation, is applied as a key to the problem of unitary and apparently inert matter. In all this there is more than mere allegory, allegory at its most literal, the consistent expression of meaning in a different code from that of normal language and direct perception. Sometimes the nature of the code itself, as in the erotic allegory of the Church as the Bride of Christ, adds a powerful emotional tone to the 'real situation'; in this instance the Church becomes the proper object of an almost physical adoration. But in other respects allegory can do little, is an affectation of literature rather than a conceptual and imaginative mode in pre-literate societies. Few instances of myth are pure allegory; indeed myths tend to be fantastic, to be contra-logical, to reject the dull and routine sequences of ordinary life. One of the ways in which they illuminate experience is precisely by breaking down the divisions imposed by reason, by showing up new aspects of a complex situation through reflecting upon it the unfamiliar glow of other events at first sight quite distinct.

In a sense this is what the structuralist theory of myths claims to detect. It is important to pass by Lévi-Strauss' examination of the Oedipus myth if one wants to understand his ideas at their best and most true; and if one cannot go beyond that initial paper on 'The Structural Study of Myths' then it is more fruitful to look at his example drawn from the Pueblo creation-myth, where the emphasis on carrion-eating animals as a mediating type between beasts of prey and animals that feed on grass and so on seems to suggest a possible mediation between death and life in general.[8]

8. C. Lévi-Strauss, *Structural Anthropology* (New York 1963), p. 216.

A not dissimilar mode of operation, this time beyond Lévi-Strauss' own area of study and interest, is presented by ancient Mesopotamian tales, which (as I have suggested elsewhere) tend to manoeuvre two ostensibly distinct mythical situations so as to make each refract light on the subject of the other.[9] In the Akkadian Etana-tale the animal fable of the eagle who lives at the top of a tree and breaks his compact with the snake dwelling at its foot, not to devour each other's young, is worked into the story of how a childless king ascends to heaven on an eagle's back to gain the plant of birth. It is not just that the snake is made to reveal to him how to catch the eagle; rather the idea of improper displace-ment (from on top of the tree to the snake's nest in the earth below) is somehow applied to the complex relation between a mortal king, the god he represents on earth, his own death, and the question of a successor. In this exploratory kind of myth the 'aetiology', if we must use the word, consists in making and revealing unexpected juxtapositions, either between two imaginary situations that can then be seen to bear on a real one, or between a real situation and an imaginary one with which it does not overtly correspond. What is achieved, a feeling rather than a conclusion, is not so much a cause or an explication as an apparent clarification: for example that a situation is not after all insoluble, or that it does not really matter, or that it does not really exist, or that sooner than being like X and therefore intolerable it is like Y and therefore accept-able or even rather nice. My own opinion is that this is an essential mode of speculative or problematic myths, since it is undamaged by (and indeed depends on) those fantastic and dream-like disloca-tions that characterize many pre-literate traditional tales that are neither folktales nor obvious legends; whereas other types of aetiological myth, whether superficial and concrete or explicative in a more strictly allegorical manner, do not accord with that kind of fantasy and are indeed disrupted by it.

The second of the trio of equivocal categories is ritual. It is for-tunately unnecessary to give a full presentation of the myth-and-ritual theory in its more extreme form. That theory has always had a certain appeal for classicists since the time of Jane Harrison, the learned authoress of *Themis*, and Francis Cornford, who was still propagating a version of it at the end of his career; and there are

9. *Myth: its Meaning and Functions in Ancient and other Cultures*, pp. 117f.

still serious scholars like Walter Burkert and M. L. West who think that all or most myths are in some way or other intimately associated with rituals.[10] Biblical scholars of the S. H. Hooke school are the most fully committed to the theory, and it is indeed the case that rituals were a particularly pervasive element of religious and social life in the ancient Near East. Folklorists, on the other hand, have little use for the myth-and-ritual idea; but many anthropologists still tolerate it in one special form. The idea adopted by Durkheim that myth is the *legomenon*, the thing said, ritual the *drōmenon*, the thing done, was enthusiastically endorsed by Jane Harrison and other members of the so-called Cambridge School; and it is still used in Clyde Kluckhohn's much cited article 'Myths and Rituals: a General Theory'[11] – a general theory that is not very different, except for an increase in functionalism and Freudianism, from the view urged by Jane Harrison in her *Prolegomena to the Study of Greek Religion*. I do not wish to question the thesis that some myths and some rituals 'satisfy a group of identical or closely related needs of individuals', although I resist Kluckhohn's implication that all or most myths are of this kind. What interests me more is the conception of ritual involved in the theory. Obviously he was not just thinking of religious rituals, but about all kinds of formalized and often collective expression by means of action. These include dancing, processing, all kinds of expressive gesture; they might also include participation in a performance, led by a priest or other individual, of a symbolic act or sequence of acts, often connected with fertility or initiation and occasionally taking the form of a ritual drama. Finally a story is often *acted out* in an almost ritual manner by its teller in a pre-literate society, even if it has no other ritual connection or implication. I suggest that most of these kinds of action are distinct in their motives and sources, that the differences are crippling for any 'general theory', and that they are disguised by the imprecise connotations of the term 'ritual' itself.

I want now to offer an analysis of some of the main types of ritual, with the aim of making clear how different they are; and to

10. F. M. Cornford, *The Unwritten Philosophy* (Cambridge and New York 1950), pp. 95ff.; W. Burkert, *CQ* n.s. 20 (1970), 15ff.; M. L. West, *Hesiod, Theogony* (Oxford 1966), p. 200 *init*.
11. *Harvard Theological Review* 35 (1942), 45–79.

point out what kinds of myth, if any, are likely to be associated, and in what way, with each type.

The first type (although the order is obviously arbitrary) consists of secular ritual behaviour in a ceremonial sense. The ceremonial quality of life varies enormously from society to society: it is marked among North American Indians, for example, but unmarked (except for politically engendered flag-worship and the like) among most other North Americans. Ceremonial occasions do not of themselves generate myths, although they tend in pre-literate societies to encourage the telling of tales and their becoming traditional – either for tribal and charter purposes or as aristocratic entertainment in the way in which Demodocus and Phemius entertained the chieftains after dinner in Phaeacia and Ithaca. In exceptional cases a predominant ceremonial, like the elaborate *kula* exchange practised by the Trobriand islanders and described in Malinowski's fascinating *Argonauts of the Western Pacific*, becomes a focus for myths drawn originally from other areas of experience.

A second and far more important type consists of primarily secular rituals associated with special and occasional events, either seasonal on the one hand or social and biological on the other.

Among seasonal rites, those that are celestial or calendaric (festivals of midsummer and midwinter in particular) are often sparse in mythical association, as in the case of Carnival. Others are more directly connected with agrarian fertility, and these rituals of sowing, of harvest, of purification, of making the seed grow underground, tend to be accompanied by myths. Some of these myths are patently generated by the ritual, and are variously aetiological in character. Yet even here (and many such rituals are devoid of myths, in Greece at least) the connection of rite and myth may be very loose. In the Delphic festival of the Septeria, for example, a hut was burned, then a group of boys fled to Tempe and later returned in triumph – this looks like a scapegoat ritual in part, but the Delphians themselves were content to explain it, quite improbably, as reproducing Apollo's victory over the dragon Python.[12] And in other cases the accompanying myth is not engendered by the ritual at all, but is a parallel but independent response to the fear of infertility and starvation. The disappearing-

12. Plutarch, *Moralia* 418 A–B.

god myth that was so widely spread over the Near East, and is represented by the Sumerian tale of Inanna's descent to the under-world or by the various versions of the death of Dumuzi–Tammuz, is an example of the kind of myth that can accompany a fertility-ritual without being generated by it.

The second kind of primarily secular ritual consists of responses to human, rather than seasonal, events: to birth, puberty, initia-tion, marriage and death. These 'rites of passage' take characteris-tic forms, some of which, like transvestism (as part of a temporary reversal of normality), can generate either a myth, like that of Achilles disguised as a girl in Skyros, or a different ritual, like that implicit in the priest of Heracles dressed as a woman in Cos.[13] These are in no sense explicative, but simply reflect in a different medium an oddity of the original rite. A more important associa-tion of myths with this sort of ritual is that initiation-ceremonies (most notably) provide an important occasion for reciting charter-type myths concerned with the customs of the tribe, clan, family or particular age-class into which initiation is being effected. We cannot clearly observe this tendency in ancient Greece, but it is a familiar aspect of such ceremonies in surviving tribal societies.

The third and last group is composed of religious rituals, and these consist, primarily but not exclusively, of rituals connected with cult. Yet even cult-rituals fall into two distinct types. The first contains actions connected with the making of offerings or sacrifices and the maintenance of the sacred place or its cult-image, for example by sweeping the floor or renewing a sacred garment – services that are better illustrated in the temple documents of Egypt and Mesopotamia than in anything that survives from ancient Greece. That is one important type of cult-ritual, and it is germane to observe that it is not commonly accompanied by a myth. The actions, for one thing, are too ordinary. A second kind, on the other hand, consists in the formal reciting of prayers and hymns; and hymns in particular tend to include the narration of episodes from the life and actions of the deity. The divine history is itself a traditional narrative, a myth. What is remarkable is that in this case further ritual actions can be generated by the myth (the divine biography) and not *vice versa*. The Homeric Hymn to Demeter, whatever its exact cult status, probably resembled in

13. Apollodorus III. 13. 8 (Achilles); Plutarch, *Moralia* 304 c–e (Cos).

many respects hymns that were actually sung to the goddess: it describes the whole episode of the abduction of her daughter Persephone, Demeter's sorrow and withdrawal of fertility, her wanderings, her arrival at Eleusis, the restoration of the maiden, and the foundation of the secret cult at Eleusis itself. There are no reasons for thinking that the myth as a whole was originally based on ritual; conversely there are grounds for believing that certain of the *drōmena*, the things performed in the secret rites, were founded upon, and dramatically illustrated, the events recorded in the myth – as Clement of Alexandria put it, 'Deo and Kore have turned into a drama for initiates, and Eleusis celebrates with torches their wandering and rape and mourning' (*Protrepticus* II. 12).

The result is that cult-rituals can be divided in the first instance into those concerned with the tendance of the god primarily by ritual and mimetic *actions*, and those concerned with propitiation and worship by the ritual *recital* of prayers and hymns. The first category does not naturally generate myths, and in the second the narrative content of hymns and prayers tends to encourage a derivative dramatic ritual. In other words, specifically religious rituals are not often, in themselves, the prime causes of myths, nor are myths primarily 'aetiological' of religious rituals.

It is not claimed that this brief analysis is exhaustive; but it does, I think, suggest the deficiencies of the widespread assumption of a single kind of relationship between myths and rituals, or the claim that all myths have ritual counterparts. Certain kinds of seasonal festival are often devoid of mythical elements, and so are some fertility-rituals and most cult-rituals of the feeding, sweeping and anointing type. Some rituals depend on myths, rather than *vice versa*, and many myths (as we can see from obvious examples like Oedipus or Perseus) are devoid of ritual aspects except for what might be implied by heroic cults. To take some specific Greek instances, it is remarkable that so strange a ritual, and one that affected so many people, as the annual passage of offerings wrapped in straw from country to country, from the mythical Hyperboreans in the far north to the Scythians, then across to the Adriatic and down to Dodona, then eastward again to Euboea and Tenos and Delos, where finally they were offered to Artemis and Apollo – it is remarkable that this elaborate performance (described by Herodotus, IV. 33–5) seems to have engendered no more in the way of myths than the mention of the obscure Hyperboreans themselves and one or two obvious deductions based on the supposed tomb of two Hyperborean girls in Delos. Again, many of the Attic festivals on which we are relatively well informed had little or nothing of narrative and mythical accompaniment beyond what was implied by their mere association with a particular deity. Even the intriguing and bizarre events of the Arrhephoria and the Thesmophoria, festivals of obvious fertility implications, did not give rise to close or elaborate mythical parallels.[14] In the former, two (or four) young Athenian girls lived for a time on the Acropolis close to Athena's temple; on the appointed night the priestess gave them objects to carry on their heads down to a precinct below, which was approached through a sort of ravine; neither they nor the priestess knew what these objects were; at the precinct they handed over the objects and received others, still wrapped up and unknown, which they carried up to the Acropolis again; then they were discharged. There is admittedly a myth, specifically set in Athens, that we can see to be loosely related to this ritual: the tale of King Cecrops' daughters. There were three of them, and their names suggest various aspects of fertility or at least moisture; they were given a box by Athena and told not to look inside it; two of them did so, and saw there the snake-like figure of the embryonic Erichthonius, formed by the seed of Hephaestus which fell on the ground when he tried to rape Athena; they went mad and threw themselves off the rock to their death. Now the box and the seed are motifs familiar from other myths, the latter being strange to the ritual of the Arrhephoria and the former doubtful; and the whole story looks most like a loosely-woven deterrent tale designed to prevent the little Arrhephoroi from prying into their mysterious bundles.[15] Certainly the relation of the myth and the ritual does not resemble an aetiological one in any ordinary sense. Not dissimilarly, in the festival of the Thesmophoria pigs were placed in

14. Pausanias 1. 27. 3 (Arrhephoria); scholiast on Lucian, pp. 275f. Rabe (Thesmophoria; I accept Burket's argument, in the article cited in the next note, that the burying of pigs belongs to the Thesmophoria and not the Skira, *contra* L. Deubner, *Attische Feste* (Berlin 1932), pp. 40ff.).

15. Apollodorus III. 14. 6. W. Burkert (*Hermes* 94 (1966), 10ff.) argues carefully for a close correspondence between the myth and the ritual, and connects both with initiation; but in my opinion there are considerable difficulties in this interpretation.

underground chambers and left to rot, to be eventually removed by specially named and chosen matrons and then mixed with the seed-corn. The feeble mythological reason adduced for this (not that we really need one, since the pig is an obvious symbol of fertility) is that a swineherd called Eubouleus, which is actually a name of Hades or Plouton himself, had cast himself and his swine into the chasm through which Persephone was reft into the underworld.

It is significant, indeed, that the clearest cases in which a complex myth grows out of a known ritual are precisely those in which the ritual entailed doing something with dolls, statues, or puppets, and so carried its own inherent implication of some specifically human origin. In all probability, however, such dolls and puppets were not originally meant to represent particular people, mythical or otherwise. Casting puppets into a fire seems to have been either a scapegoat ritual or some other kind of fertility rite (derived, it has been suggested with only a modicum of plausibility, from a memory of human sacrifice). Three well-known examples confirm the general conjecture. In the Attic country festival of the Aiora, puppets were tied to trees and swung about, and this was said to represent the girl Erigone who hanged herself from a tree because of her father Icarius' curious death.[16] In a ritual called the Daedala at Plataea a sacred oak was cut down, dressed as a bride, and taken to the top of Mount Cithaeron in a cart; every fifty-nine years all the images were burnt.[17] This was associated, rather casually as it seems, with a version of Zeus' quarrelling with Hera: she left him, and he made her jealous and got her back by dressing up an oak tree as his intended new bride. At the top of another mountain, Oeta, the remains of an often-rekindled ancient pyre were excavated some fifty years ago, and among them were found figurines of human form.[18] That must have been another fertility or New-Fire ritual, but with it there somehow became associated the myth that Heracles at his death became a god – that is, he had himself carried to the top of Mount Oeta and cremated there.

More broadly I would suggest that those rituals which involved certain individuals in very unusual actions, or those that included

16. Apollodorus III. 14. 7; Hyginus, *Fabulae* 130. 3.
17. Pausanias IX. 3. 1ff.
18. M. P. Nilsson (see above, n. 1), p. 131.

models of human beings, or finally those that required some kind of abnormal behaviour from a large part of the community (like the women of Lemnos who at a certain time of year induced, probably, a bad smell to keep their husbands away),[19] tended to generate mythical explanations or counterparts. Other kinds of ritual – and there are plenty of them – did not. That may seem a poor kind of conclusion to the consideration of rituals, but, against the background of myth-and-ritual dogmas exercised by anthropologists, Near-Eastern experts and some classicists, it is highly significant if true.

The third of the three ambiguous and confusing concepts is that of 'charter'. The term is Malinowski's: 'Myth...is not an idle tale, but a hard-worked active force; it is not an intellectual exploration or an artistic imagery, but a pragmatic charter of primitive faith and moral wisdom.'[20] Malinowski was here reacting violently against the nature-myth school on the one hand and its intellectualist opponents, especially Andrew Lang, on the other. Disillusioned with the *a priori* nature of previous mythological theories, he claimed that only the anthropologist – and not the psychologist, the philosopher, the sociologist or the classicist – could understand myths, because only he has the myth-maker at his elbow. There is a certain truth in all this, and undoubtedly Malinowski's assertion of the *pragmatic* function of myth in society has been salutary. But anthropologists, at least, have been too easily persuaded that all they need do is follow Malinowski in this respect – although they have thrown him overboard in practically every other. With an occasional glance over their shoulder at classical myths, which they persist in regarding as some kind of universal paradigm, they pursue the assumption that myths must be charters of beliefs and institutions, that they provide a record and validation of titles, lands, families, privileges, customs, and of course rituals. More serious, they assume with Malinowski that this is the only kind of thing that myths do; that, as he put it in reaction against Andrew Lang's idea of myth as a kind of primitive science, 'Melanesians...do not want to "explain", to make

19. Cf. G. Dumézil, *Le Crime des Lemniennes* (Paris 1924), *passim*; W. Burkert, *CQ* N.S. 20 (1970), 7 and 10–12.

20. B. Malinowksi, *Magic, Science and Religion* (Garden City, N.Y. 1948–), p. 101; reprinted from *Myth in Primitive Psychology* (1926).

"intelligible" anything which happens in their myths – above all
not an abstract idea. Of that there can be found to my knowledge
no instance either in Melanesia or in any other savage community.'[21] One reason why Lévi-Strauss is so unpopular at present
with Anglo-American anthropologists is that he infringes this
Malinowskian rule on which so many of them have been reared.

While admitting the possible utility of the charter function of
myth as one common type, especially in tribal societies, let us now
glance at some of the confusions implicit in the concept, confusions
that have permeated not only Malinowski's treatment but also
that of his successors. First, the idea of 'charter' or 'validation' is
itself misleadingly loose. A myth that validates a claim to tribal or
family land often works in a quite different way from one that
confirms an institution like kingship or a rule like the prohibition
of incest. The former kind typically operates by recounting how a
mythical founder or culture-hero gave the land to an ancestor; the
latter might function by stressing the dire consequences, on a
particular mythical occasion, of doing the reverse of what is
prescribed by present custom or institution. This second type is
argumentative in essence – not, like the first, dogmatic: it justifies
the *status quo* by pointing out the danger or absurdity of its contrary.

Elsewhere Malinowski wrote of charter myths as warranting the
belief in immortality, eternal youth, and so on, and serving as 'an
explicit act of faith born from the innermost instinctive and emotional reaction to the most formidable and haunting idea'.[22] In
other words they serve to formulate and express wishes and attitudes pertaining to the most crucial concerns of life, but not as any
'intellectual reaction upon a puzzle'. And yet, whatever one thinks
about the role of intellectual and emotional elements in myths
about death (for instance), it is surely the case that such myths
tend to be seriously different in form, method and intention from
those that validate claims to lands or social institutions; and it is
merely confusing to group the whole lot together under the heading
of 'charter'. The myth is no longer confirming or recording an
established and concrete social fact, but reflecting and indeed
helping to shape an abstract attitude. In the former instances
'charter' overlaps the simpler kinds of 'aetiology', since the myth
tends to provide validation by giving a fictitious explanation of

21. *Op. cit.* p. 109.   22. *Op. cit.* p. 110.

how it is that such-and-such a clan has always possessed such-and-such lands. In the latter the mythical function overlaps a radically different and problematic aspect of aetiology; for like Lévi-Strauss and unlike Malinowski, I am convinced that certain myths, in many societies at least, *do* contain solutions, of a kind, to problems – or perhaps it would be truer to say that they provide a certain kind of palliation of preoccupations.

Other ambiguities in this charter concept, although implicit in Malinowski himself, are most clearly exemplified in an eclectic follower, Mircea Eliade. Eliade maintains that

> Myth narrates a sacred history; it relates an event that took place in primordial time, the fabled time of the 'beginnings'. In other words, myth tells how, through the deeds of supernatural beings, a reality came into existence...Myth, then, is always an account of a 'creation', it relates how something was produced, began to be...myths describe the various and sometimes dramatic breakthroughs of the sacred (or the supernatural) into the world.[23]

It is of course clear that myth is not, in spite of Eliade's confident assertions, 'always an account of a "creation"'. Many myths, those of Oedipus, Heracles and Gilgamesh among them, are not of this kind. Some of Malinowski's Trobriand myths can be accommodated to that description only with great strain. In many parts of the world founders or culture-heroes operate on a deliberately non-supernatural level, so that existing features are established by citing an event from a past that is not particularly sacred. In ancient Greece the founding of games does not take us back into a sacred and creative past, but to an intermediate stage between a divine or golden age and the full light of history. Admittedly that provides a link between the human present and the immortal past; this is important – but so, I suspect, is the choice of an era when fantasy could be given a free rein. No one could doubt that Heracles is a genuinely mythical figure; yet neither his ubiquity, nor his enormous variety of character and functions, depends on any notably sacred quality. It is true that Greek instances are often not the most typical or revealing; but other cultural sets of myths (one thinks of Adapa and Etana among Akkadian myths, Rama

23. *Encyclopædia Britannica* (1969 ed.) vol. 15, 1133f., s.v. Myth.

and Krishna among Hindu, Geriguiaguiatugo and related figures among those of the Brazilian Bororo) suggest that the re-establishment of the full creative period is not the prime intention of many important traditional tales. This emphasis on the sacred quality of myths is partly a response to a further widely-held but erroneous assumption, that all myths are about gods in some important sense. But 'sacred', like 'ritual', is an ambivalent term, as most attempts to explain the origins of religion indicate. Many myths do concern gods, although some do not; but that is largely because most people are polytheistic, and polytheism of itself generates traditional narrative. The presence of gods in myths does not necessarily make those myths sacred in any strict religious sense. In so far as all myths can usefully be described as 'sacred' at all, it is because of their function as preservers of the tradition among people for whom tradition is the highest social value – because of their solemn role in society, a role that endows them with a loosely sacrosanct tone and status.

Even apart from this additional ambiguity over the meaning of 'sacred', and the doubt whether all myths really do reach back into an essentially supernatural and creative past, there is the further question whether myths in their charter aspect are also necessarily magical in some sense. Eliade simply assumes that they are, and writes of the aboriginal Australians that 'The myths teach them how to repeat the creative acts of the supernatural beings and hence to ensure the multiplication of such-and-such an animal or plant'.[24] This is a familiar idea, and I certainly would not deny that many Australian myths were used as a magical stimulus of reproduction and growth. Whether the myths always achieve this result by teaching an effective mimetic ritual, as Eliade here implies, is more questionable; and in fact he switches position on this point with startling suddenness, and is soon claiming that the magical control is produced not by *mimesis* but because 'knowing the origin...is equivalent to acquiring a magical power' over an object.[25] This is a quite different conception, which reminds us that the cavalier use of terms and concepts is not restricted simply to 'aetiology', 'ritual', 'charter', and 'sacred'. In any event it is important to perceive that only some myths in some societies can be seen to possess any kind of magical function, either directly or

24. *Op. cit.* p. 1134.   25. *Ibid.*

indirectly; and that these magical functions are moreover often radically distinct from charter functions in which the myth simply reasserts the tradition in graphic terms. This whole group of possible mythical operations, which are undoubtedly important in tribal, pre-literate and highly traditional societies, deserves some better classification than can be provided under this obscure and cumbrous heading of 'charter myths'.

What are the reasons for the confusion that evidently exists in the study of mythical functions, and for the equivocal range of meanings of ritual, charter, aetiology, and other important concepts like folktale, saga, and nature as opposed to culture? Is it a necessary consequence of the irrationality of myths themselves? Of course not. Partly, rather, it is due to the old entanglement of the study of myths with that of religion; but partly it arises out of the interdisciplinary spread of mythology, which encourages everyone to leave some of the basic discriminations to someone else. Psychologists and Biblical scholars, for example, seem to feel free to form their own particular theories of myth until such time as anthropologists or philosophers can prove them wrong. Meanwhile the anthropologists are keeping half an eye on the classicists (because they cannot entirely exorcize the ghost of Frazer), and the other half on revenant philosophers from among their own ranks, like Lévi-Strauss. The classicist, on the other hand, usually does not concern himself with these matters at all – or, when he does so, is content with old masters like Cornford and Nilsson or fluent new prophets like Eliade and Kerényi, behind whom lurk respectively Malinowski and Jung. The classicist's most familiar attitude is the egregious one that what counts is the myths themselves; that when one is not reading them in Homer, Pindar or Sophocles one might as well read summaries in the purely descriptive pages of Apollodorus or H. J. Rose. And when the classicist comes to give a course on Greek mythology (for which there is an increasing demand in America, at least), what he tends to do as a substitute for theorizing, and beyond the mere paraphrasing of the main classical myths, is to run through the list of theorizers of the past: Theagenes, Euhemerus, the Stoic and Neoplatonic allegorizers, Tylor, Frazer, Max Müller, Andrew Lang, Freud, Malinowski, Jung, Cassirer... I am not suggesting that this procedure is devoid of value and interest. None of the old theories has been satisfactory, all have been too universalistic, but many have had their points, and in any case it clears the air to identify a number of paradigm errors. But somehow the rehearsal of these names often becomes, itself, an empty ritual, symbolizing an excessively doxographical and insufficiently analytical approach to the whole subject. It is as though all these old theories of myth are seen as individual pieces on a chess-board. Different values are assigned to them: some are knights, some bishops, most are pawns – but even a pawn, if properly played, must have his day; and the hidden assumption seems to be that when the board is complete, given a few more vague and general theories or a few new descriptive surveys, then the game will be ended and the problems of myths finally resolved. But this is not how it is at all – in reality the game will hardly have begun. The study of myth cannot proceed by mere agglomeration; and on my board, at least, the queen, the chief instrument of clarification and destruction, is to be, precisely, the application of order to our primary categories and concepts, to charter, ritual, aetiology and the rest. That will still leave an enormous amount to be done, and at this point imagination becomes no less important than analysis. But at least we might begin to perceive the problems clearly, and as they are.

Divine and human action in Sophocles: the two burials of the Antigone

MARSH McCALL

SIR RICHARD JEBB called attention long ago to a problem of motivation in Antigone's presumed double burial of Polynices, and he remarked, 'I have never seen this question put or answered'.[1] Were he alive, he might well wish he had never raised the question, so frequent and various have been the answers proposed during the intervening three-quarters of a century. It has even been suggested that concern for the question is irrelevant to the text or fostered merely to produce 'original' literary criticism.[2] The number of able scholars who have dealt with the problem of the double burial, however, would appear to reflect a real uneasiness about the true meaning of the text.

In 1931, S. M. Adams suggested that not Antigone but the gods effect the first burial of Polynices.[3] The idea was met by a flurry of rebuttals,[4] indeed with almost as much suspicion as the earlier theory of Rouse that Ismene performs the first burial.[5] Adams persisted, however, and repeated his proposal as part of a longer article on the Antigone, which became a chapter in his Sophocles the Playwright.[6] Reviews of the book either passed over the theory[7] or

1. R. C. Jebb, Sophocles, Antigone[2] (Cambridge 1891), p. 86, note on v. 429. Jebb's text is used throughout.
2. This is essentially the charge of E. T. Owen, 'Sophocles the Dramatist', Univ. of Toronto Quarterly 5 (1936), 228–9.
3. S. M. Adams, 'The Burial of Polyneices', CR 45 (1931), 110–11.
4. See K. W. Meiklejohn, 'The Burial of Polynices', CR 46 (1932), 4–5; M. K. Flickinger, 'Who First Buried Polynices?', Philological Quarterly 12 (1933), 130–6.
5. W. H. D. Rouse, 'The Two Burials in Antigone', CR 25 (1911), 40–2.
6. S. M. Adams, 'The Antigone of Sophocles', Phoenix 9 (1955), 47–62; Sophocles the Playwright (Toronto 1957), ch. 3.
7. R. Lattimore in AJP 80 (1959), 100–2; P. T. Stevens in CR n.s. 10 (1960), 21–3.

responded negatively, the most favorable comments being 'controversial' or 'interessant'.[8]

During the past thirty years, however, a movement toward belief in some sort of divine assistance in the burial of Polynices has been discernible. Reinhardt believes that in general the divine and human spheres intermingle in Sophocles and discusses Polynices' two burials in this light.[9] Kitto makes much the same suggestion, adding that in Sophocles to resist 'an affront to common humanity' is to work in concert with the gods.[10] Sheppard comes even closer to Adams' position: 'Is it not possible that heaven has really intervened, sending a dust storm in the night...?'[11] Kirkwood has his own explanation of the two burials,[12] but he refers to the Adams theory as 'far more in accord with the sense of the play' than other theories which he rejects altogether.[13] Even Knox, who argues firmly against Adams' solution, recognizes 'the aura of divine help which surrounds the first burial and compares the open protection by the gods of the bodies of Sarpedon and Hector in the *Iliad*.[14] While all these writers retain Antigone as the agent of the first burial, they still sense in Sophocles' text some more than human power at work.

If Antigone alone performed both burials, then Sophocles felt that two burials supply something to the development of the play which a single burial would not. It has never been argued persuasively that the second burial is required for religious purposes. The guard explicitly credits the first burial with all necessary

8. H. Musurillo in *CW* 52 (1958), 58; Wasserstein in *Gnomon* 32 (1960), 178. H. F. Johansen, 'Sophocles 1939–1959', *Lustrum* 7 (1962), 186 says that Adams is preposterous; but he finds the whole problem 'uninteresting'.

9. K. Reinhardt, *Sophokles* (Frankfort 1933), pp. 82–6.

10. H. D. F. Kitto, *Form and Meaning in Drama* (London 1956), p. 155.

11. J. T. Sheppard, *The Wisdom of Sophocles* (London 1947), p. 51.

12. G. M. Kirkwood, *A Study of Sophoclean Drama* (Ithaca 1958), p. 72, 'Physically there were two burials; dramatically there was only "burial" divided in two in order to achieve two separate purposes.'

13. *Ibid.* p. 71, n. 34. In his bibliography of Sophoclean scholarship 1945–1956 in *CW* 50 (1956), 168, Kirkwood says of Adams' *Phoenix* article that, whether right or wrong, the theory of divine burial finds 'support for its spirit in many passages of the play'.

14. B. M. W. Knox, *The Heroic Temper: Studies in Sophoclean Tragedy* (Berkeley 1964), p. 69. One might mention also the gods' actual burial of Niobe's children at *Il.* xxiv. 610–12. Knox himself is hard put for an explanation of the second burial, 'perhaps a sense of inadequacy of the first attempt is what brings her back a second time'.

observances.[15] The purpose of the second burial must be dramatic. More 'dramatic' solutions for Antigone's return to her brother have been proposed than can be noted here. For the most part, however, they may be grouped under the following headings. (1) Antigone's return signifies her ἁμαρτία, the stubbornness which forms her tragic flaw.[16] (2) Antigone in some way *wants* to be caught.[17] (3) The Athenian audience does not really notice, or at least does not question, the two visits.[18] (4) It is simply a natural and dutiful act of devotion for Antigone to return to her brother, especially on learning that he has been uncovered.[19] (5) Two burials increase the suspense of the play and serve to show Antigone triumphant before we see her defeated and captured.[20] Clearly these categories impinge upon one another, and writers have not always restricted themselves to one alone.

The first three are perhaps least satisfactory. (1) and (2) involve highly dubious interpretations of the play, with (1) harking back to the Hegelian theory of the equal rightness and wrongness of Antigone and Creon, while (2) inserts an immolation motif into the play which does not seem to exist; (3) appears to be an attempt to avoid the whole problem by attributing (somewhat brazenly) to the Athenians a naïveté which we have outgrown. (4) is initially appealing, but eventually it must either lead us back to (1) or (2),

15. 247, κἀφαγιστεύσας ἃ χρή. See T. von Wilamowitz, *Die dramatische Technik des Sophokles* (Berlin 1917), p. 31. Jebb's suggestion (at v. 429) that perhaps the χοαί were neglected during the first visit and formed the basis for the second is made only half-heartedly. It has been taken up again, however, by A. O. Hulton, 'The Double Burial of the *Antigone*', *Mnemosyne* 16 (1963), 284–5.

16. Meiklejohn (above, n. 4); M. K. Flickinger, 'The ἁμαρτία of Sophocles' Antigone', *Iowa Studies in Class. Phil.* 9 (1935).

17. G. Norwood, *Greek Tragedy* (London 1920), p. 140; J. Cowser, 'The Shaping of the *Antigone*', *PCA* (1939), 38–40 (summary).

18. W. M. Calder, *CPh* 53 (1958), 129, n. 4, in a review of Kitto's *Form and Meaning in Drama*. Calder, in opposition to Adams and in support of Antigone's performance of the two burials, declares with a pleasant insouciance, 'I know no unprejudiced spectator who has thought otherwise'. The views of Owen (above, n. 2), and Kirkwood (above, n. 12), p. 70 also fall partly under this heading and partly under (5).

19. C. M. Bowra, *Sophoclean Tragedy* (Oxford 1944), p. 93; J. L. Rose, 'The Problem of the Second Burial in Sophocles' *Antigone*', *CJ* 47 (1952), 219–21; A. T. von S. Bradshaw, 'The Watchman Scenes in the *Antigone*', *CQ* N.S. 12 (1962), 200–11. Hulton, op. cit. (n. 15), also thinks partly along this line.

20. A. J. A. Waldock, *Sophocles the Dramatist* (Cambridge 1951), pp. 126ff.; Kitto (above, n. 10), p. 152; A. Lesky, *A History of Greek Literature*, tr. J. Willis and C. de Heer (London 1966), p. 280.

or else treat Antigone as not centrally committed to the public relevance of her act.

(5) is dramatically the strongest of the above solutions, but it too is subject to certain questions. First, as the younger Wilamowitz realized, it still leaves unanswered the problem of internal motivation.[21] Sophocles may well have wished to create in his audience a feeling of suspense until the moment that Antigone is led in by the guard. He may equally well have wished to show a just burial effected and Creon enraged, before the upholder of the ἄγραπτα νόμιμα confronts the representative of the state. But none of this will explain why, *within* the play, Antigone herself is impelled to repeat the burial.

Two other questions may also be asked. If the second burial is only a dramatic device, why does its character seem so different from the first burial? There, Antigone accomplishes her mission with stealth; the guards are wholly unaware of her presence.[22] At the second burial, on the other hand, once the dust storm has lifted, Antigone is perceived making no effort either to hide herself or to keep silent. She conducts the first burial with caution, the second with abandon. Her approach to the second burial might be used to support the theory that she desires capture, but then why does she wait until a second burial to expose herself? The difference in the *modus operandi* of the two burials must be taken as a dramatic inconsistency in any theory involving Antigone's performance of both of them, unless we say that she was required religiously to return and lament over the body, and by so doing reveals herself. This has been argued[23] but, like other solutions of a religious nature, without compelling evidence.

Secondly, why does Antigone make no mention of the double act of devotion to her brother in the scenes from her capture to her final exit? One would think that in her defiance of Creon and in the maintenance of the higher justice of her actions such a mention

21. Wilamowitz (above, n. 15); while viewing all of Sophocles as a series of brilliant dramatic scenes, Wilamowitz was still honest enough to admit uneasiness over a purely external dramatic interpretation of the two burials.

22. I assume for the moment that the guard has already been set when Polynices is first buried; why this must be so if Antigone is credited with the first burial will be discussed below.

23. E. Struck, 'Der zweimalige Gang der Antigone zur Leiche des Polyneikes', *Gymnasium* 60 (1953), 327–34.

would find natural and emphatic expression. Yet it never occurs. At 442, when Creon first addresses Antigone after the guard's reluctant indictment of her, *he* uses a generalizing plural, τάδε, to refer to her actions (he of course is quick to attribute both burials to her), and she assents to his words, but he seems to be thinking mainly of the second burial,[24] and in any case τάδε can signify singular as easily as plural.[25] At 542, Antigone rebuffs her sister with a reference in the singular to what she has done, ὧν τοὔργον, ῞Αιδης χοἰ κάτω ξυνίστορες. A few lines later, 546–7, she uses a generalizing plural, μηδ᾽ ἃ μὴ ᾽θιγες / ποιοῦ σεαυτῆς. At no point is there anything like an explicit reference by Antigone to a double burial. The guard's words at 434–5:

κοὶ τάς τε πρόσθεν τάς τε νῦν ἠλέγχομεν
πράξεις· ἄπαρνος δ᾽ οὐδενὸς καθίστατο,

have regularly been taken as in effect an admission by Antigone of both burials, but Adams pointed out that the Greek means only that Antigone 'took the stand of making no denial of anything; she owed no answer to these men',[26] and Antigone's proud indifference does indeed underline her distance from the vociferous guards and their natural concern for an immediate solution.[27]

If we are unconvinced by the various explanations of how and why Antigone performed the two burials of her brother, must we then conclude that Sophocles has created a dramatic sequence that does not admit satisfactory interpretation? Perhaps so, but first let us follow the text through once again.

The prologue of the play between Antigone and Ismene undoubtedly plants a firm conviction in the mind of the audience that Antigone is about to set off to bury her brother. Such verses as 71–2:

κεῖνον δ᾽ ἐγὼ

θάψω,

24. Jebb, *ad loc.*, translates 'this deed'.
25. Cf. just below at 450, where Antigone uses it to refer to Creon's edict. At 248, Creon uses τάδε to refer to the first burial alone.
26. Adams, *Sophocles the Playwright*, p. 49.
27. Meiklejohn (above, n. 4), claims that the Greek *does* mean that Antigone admits both burials; by contrast, Knox (above, n. 14), p. 176, n. 3, while staunchly opposing Adams' theory, still grants: 'It is of course literally true that, as he [Adams] says, "the Greek does not mean and cannot mean that she confessed to both burials".' Knox goes on to argue, however, that in the context the audience would certainly conclude that Antigone has confessed to both burials.

80–1:

σὺ μὲν τάδ’ ἂν προὔχοι’· ἐγὼ δὲ δὴ τάφον
χώσουσ’ ἀδελφῷ φιλτάτῳ πορεύσομαι,

and 91:

οὐκοῦν, ὅταν δὴ μὴ σθένω, πεπαύσομαι,²⁸

are quite unmistakable. When does the prologue take place? Ismene says that the Argive army has fled ἐν νυκτὶ τῇ νῦν (16). Jebb translates 'in this last night' and places the scene at daybreak, as do almost all commentators. This chronology has been attacked recently, however, and the phrase has been taken to mean 'in this present night', with the prologue also taking place while it is yet night.²⁹ Parallels have been adduced for both interpretations of ἐν νυκτὶ τῇ νῦν, but even *were* the phrase to be translated 'in this present night' it does not necessarily follow that the *scene* must be regarded as occurring at night. Ismene's words refer to the time of the flight of the Argives, not to her present conversation with Antigone, and it would seem equally easy for someone talking *at daybreak* of events of the past few hours to say either 'in this last night' or 'in this present night'. The phrase does not in itself conclusively set the time of the prologue. Once this is realized, it is clear that the prologue contains no statement at all to counteract the natural assumption of the audience that it is viewing a daytime scene. If an Athenian audience was supposed to think otherwise, explicit and stressed information was set before it, as for instance at the beginning of the *Agamemnon* where the watchman talks in detail of his starry vigil.³⁰ There is nothing comparable in the prologue of the *Antigone*. Furthermore, the first verses of the parodos hailing the rising sun are so forceful and follow so directly upon the prologue that it is more natural to feel that Ismene and Antigone also have conversed at the break of day than to insert a

28. This phrase, together with Ismene's preceding statement, ἀλλ’ ἀμηχάνων ἐρᾷς, has sometimes been taken to indicate that Antigone has no hope of accomplishing her purpose and is simply throwing away her life blindly (see Norwood (above, n. 17), p. 140). This seems to me a perverse reading of the Greek.

29. Bradshaw (above, n. 19), pp. 201ff. This is a most careful study, but its many interesting conclusions seem suddenly less persuasive when the writer asserts (209f.) that Creon is the single tragic hero of the play.

30. Further examples are the opening scenes of *IA*, *Rhesus*, Euripides' *El.*, and *Clouds*. Bradshaw (above, n. 19), p. 203, adds *Choe.* and *Eum.*, but these are doubtful, in part precisely because they contain no specific words such as those which set the time of the other plays.

lapse of time. Jebb's chronology, therefore, should be followed, no matter which way ἐν νυκτὶ τῇ νῦν is translated. The prologue occurs at daybreak.

Antigone departs to bury her brother. The vigorous parodos is followed, in the first episode, by Creon's pronouncement of his edict to the chorus, an edict first issued prior to the prologue – hence during the night, at some point between the Argive retreat and daybreak. To the chorus's obvious reluctance to oversee enforcement of the edict, Creon retorts that there are already watchers over Polynices, ἀλλ' εἴσ' ἕτοιμοι τοῦ νεκροῦ γ' ἐπίσκοποι (217), and that the chorus need only take care not to side with transgressors. The chorus expresses doubt that there will be any, whereupon Creon for the first time voices his deep and unheroic fear that money may prompt an attempt at burial (221–2).

When the guard enters to report that just such an attempt has been made – and with success, the audience immediately thinks of Antigone, and the first references to the perpetrator of the deed do not lessen this assumption. The guard claims, οὔτ' εἶδον ὅστις ἦν ὁ δρῶν (239), and again, τὸν νεκρόν τις ἀρτίως / θάψας βέβηκε (245–6); Creon demands, τίς ἀνδρῶν ἦν ὁ τολμήσας τάδε; (248). The references are indefinite, but singular and personal. In the guard's reply to Creon's demanding question, however, a new element suggests itself. The normal signs of burial, even a symbolic burial such as this one, are absent: no marks of pickaxe or mattock, no removal of earth, no moisture such as might be caused by libations. Altogether, as the guard says, ἀλλ' ἄσημος οὑργάτης τις ἦν (252). The reference is still indefinite, singular, and personal, but a quite different tone is sounded. No longer is it simply a matter of some unknown violator of the edict; whoever it was acted without trace.

Taken by itself, the phrase could well be interpreted as nothing but defensive exaggeration by the guard. His next words, however, unconsciously make much more explicit the air of mystery which has begun to surround the burial:

> ὅπως δ' ὁ πρῶτος ἡμῖν ἡμεροσκόπος
> δείκνυσι, πᾶσι θαῦμα δυσχερὲς παρῆν (253–4).

ὁ πρῶτος...ἡμεροσκόπος is a strong phrase, and 'the first *day-watcher*' surely suggests that there had been also a watch while it was night.[31] Nothing else will explain adequately the use here of the compound ἡμεροσκόπος[32] and the emphatic πρῶτος. The simpler word ἐπίσκοποι has already been used by Creon (217) to refer generally to the watch he has set. Now the guard says that of these the first to take up the watch by day, i.e. at the same time as the prologue, reported the carrying out of the burial. Polynices, then, was first buried during the night – before Antigone and Ismene met and certainly before Antigone set out on her own burial mission.

Can it be reasonably claimed that Sophocles' Athenian audience would have grasped this crucial double fact which has escaped so many, both ancient and modern?[33] Certainty is perhaps not possible, but one may with some confidence answer affirmatively. A daybreak scene opens the play; Antigone goes off to bury her

31. To be sure, Jebb, *ad loc.*, says of ἡμεροσκόπος, 'The man who took the first watch of this day was the first who had watched at all.' His next words, however, 'If a sentinel had been near the body, Ant. must have been seen', show that he has been forced to this position by his attribution of the first burial to Antigone.

32. Of other instances of the term, some are quite restrictive. Xenophon (*HG* I. 1. 2) says that ὁ τῶν 'Αθηναίων ἡμεροσκόπος observed Dorieus sailing into the Hellespont ἅμα ἡμέρᾳ. Aeneas Tacticus (VI. 1ff.) notes of ἡμεροσκόποι that they should be sent out at dawn or even earlier, while it is yet dark. More generally, jays are spoken of at *Av.* 1174 as the φύλακας ἡμεροσκόπους of Nephelococcygia. The messenger tells Eteocles (*Septem* 66) that his eye will serve as a πιστὸν ἡμεροσκόπον of the enemy's movements. The word is used twice in Herodotus (VII. 183, 192) of the guards left on the heights of Euboea to watch the Persian fleet, and again (VII. 219), more narrowly, of the watches who at dawn told the Greeks at Thermopylae of the Persian circumvention of the pass during the night. The technical term for 'night-watch', it may be added, is νυκτοφύλαξ (Xen. *An.* VII. 2. 18, VII. 3. 34).

33. The writer of the third hypothesis, for instance, says flatly, καὶ δὴ λαθοῦσα τοὺς φύλακας [Antigone] ἐπιβάλλει χῶμα. Philostratus, *Imagines* II. 29, sees half the truth and places the first burial at night, but creates a florid scene in which Antigone by the light of the moon raises up Polynices in her arms and buries him by the side of Eteocles. Knox, Bradshaw, and Masqueray are among the few modern scholars who have recognized that the first burial must take place at night. Bradshaw (as we have seen) and Knox (above, n. 14), p. 83, then force the prologue also into a night setting, thus enabling Antigone to carry out the burial. Masqueray asks exactly the right question: *Sophocle*, vol. I (Paris 1922), p. 86, n. 1, 'elle [the first burial] a été commise dans les dernières heures de la nuit. Mais comment Antigone a-t-elle bien pu s'y prendre, puisqu'elle n'a quitté Ismène, v. 99, que lorsqu'il faisait jour?' Sheppard (above, n. 11) is equally probing, 'How could Antigone have reached the body in the darkness? She had set out, we had imagined, after dawn.' Neither, however, proceeds to the necessary answer.

brother as the chorus addresses the rising sun; the guard reports a burial, assumed to be effected by Antigone; then he describes how mysterious the burial was and, employing an unusual compound, follows with an emphatic verse which says that the burial was discovered fully accomplished at daybreak, a time when Antigone is only just undertaking her mission. Surely Athenians who almost twenty years earlier had been able to appreciate the delicate shadings of guilt and counter-guilt in the *Oresteia*, who had since then entered the first phase of the sophistic revolution, and who, thirty years later, would gain freedom from their Sicilian captors by reciting extensive passages of Euripides[34] may be thought capable of registering, as the guard's speech develops, first surprise, then disbelief, that Antigone can be the one who has buried her brother.

The alternative which is subtly urged on the audience in the remainder of the scene between the guard and Creon is neither discredited in the second guard scene when the captured Antigone is led forward nor is out of harmony with the spirit of the whole play: in this first burial the gods have been present. We should not expect such an idea to be delivered frontally by any single character in the play. It emerges rather by repeated implication and suggestion – as indeed it must.

After the guard firmly places the burial of Polynices during the night, unaware that by so doing he has eliminated Antigone as the agent, he goes on to relate more details. The body, he says, was covered lightly with dust, as if by someone avoiding pollution, and had not been molested by any dog or preying beast:

> λεπτὴ δ' ἄγος φεύγοντος ὡς ἐπῆν κόνις.
> σημεῖα δ' οὔτε θηρὸς οὔτε του κυνῶν
> ἐλθόντος, οὐ σπάσαντος ἐξεφαίνετο (256–8).

It has been argued that 256 is inconsistent with Adams' theory.[35] Why should the gods, if they are to be associated with the burial, be bothered about avoiding pollution? Such a concern is of the human sphere, not of the divine. A closer inspection of the verse, however, reveals that this is one of two noteworthy instances in the play in which the guard applies his own, not necessarily correct, interpretation to events. He still thinks in terms of a human agent. Of course. He does not know that his own testimony has dis-

34. Plutarch, *Nicias* 29.   35. Flickinger (above, n. 4), p. 132.

qualified the one human being who intends to perform the burial.
For him the religious intensity and mystery that seem to have
surrounded the burial can be expressed meaningfully by a simile
of a dread curse avoided. But the simile is only his, and his knowledge is incomplete, though ironically he states a deep truth in his
half-ignorance. Incomplete knowledge and dramatic irony are
pervasive elements in Sophocles' genius, and they strikingly mark
this scene. It is quite clear from the beginning of the play that to
refuse Polynices burial is a wrong, unredeemed by any appeal to
the stability of the state. So wrong is such a refusal that it does
create a sort of pollution, as Teiresias declares firmly later in the
play. Thus the guard is confirming a central theme of the play
when he compares Polynices' burial to avoidance of an ἄγος. *He*
cannot progress beyond belief in a human burial, albeit mysterious.
The audience, pondering an alternative to Antigone, may be
thought of as reacting sympathetically to the guard's simile, then
as feeling a tremor of excitement as he mentions the last detail of
the burial, the preservation of the corpse. Polynices has been protected since his death, in just the same manner as other famous
heroes, for instance Sarpedon and Hector, were protected – and it
was the gods who protected *them*! As the guard ends his report of
the burial and moves from mystery to rationality, λόγος (λόγοι δ'
ἐν ἀλλήλοισιν ἐρρόθουν κακοί, 259), the audience may perhaps be
pictured as drawing a comparison of its own: Polynices has been
buried and a wrong righted, as if by the gods.

The audience's awesome musing is reinforced as soon as the
guard has finished his tale of the mutual accusations among his
fellow guards and how the lot fell to him to bear the news to
Creon.[36] The coryphaeus immediately addresses the king in polite
but precise tones:

> ἄναξ, ἐμοί τοι, μή τι καὶ θεήλατον
> τοὔργον τόδ', ἡ ξύννοια βουλεύει πάλαι (278–9).

Every word in the first verse is trifling until the last, which is strong,
and is made even more so by its position, both metrical and
rhetorical: 'Lord, to my mind – may I say it – is it not possible
that perhaps *god-imposed* is this action? My thoughts have counseled

36. One function of these twenty verses by the guard surely is to prolong and
increase the audience's suspenseful anticipation.

this long.' The chorus in Sophocles is often separated from the truth by its unheroic vision and its common, though honest, morality. In this instance, however, the simple directness of its response makes it, as it were, a bellwether to the audience. The chorus has heard the same facts as the audience, but without preconceptions of Antigone's involvement. Its first words altogether neglect mankind and focus on the gods, though carefully mentioning them only through the indirect means of a compound adjective. The chorus's reaction to the guard's speech is presumably a natural one, and the audience's own growing thoughts of a divinely wrought burial are considerably furthered.

Creon, enraged at the coryphaeus' suggestion, delivers a violent tirade in answer, during which the dramatic irony of the scene continues to mount. After an opening volley of contempt, he states:

λέγεις γὰρ οὐκ ἀνεκτά, δαίμονας λέγων
πρόνοιαν ἴσχειν τοῦδε τοῦ νεκροῦ πέρι (282–3).

Unendurable the chorus's words may be, but they are so only to one who has been blind to the true will of the gods. The audience already recognizes Creon to be in error in his position toward Polynices and thus toward the gods. Yet it is he alone who can bring himself to mention the gods directly, and the combination of his mistaken outlook and fervent denial of divine involvement produces something like the rhetorical effect of a double negative – that is, an affirmation of the chorus's suggestion. The remainder of Creon's speech deepens the impression that we come close to the truth by inverting his statements. His repetition of the theory that bribery lies at the root of the burial is a case in point. The audience knows well that even were Antigone the one who first buried Polynices such a theory would be a debasement of her motives. As an unknowing reference to a burial involving the gods, the theory approaches sacrilege. The irony of Creon's rantings reaches full force in his fierce vow to the guard:

ἀλλ' εἴπερ ἴσχει Ζεὺς ἔτ' ἐξ ἐμοῦ σέβας,
εὖ τοῦτ' ἐπίστασ', ὅρκιος δέ σοι λέγω,
εἰ μὴ τὸν αὐτόχειρα τοῦδε τοῦ τάφου
εὑρόντες ἐκφανεῖτ' ἐς ὀφθαλμοὺς ἐμούς,
οὐχ ὑμῖν Ἅιδης μοῦνος ἀρκέσει (304–8).

8

In effect, he is swearing by Zeus to bring the gods to the tribunal, to judge and punish the divine will. The error of his position is indicated tellingly, and the irony of his self-conviction is not lost on the audience.

The scene is now complete. The guard has told the story; the chorus has drawn the simple, yet marvelous, conclusion;[37] Creon has reaffirmed it by his very opposition. A final, lighter touch is added as the guard retreats from the stage:

καὶ νῦν γὰρ ἐκτὸς ἐλπίδος γνώμης τ' ἐμῆς
σωθεὶς ὀφείλω τοῖς θεοῖς πολλὴν χάριν (330–1).

Owing thanks to the gods is a standard phrase, not especially religious in feeling. Here, it not only exemplifies the Greek penchant for a quiet aftermath to a climax but also receives a certain ironic significance: a prosaic mention of the gods comes from the very character who unwittingly has just cast them in a solemn role.

The first stasimon which now follows, regarded in the light of the more than human scene that has been unfolded, takes on hues of sharp contrast. Man is variously amazing. Death alone he cannot outdo. His city stands high so long as he reverences its laws and the gods' justice. Such are man's dimensions and limits, and the ode works both as a contrast to the loftier realm manifested in the previous scene and as a transition to the rest of the play, which will illustrate specifically the fruits reaped by Creon's obtuse view of a city's laws and the gods' justice.

The second burial of Polynices subdues but does not negate the miraculous aura felt by the audience to mark the first burial. The scene in which the guard returns with the captured Antigone is comparatively straightforward. She has been taken in the act, and no mystery surrounds the details of the second burial. The guard assumes throughout the scene that Antigone is also responsible for the first burial, as he states upon entering, ἥδ' ἔστ' ἐκείνη τοὔργον ἡ 'ξειργασμένη (384). There is no reason for him to think otherwise. Despite his report of the uncanny circumstances of the first burial,

---

37. Meiklejohn (above, n. 4), wrongly reverses the sequence when he says that the guard suggests divine intervention and the chorus follows his suggestion. The case is rather that the chorus is the initiator of the suggestion. The guard does not know what to make of the strange anonymity of the burial.

his king dismissed him roughly to find a human culprit. Antigone has now been caught, and as the guard later narrates (434–5) she has not denied the first burial. If only in self-preservation, it is natural for him to assign both burials to his one tangible captive and, as has been noted, he is not aware that Antigone only set out on her mission after the first burial was accomplished. Creon also is unaware of this fact, and so the scene develops on the assumption of the guard's opening statement. Only Antigone can change that assumption, and she chooses not to do so. On the other hand, we have seen that neither her stance toward the guards at 434–5 nor her later references to her deed constitute admission of involvement in the first burial. If anything, they suggest the opposite.

Her actual performance of the second burial, as has been noted, also jars with the secret aura of the first burial, but in this context two remarks of the guard have been adduced as evidence of Antigone's responsibility for both burials. After he describes how at noon the dust storm arose[38] and, upon subsiding, revealed Antigone at the side of her brother, he continues:

κἀνακωκύει πικρᾶς
ὄρνιθος ὀξὺν φθόγγον, ὡς ὅταν κενῆς
εὐνῆς νεοσσῶν ὀρφανὸν βλέψῃ λέχος·
οὕτω δὲ χαὔτη, ψιλὸν ὡς ὁρᾷ νέκυν,
γόοισιν ἐξώμωξεν (423–7).

The image is of a mother bird who has left her nest full and returns to find it empty. Correspondingly, it might seem, Antigone has returned to find *her* once buried Polynices unburied.[39] It is a beautiful and moving picture, but it is not evidence for what has actually happened, since for the second time the guard's own interpretation of events is decisive in his choice of language. To him it appears that Antigone is acting in precisely this manner, but only because he assumes the first burial to be hers. *His* image must not be thought to express the way in which Antigone herself, as

38. This paper in no way argues actual divine participation in the second burial. But in light of the mystery of the first burial, the guard's language describing the dust storm, οὐράνιον ἄχος (418) and θείαν νόσον (421) surely suggests the continuing force of the gods in the play.

39. Cowser (above, n. 17); Rouse (above, n. 5); Hulton (above, n. 15).

she beheld her brother, necessarily would have described her feelings.[40] Similarly, the guard's next words, still referring to Antigone:

$$\text{ἐκ δ' ἀρὰς κακὰς}$$
$$\text{ἠρᾶτο τοῖσι τοὔργον ἐξειργασμένοις (427–8),}$$

initially seem to mean, in the light of the bird image, that Antigone cursed those who had undone *her* handiwork.[41] This, however, is only an inference. The Greek merely says that she cursed those who did the deed, i.e. who uncovered the body.[42] Neither of these remarks by the guard, then, should be used to argue that Antigone effected the first burial. Both exist easily in a theory which assigns only the second burial to her.

No one, I think, denies that a central issue in the *Antigone* is the code of the individual and the family against the demands of the state, and that Antigone in her defence of the individual claims for her side the higher justice of the gods. If we abide, as surely we must, by the interpretation that on this issue, and as Sophocles presents the arguments in *this* play, Antigone is in the right and Creon in the wrong, then an equally central theme, as many have recognized, is the confirmation of the individual by the gods, and Sophocles has chosen a magnificent way to express it. In contrast to the clear-cut participation of the gods in other tragedies, such as the *Ajax*, to go no further, the hand of the gods in the burial of Polynices never quite becomes visible. In the first guard scene, the audience is led to the very edge of exclaiming, 'The gods have done it!' The first stasimon and the second guard scene divert this exciting response into more normal channels of thought, but it is never far below the surface. Antigone does not reject the guard's accusation of the first burial. She is willing, even eager, to accept responsibility for all that has to do with her brother's burial. In addition, though more aware than the other figures in the play,

40. This point is mentioned by J. E. Harry, *Greek Tragedy* (New York 1933), p. 119, but without emphasis and in the different context of a discussion, almost a tacit acceptance, of Rouse's theory that Ismene first buried Polynices.

41. Hulton (above, n. 15).

42. Fraternal love is the chief prompter of this curse. In addition there is a visual spur if we may suppose that Antigone, as she waited through the morning hours for an opportunity to approach her brother, saw the guard return from his first scene with Creon and, with his fellow guards, sweep bare Polynices' body.

even she does not see fully what has happened. Only the audience knows the exact sequence of events, the impossibility of Antigone's participation in the first burial, and the ensuing suggestiveness of the first guard scene. It is the sort of suggestiveness which may be pushed aside in the stir of the actual performance but which returns afterward to haunt the imagination. The *Antigone* moved the Athenians profoundly; Sophocles may even have been elected *strategos* as a result. The remarkable thought of a divine burial is no small part of the play's power, and both deepens the significance of Antigone's appeal to the ἄγραπτα νόμιμα and makes even more satisfying, not to say inevitable, Creon's eventual acquiescence in Polynices' burial.[43]

43. I wish to thank Professor Cedric Whitman for seminal help on the ideas of this paper, Professor Zeph Stewart for criticism of an early draft, and Professor Bernard Knox for constructive opposition to many of my views. The substance of the paper was read on 29 December 1966, before the American Philological Association. I am more than delighted to see it appear in a volume which honors my former professor, Eric Havelock.

Menander's *Samia* in the light of the new evidence*

HUGH LLOYD-JONES

IN JUNE 1969, the Bodmer Library at Cologny, near Geneva, brought out a photographic facsimile and a transcription of those pages of the codex containing Menander's *Dyskolos* which contain large fragments of the *Samia* and *Aspis* of the same author (Papyrus Bodmer xxv and xxvi). In July Dr Colin Austin, who has collaborated with Professor Rodolphe Kasser in the preparation of these volumes, published a critical edition of both works; a commentary in a separate volume soon followed (*Menandri Samia et Aspis*, I et II, in the series *Kleine Texte für Vorlesungen und Übungen*, Berlin, Walter de Gruyter, 1969, 1970). The reader of this article will be well advised to have in hand the facsimile and Dr Austin's text, or at any rate the latter. In it I am concerned not to discuss the critical problems in which the text abounds, but to attempt a general survey of the *Samia*, offering at the same time a translation of most of the new material. For detailed explanation of the text, I refer the reader to Dr Austin's work. 341 lines (or parts of lines) of this play are contained in the famous Cairo papyrus published by Lefèbvre in 1905, together with one line known from a quota-

* This article is based on a paper read at the Fifth International Congress of Classical Studies at Bonn in September 1969. Its publication has been unfortunately delayed.

Bibliography: E. W. Handley, 'Menander's *Aspis* and *Samia*: Some Textual Notes', *BICS* 16 (1969), 102ff.; Colin Austin, 'Notes on Menander's *Aspis* and *Samia*', *ZPE* 4, Heft 3 (1969), 161ff.; F. Stoessl, 'Die neue Menanderpublikationen der Bibliotheca Bodmeriana in Genf', *Rh. Mus.* 112 (1969), 193ff.; M. Treu, 'Humane Handlungsmotive in der *Samia* Menanders', ibid., 230ff.; H. J. Mette, 'Moschion ὁ κόσμιος', *Hermes* 97 (1969), 432ff.; W. G. Arnott (1) *Gnomon* 42 (1970), 10ff.; (2) *University of Leeds Review* 13 (1970), 1ff.; (3) *Arethusa* 3 (1970), 56ff.; D. Del Corno, *Atene e Roma* N.S. 15 (1970), 65ff.; J.-M. Jacques, *Ménandre*, Tome Ie, *La Samienne* (Budé edition), 1971 (whose introduction contains an excellent general discussion of the play); Christina Dedoussi, *The Samia*, 'Ménandre', *Entretiens de la Fondation Hardt*, no. 16 (1970), 159ff. (which I saw only at the proof stage).

[119]

tion.[1] We now have 738 lines altogether, and it seems likely that about 158 lines are missing.

In order to evaluate our new gains we may begin by recapitulating what was known about the play when we had only the portion of the text in Cairo. The 341 lines of the *Samia*[2] there preserved are contained in a single quaternion, whose middle folio – four sides, including, as we now know, 131 verses – and whose last page – two sides, including 51 verses – are missing. Until very lately scholars had not agreed as to where the portion of the text preserved in the Cairo manuscript began. It starts soon after the beginning of an act; the Teubner editor, Alfred Koerte, and most scholars thought this act was the third, but Wilamowitz[3] held that it was 'undoubtedly' the fourth and A. W. Gomme[4] in 1936 argued that it was the second. Since 1961 we have known from a mosaic pavement with illustrations from Menander found in Mytilene[5] that the majority was right. The Cairo papyrus starts just after the beginning of the third act, has a gap of 131 lines just before the beginning of the fourth and breaks off more than halfway through the fifth.

Let us take first the question of the title. The view that the play in the Cairo manuscript was the *Samia* rested until eight years ago simply on a couple of references to its heroine; the single fragment

1. A valuable aid to the understanding of the parts of the play preserved in the Cairo manuscript is the commentary in demotic Greek by Dr Christina Dedoussi (*The Samia of Menander*, Athens 1965); see the review by Colin Austin in *Gnomon* 39 (1967), 121ff.

2. See Koerte–Thierfelder's Teubner *Menander* I, 1959 edn, xxxvii ff.; Koerte, *R.-E.* xv 1 (1931), 725–6; cf. K. Kunst, *Studien zur griech.-röm. Komödie* (1919), p. 67; *Wiener Studien* 43 (1922/3), 147ff.; E. Wüst, *Philologus* 78 (1923), 193; T. B. L. Webster, *Studies in Menander* (2nd edn 1960), pp. 40ff.

3. Wilamowitz, *S.B. Berlin* (1916), pp. 66ff. = *Kl. Schr.* I, 410ff., esp. p. 74 = 425. Cf. E. Capps, *Four Plays of Menander* (1910); Wüst, loc. cit. (above, n. 2), 197.

4. Gomme, *Cl. Quart.* 30 (1936), 70ff., A. Barigeazzi, *La Formazione Spirituale di Menandro*, pp. 116ff., took this view in 1965. Cf. J. Van Leeuwen, *Menandri Fabularum Reliquiae* (1919), p. 98; F. G. Allinson, *Menander* (L.C.L.; 1919), p. 131.

5. It is illustrated on the jacket, and also opposite p. 1 of Dr Dedoussi's edition; see Austin's review, cited in n. 1 above, pp. 122–3. A coloured reproduction is on the front page of the Bodmer *Samia*. See now the splendid publication of S. Charitonidis, L. Kahil and R. Ginouvés, *Les mosaïques de la maison du Ménandre à Mytilène*, Sechstes Beiheft zur Halbjahresschrift *Antike Kunst* (1970), pp. 38ff. with Plate 4.

of that play preserved in a quotation did not coincide with any portion of the Cairo text, and Wilamowitz thought the title of the work wholly uncertain. The Mytilene mosaic gave the first clear evidence that the play in question was Menander's *Samia*. But at first sight the Geneva manuscript presents us with a new problem regarding the title of the work. The new portions of the text show coincidences with two fragments, one three lines and one two lines long, quoted in Stobaeus and assigned in the Teubner *Menander* to the *Knidia*, 'The Woman of Cnidos'.[6] No Cnidian woman appears in this play. But if we look at the apparatus criticus to each of these fragments, we find that in both cases Κνιδία is a conjecture, and that it is wrong.

The first fragment is given by the only two manuscripts of Stobaeus that contain it to Μενάνδρου Κνηδία: the second is given by one manuscript to Μένανδρος Κηδείαι, by the other to Μενάνδρου 'Ακηδεία (*sic*). The late Alphonse Dain, who in *Maia* 15 (1963), 292 offered some advance information about the Bodmer manuscript, took 'Ακήδεια to be correct; this encouraged H.-J. Mette, *Lustrum* 10 (1965), 167–8, to imagine that the prologue was spoken by the goddess Akedeia, 'Incuria'.[7] Sorry as I am to deny belief in this fascinating divinity, I must point out that the correct reading is obviously Κηδεία, 'The Marriage Alliance', an expression used by Xenophon, Aristotle and Polybius, as well as by Euripides (see LSJ, s.v.).

The central subject of the play is the alliance between the two families whose houses are visible on the stage, which the two fathers wish to cement by the marriage of Demeas' adopted son Moschion to Nikeratos' daughter Plangon. All the characters both old and young are eager to bring about the marriage, but one mischance after another causes it to be put off. Gomme (loc. cit. 72) says that 'had it been an eighteenth-century play, it might have been called "Chrysis, or the Wedding Postponed"'. 'The Samian Woman, or The Marriage Alliance' is a good ancient equivalent.

The houses on either side of the stage belong to two middle-aged Athenian citizens, Demeas and Nikeratos. Demeas is a rich man, as the new material abundantly confirms; he has an adopted son

6. Frs. 248–9 K.–T.
7. Mette still believes in 'Akedeia' at *Hermes* 97 (1969), 435, and in his supplement to Koerte's *R.-E.* article 'Menandros' (Sp. 860).

called Moschion, perhaps in his early twenties, and a Samian
mistress called Chrysis who keeps house for him. Nikeratos is a
poor man; he is married and has a daughter called Plangon. The
third act starts with a long soliloquy in which Demeas describes
how he has remained unnoticed in the storeroom of his house while
Chrysis and the servants have been making preparations for his
son's wedding. The Cairo text begins with what is l. 216 of the play
as we now have it; which has turned out to be the eleventh line of
Demeas' soliloquy. While busy with these preparations, the
women have been neglecting an infant; Moschion's old nurse has
hurried in and reproached another woman with neglecting it on
the occasion of its father's wedding. The other woman has warned
her to be quiet, since the master is at home; and a little later
Demeas has seen Chrysis holding the infant and giving it the
breast. Chrysis has persuaded him against his will, he says, to allow
a child of hers to be brought up instead of having it exposed, as a
citizen whose concubine gave birth had a perfect right to do. He
now guesses that she has found herself pregnant by his son Moschion, and in order to preserve the child has tried to persuade
Demeas that it is his own.

Demeas' slave Parmenon now enters (l. 283 of the complete
text, 68 in the Teubner edition), accompanied by a cook whom he
has hired to cook the wedding dinner and by other attendants,
who are carrying provisions from the market. After a brief comic
passage that involves the cook, they are about to enter the house
when Demeas detains Parmenon (295ff. = 8off.) and asks him
who is the father of the child. Parmenon says that it is the child of
Demeas and Chrysis, but not in a way that allays Demeas' suspicions. Demeas flies into a temper, threatens the slave with severe
punishment, and is about to carry out his threat when he suddenly
checks himself; Parmenon makes off, and Demeas delivers another
reflective monologue (326ff. = 111ff.). Since Moschion has lately
shown himself eager to marry, Demeas says, he must have been an
unwilling partner in the liaison with Chrysis; he must have taken
advantage of a drunken moment to seduce him. But as for Chrysis,
she has shown herself in her true colours, and he must steel himself
and dismiss her from his house.

The cook returns looking for Parmenon (357), and during the
scene between Demeas and Chrysis that follows he makes ridicu-

lous efforts to come between them.[8] Demeas violently expels Chrysis from his house, together with an old slave-woman who is carrying the child; he makes no mention of her supposed affair with Moschion, but allows her to suppose that he has suddenly become furious at the request to be permitted to bring up the child which when she first made it he had granted.

The nextdoor neighbour Nikeratos now arrives (399ff. = 184ff.), bringing a sheep to be sacrificed for the wedding feast; it is a lean sheep, for he is a poor man, and complaint of the leanness of a sacrificial sheep is a stock joke in the New Comedy. He finds Chrysis outside the door, and learns from her that Demeas has expelled her on the child's account. He was angry not at once, but after an interval, she says; he first gave orders to get ready for the wedding and then suddenly burst in and turned her out. At this point (after l. 416) occurs the big gap in the Cairo text, amounting as we now learn to 131 lines.

The Cairo text begins again well inside the fourth act (546 = 202), during a scene in tetrameters, the metre so often reserved for episodes of unusual speed and animation. Demeas is on the stage together with Nikeratos, who is in a state of violent excitement. Demeas in an aside says that his neighbour has threatened to burn the child, that he has come rushing in like a whirlwind or a thunderbolt, and that he, Demeas, is to blame for not having foreseen the other's indignation. Nikeratos complains that Chrysis has persuaded his wife and daughter to admit nothing and refuses to give up the child; he now threatens that he will murder her. He rushes back into the house and out comes Chrysis, hotly pursued by him. When Demeas tries to restrain him, he complains that Chrysis refuses to give up the child. 'That's ridiculous', says Demeas, 'it is mine' (579 = 234). Denying this, Nikeratos says he will pursue Chrysis into the house and do away with her. At last Demeas manages to persuade him to put questions to himself instead. 'Has your son made a fool of me?' asks Nikeratos (585–6 = 240–1). 'You are talking nonsense', says Demeas, 'he shall take the girl, but it is not as you think.' Then he suggests to his friend that they take a walk, so that Nikeratos can pull himself together.

8. See Austin, *Gnomon*, loc. cit. (in n. 1), 123. Radermacher and Van Leeuwen, who saw that the cook must be a speaker in this scene, have been vindicated against Wilamowitz by the Mytilene mosaic.

Nikeratos must know how in the tragedy Zeus turns to gold and drips through a roof to seduce Danae; Nikeratos should look at his own roof to see if it is leaking. Nikeratos is less important than Akrisios, king of Argos, Danae's father; if Zeus seduced Danae, what may he have done to Plangon? 'Ah me, Moschion has tricked me', exclaims Nikeratos (598–9 = 253–4), and again Demeas assures him that Moschion shall marry the girl. Finally he manages to calm down his friend and send him off to help in the preparations for the wedding.

The fifth act starts with a soliloquy by Moschion (616ff. = 271ff.). He is relieved to be acquitted of the suspicions that have hung over him, but is angry with his father for having thought him capable of an intrigue with Chrysis. Were it not for his oath, his love and habit – things to which he has become enslaved – he would go off and earn his living as a mercenary. As it is, Eros will not allow this; but he would still like to give his father a fright.

Now Parmenon enters, at first not seeing Moschion, and delivers a soliloquy (641ff. = 296ff.); with hypocritical self-righteousness he reproaches himself with having run away and hidden when he had no real reason to be afraid. His young master seduced a citizen's daughter and got her with child; this was not his, Parmenon's, fault. The child was introduced into the house; it was not he, but Moschion, who brought it. Someone in the house acknowledged the child; what harm had he, Parmenon, been guilty of? Well, it is not pleasant to be punished, whether one has deserved to be or not.

At this moment (657 = 312), Moschion attracts the slave's attention. He tells him to fetch the sword and military cloak which he will need as a mercenary, explaining in an aside that he means to scare his father. At this point (670ff. = 325ff.), the metre changes to tetrameters, which continue for the remainder of the play. Parmenon tells Moschion that he seems to be out of date in his information, and asks him to come in and join the wedding party; it is time for him to go and fetch the bride. Furious at the slave's presuming to give him orders, Moschion strikes him in the face (679 = 334),[9] thus proving Parmenon's earlier self-satisfaction

---

9. Austin, *Gnomon*, loc. cit., 126–7 and L. A. Post, *AJP* 88 (1967), 103 are right in this matter against Dedoussi; Austin aptly quotes Terence, *Ad.* 559, *em vide ut discidit labrum.*

to have been premature. He starts off to fetch Moschion's equipment, but stops to say that he has noticed that the feast has
actually begun. For a moment Moschion hesitates; suppose his
father does not, after all, implore him to forgive him and remain
at home, but simply allows him to depart? This is where the Cairo
text breaks off (686); we now learn that it does so 51 lines before
the end.

Let us now turn to the new material. The opening pages of the
Geneva manuscript are by no means perfectly preserved. They
contain a number of lacunae, so that of the first two acts we possess
only 205 out of about 360 verses, and some of those are incomplete.
Still, we are more or less able to follow the action during this
opening section of the play, and of the last three acts, though some
lines are incomplete, only two or three lines are missing altogether.

The text starts apparently some six lines after the beginning of
the play; Moschion is the speaker of the prologue speech. Something, he tells us (3), is painful, for he has done wrong. 'I think I
can do this reasonably', he says a little later (5ff.), 'if I describe
his whole character.' The person whose character he goes on to
describe turns out to be his adoptive father Demeas. He must
therefore have been mentioned in the lost portion of the text; the
play may have begun, like the *Aspis*, with an assertion that the
speaker is extremely miserable. 'During the time that followed',
he says (7ff.), 'as a boy I enjoyed many luxuries; I shall not tell
you of them, well though I remember. Immature as I still was, he
did me all these kindnesses. When my name was entered on the
civic roll,[10] I was just like anybody else; I was, as they say, one of
the many; but now I am unhappier than any other person. Yes,
we are only mortals! What marked me off from others was the
money I had to spend[11] and the display I made; he kept hounds
for me, and horses; I spent lavishly in command of my tribe's
cavalry; I was able to give moderate help to any of my friends who

10. In l. 10 I have adopted Austin's early suggestion ἐν]εγράφην, 'I was
entered on the citizen roll', as young Athenians were entered at eighteen; so
now Handley, Arnott, Treu. See P. Oxy. 2654 (a fragment of Menander's
Karchedonios, Part xxxiii, p. 7); the discussion of this practice in Aristotle's
Ath. Pol. referred to in Turner's note *ad loc.* is contained in ch. 42 of that work.

11. In l. 13 I take χορηγεῖν in the general, not the special, sense. In l. 17,
'to be a human being' implies, as often in Menander, 'to show human kindness'.

were in need. Owing to him I could be human. All the same, I
paid him back well for all this: I behaved myself. After that it came
about – yes, while I'm about it, I'll tell you our whole story, since
I happen to have time to spare – that he fell in love with a Samian
hetaira, the sort of thing, perhaps, that can happen to any man.
He tried to conceal it, he was ashamed of it; I noticed it despite his
efforts, and reckoned that if he did not get the hetaira into his
power, he would have trouble from rivals who were young, and
that he was ashamed to do this because of me.'

When the text continues after a break of some 22 lines, Moschion
has presumably fulfilled his promise to describe the character of
his adoptive father; later (p. 143) I shall hazard a guess at part of
what he may have said. He must also have referred to Nikeratos
and his daughter (cf. 36) and mentioned that Demeas and Nikeratos are absent (cf. 53). He has now passed on (30ff.) to an account
of his own seduction of Plangon, the daughter of the nextdoor
neighbour Nikeratos, who must have been mentioned in the preceding gap (note l. 36). 'The girl's mother', he said (35ff.), 'was
on friendly terms with my father's Samian; she was very often in
their house, and they in ours. Well, I came rushing back from the
country and found them assembled in our house for the festival of
Adonis, with some other ladies. The feast provided great amuse-
ment, naturally; and as I was there with them I enjoyed a show
without having to leave home;[12] you see, the noise they were
making was keeping me awake. They were bringing up plants on to
the roof, dancing and enjoying the midnight festival, all in different places. I don't like to tell the rest of the story; perhaps I'm
ashamed to. Of course it's no use; all the same, I am ashamed.
The girl became pregnant; when I've told you that, you know
what happened before. I didn't deny that it was my fault, but went
to see the girl's mother without waiting to be sent for; I promised
I would marry her when my father came back at last, and took an
oath to that effect. The child was born, and I took it, not long ago.
Then quite by chance Chrysis (gave birth?); we call that...' Here
begins a gap of about 28 lines; somewhere in the gap the prologue
must have ended.

The revelation that Moschion observed that Demeas was
secretly in love with Chrysis and urged him to take her into his

12. In l. 43 Kassel's οἴκοι is attractive.

house throws an interesting light on the relations between Demeas and his adopted son. Moschion says that Demeas was ashamed, and clearly his consideration for his adopted son would have restrained him from this action, if Moschion himself had not noticed his predicament and urged him to take action. Moschion's way of speaking of his adoptive father shows a real gratitude and delicacy of feeling. Delicacy of feeling, combined with the awkwardness of immaturity, is also shown by his rueful account of how the neighbour's daughter was put in the family way. We get new light (38ff.) on the words of Demeas to Nikeratos in the fourth act (589ff.), when he reminds him of how Zeus seduced Danae and advises him to inspect his own roof for leaks. Moschion seduced Plangon during the festival of Adonis, when women used to carry potted plants up on to the roof, as they do in the Alexandrian Adonis festival described in the fifteenth idyll of Theocritus. We can now see Demeas' joke to be distinctly better than we could have realized earlier. Without the temptation offered by this unusual opportunity, Moschion would hardly have acted as he did; the awkward circumlocution by which he avoids actually saying that he seduced the girl is very much in character.

After the break of some 28 lines already mentioned, the text continues, it appears, with Chrysis alone upon the stage (58ff.). What will have stood in the lacuna? Moschion will have told how Chrysis lost her child and took charge of his, and then explained (61) that his father has returned and is expected to reach home any minute, and that he is dreading their encounter. Then the Chorus will have made its first entry, which will no doubt have been explained as the appearance of a company of intoxicated revellers.

Act II seems to have begun with a soliloquy of Chrysis, probably very brief. 'I will wait and listen to what they say', Chrysis says; the people in question turn out to be Moschion and the slave Parmenon. 'Did you see my father with your own eyes, Parmenon?' Moschion begins (61). 'Didn't you hear me? I said I had.' 'And our neighbour?' 'They are here.' 'Good for them!' 'Well, be sure to be brave and raise at once the question of the marriage.' 'How can I? I'm getting cold feet already; the moment is so near!' 'What do you mean?' 'I'm ashamed of what my father will think.' 'And what about the girl you've done wrong to, and her mother?

Why, how you're trembling, woman-man!' Now Chrysis cuts in
with 'Why are you shouting, wretch?' 'So Chrysis was here too',
says Parmenon, 'Do you ask me why I'm shouting? It's absurd;
I want the marriage to take place at once, and this fellow to stop
weeping at these doors, and to remember what he swore; I want
him to offer sacrifice, to wear a garland, to pound sesame, after
approaching his father on his own. Haven't I reason enough to
shout?' 'I'll do it all', says Moschion, 'What must I say?' 'I
think –', Chrysis begins, but Parmenon interrupts her. 'We must
leave the child where it is', he says, 'and let Chrysis look after it,
saying she has had a child herself.' 'Why ever not?' says Chrysis.
'But my father will be angry', puts in Moschion. 'He won't be
angry for ever', says either Parmenon or Chrysis, 'He is just as
madly in love as you, and that quickly makes even the most hot-
tempered of men make up a quarrel. I would endure anything
rather than have the child...a nurse in a humble lodging...'
Who is the speaker of these last lines? We may feel that the reference to Demeas' love is better suited to Parmenon. But the
determination not to have the child put out seems more like
Chrysis, who after all is an hetaira and may enjoy a liberty of
speech not permitted to the Athenian bourgeoise.

We have learned that the old conjecture[13] that Chrysis found
herself pregnant by Demeas just when Plangon became pregnant
by Moschion turns out to be correct (55–6); clearly her child must
have died at birth. It is therefore natural that Parmenon, who
despite his feigned innocence in the last act (641ff.) is like so many
slaves in New Comedy the arch-intriguer of the piece, should
suggest that Chrysis should pass off the child as her own until its
father can persuade Demeas to allow his marriage with its mother.
Clearly Demeas, though kind and generous, is exceedingly irascible, and no doubt Moschion said so during the sketch of his
adoptive father's character given in the prologue. Without Parmenon, Moschion would hardly have had either the ingenuity to
think of such a plan or the courage to put it into execution; the
plotting scene clearly brings out his characteristic blend of moral
sensitivity and youthful timidity. It also throws some light on the

13. First made by S. Sudhaus, *Menanderstudien* (1914), p. 34, n. 2; cf. Van
Leeuwen, loc. cit. (n. 4), 99 and Koerte, *R.-E.*, loc. cit. (n. 2), 726 and in his
edition, p. xxxviii (with n. 2).

character of Chrysis, particularly if the final speech is really hers. Moschion allows the slave to address him in the most impudent tone without rebuke; only when he takes him by surprise in the fifth act will he dare to reprimand the formidable and indispensable schemer. Chrysis, on the other hand, roundly rebukes Parmenon for shouting; and if she really speaks the final speech, she is confident of the love of Demeas and generously resolved to save Plangon from having to board out her infant. Probably the scene ended with Parmenon telling Moschion that he must ask his father to permit his immediate marriage with Plangon as soon as he returns home.

After a gap of some 21 lines the text resumes with Moschion the speaker (88ff.). The other two seem to have departed, for this looks like a soliloquy. So great is his distress, presumably at the thought of the interview with his father which is impending, that he talks – though not very seriously – of hanging himself,[14] and ends his speech by saying he will go off somewhere where he can be alone. First he must persuade Demeas to bring up the child which the conspirators pretend is that of Chrysis. Later he will have to raise the question of the marriage; what that means we shall inquire presently.

The next scene starts with the return of Demeas and Nikeratos from the Black Sea, where they have been absent since about nine months before the beginning of the play. Their absence was doubtless mentioned by Moschion during the missing part of the prologue after l. 29. They are both glad to be back at home. 'Don't you notice at once the change of place?' says Demeas (96ff.). 'How different all this is from the wretched conditions out there! The Black Sea! Fat old men,[15] innumerable fish, a tedious quantity of trouble, the wormwood of Byzantium; everything tastes bitter, by Apollo! – while here we have the unmixed blessings that belong to poverty. Beloved Athens, if only you could be granted all that you deserve; then we who love the city would be the

---

14. Such talk is typical of the timid young lover who takes his momentary difficulties too seriously. A similar case is that of Ctesipho in the *Adelphi* (see Donatus, *ad* Ter. *Ad.* 275, Wessner, p. 62, 17). O. Rieth, *Die Kunst Menanders in den Adelphen des Terenz*, pp. 40–1, 51 was wrong to take this threat as seriously as he did.

15. 'Fat' (παχεῖς) may imply 'rich'; see J. Taillardat, *Les Images d'Aristophane*, 5. 543.

9

happiest of men in every way.' Now he addresses the slaves who are carrying in the baggage, and rebukes another who is standing idle. 'Go in, you! Idiot, do you stand there gaping at me?'[16]

'What surprised me most, Demeas', says Nikeratos, 'of all things out there was that for long periods one couldn't see the sun; a thick mist, it seemed, obscured him.' 'No', said Demeas, 'the sun could see nothing remarkable, so that he shone the minimal amount on the people in those parts.' 'By Dionysus, that's good!' replies Nikeratos. 'Well', says Demeas, 'we'll leave that for others to worry about; but what do you say about the matter we were discussing?' 'Do you mean the business of your son's marriage?' 'Yes, I still say the same. Let's fix a day and get it done, and good luck come of it!' 'My mind is certainly made up.' 'Well, mine was made up before yours was.' 'Call me when you come out.'

The guess made long ago by Sudhaus and elaborated by Van Leeuwen[17] that the two fathers' ignorance of what has been happening in their houses can be explained only by their having been away is now triumphantly confirmed. Everyone has supposed that Moschion had expected to find it hard to persuade his father to let him marry Plangon, because of the difference between the fortunes of the two families. Why, then, has Demeas decided, apparently during the journey, to marry his son to Nikeratos' daughter? Van Leeuwen conjectured that on the journey Nikeratos had done Demeas some great service, such as saving his life during a shipwreck. Something of the kind may be right, but for all we know Demeas may have decided on a family alliance with his old friend simply because he admires his character and approves of his way of educating his daughter.

Some 14 lines later, soon after the beginning of Act II, Moschion in what looks like a soliloquy (120ff.) seems to be describing how he practised (μελετήσας), doubtless in the remote place to which he has removed himself (94), the preparations for the wedding. 'When I got out...', he says, 'I offered sacrifice, I (invited people

16. Cf. *Dysc.* 441, where I should now give the whole line to Sostratos' mother; for sharp words from a woman to a slave, cf. now *Samia* 67. H.-J. Newiger in reviewing Handley's commentary has rightly insisted that Ritchie's arguments for accepting Sostratos' mother as a character are convincing (*Gymnasium* 74 (1967), 544).

17. Sudhaus (above, n. 13), pp. 34–5; Van Leeuwen (above, n. 4), p. 98; cf. Kunst, *Wiener Studien*, loc. cit. (in n. 2 above), 147.

to) the feast, I sent for the bathwater, I (summoned) the women, I distributed the cake, I (sang) the wedding song, hummed, played the fool. Well, when I had had enough – .' At that moment he is interrupted by the entry of Demeas.

'Why by Apollo!' says Moschion, 'here is my father! Good day, father!' 'The same to you, my son!' 'Why are you looking cross?' 'Why do you ask?' replies Demeas, 'It seems I had a mistress who was a wife without my knowing it.'[18] 'A wife? What do you mean? I don't understand what you are saying.' 'It seems a bastard child has been born to me. But she shall at once get to perdition out of this house, child and all!' 'Never!' 'How do you mean, never?' replies Demeas, 'Do you think I'm going to bring up a bastard child in the house? That would be a folly not at all in my style.' 'But, in heaven's name, which of us is legitimate and which is illegitimate? Each of us is born a human being!'[19] 'You're joking!' 'No, by Dionysus', says Moschion, 'I'm serious! I think no family is different from any other; if one really thinks about it, the good man is legitimate and the bad man is a bastard as well as bad.'

Clearly Demeas has been told by Chrysis that she has had a child by him, and has been begged for permission to bring it up. His first indignant refusal will have been prompted very largely by his feeling that to rear a son by his mistress would be unjust to his adopted but legitimate son Moschion. The only person able to persuade Demeas to alter his decision will have been Moschion himself, and in the portion of the text that followed Moschion must have persuaded him.[20]

Some thirty lines later, Demeas and Moschion are still talking together. The opening lines of this page are mutilated (143ff.)[21]

18. According to Athenian notions a wife was for the procreation of legitimate children, a concubine for pleasure; that is why Demeas says he has a mistress who has turned out to be a wife.

19. The translation here takes account, by kind permission of Professor E. G. Turner, of a new fragment which he is about to publish from an Oxyrhynchus papyrus (see now *Cl. Rev.* 21 (1971), 352–3).

20. It has usually been supposed (e.g. by Sudhaus (above, n. 13), p. 36) that it was Chrysis who persuaded Demeas to bring up the child. At 332 = 117 we now read ἦν ἐπὶ τῆς αὐτῆς διανοίας ἔτι θρασύς. Demeas is clearly referring to the θρασύτης shown by Moschion in insisting on Chrysis' being allowed to keep her child.

21. Stoessl, 'Die neue Menanderpublikationen', p. 230, thinks Moschion tries unsuccessfully to tell Demeas about the child. There is no evidence for this in what we have of the text.

but the subject of the conversation is Moschion's marriage, and
when the sense becomes clear (151ff.) Moschion is asking his father
if he can arrange for the marriage to take place at once. 'How
could you', Moschion asks (151–2), 'knowing nothing of the
matter, realize that I am eager and help me?' 'Realize that you
are eager without knowing?' says Demeas, 'I understand what
matter you mean, Moschion! I will run to him at once and will
tell him to hold the wedding. Everything on our side will be ready,
since you tell me you've already sprinkled the sacral water, poured
the libation and put frankincense on the altar before you came.'
'I'll go and fetch the girl', says Moschion. 'Don't go yet', says
Demeas, 'not till I know if he will agree to our request.' 'He will
not refuse', says Moschion, 'but it is not proper for me to stay with
you and be in the way; I'm going off.' He leaves the stage, and
Demeas, after the fashion of so many Menandrian characters,
declares that Tyche must be a god, since she causes so many
matters that are obscure to turn out well. 'I did not know he was
in love...' he says, and then the text breaks off, probably just
before the end of the scene.

Clearly Demeas has astonished and delighted Moschion by
telling him that he is to marry Plangon; clearly Moschion has
astonished and delighted Demeas by readily consenting.

How does Moschion manage to get his father to consent to go at
once to Nikeratos and ask if the marriage may take place immediately? The answer is apparent from the words uttered by
Demeas after his departure; Moschion has told his father that he
is in love with his prospective bride. When Moschion says to his
father (151–2), 'How could you, knowing nothing of the affair,
realize I was in earnest and help me?', he does so, I suggest, in the
following context. He has told his father that he loves Plangon
(note ἐρῶ in l. 146 which is probably, though not certainly, the
first person singular of the present indicative of ἐράω); and he asks
his father how, if he had known nothing of this love, he could have
been expected to realize that he, Moschion, was in earnest and
help him to get his way. The manoeuvre works perfectly; Demeas
is delighted. His soliloquy may have continued for some time.

About 27 lines later begins a fragment containing very mutilated
portions of what must have been the last scene of the second act
(167–205). Clearly Nikeratos is on the stage and agrees to Demeas'

request for the marriage to take place immediately, and Parmenon (189ff.) is sent to the market with orders to buy all that will be needed for the wedding feast and to hire a cook to cook the meal. 'I'll get the money and run there', says Parmenon (195). 'Aren't you going yet, Nikeratos?' says Demeas. 'I'll go in and tell my wife to get the house ready', says Nikeratos, 'and then I'll follow him directly.' 'He'll have trouble in persuading his wife', says Demeas after his retreating figure, 'he shouldn't give his reasons or allow her to make delays...Are you still loitering? [this to the slave]. Run, I tell you.'

There follow scraps of three lines (203–5), and then a gap of about ten verses. When the text begins again, Demeas has begun the soliloquy which is in progress when the text preserved in the Cairo manuscript begins. The first line of the page (206) will have come very near the start of Demeas' soliloquy, which obviously stood at the beginning of the third act; the first line preserved in the Cairensis (216) comes ten lines later.

'Often when a ship is sailing a fair course', Demeas says, 'a great storm suddenly comes on her without warning, and her crew, who had been speeding on in perfect weather, are shattered and capsized. That is just what has happened to me now! I who had been celebrating the wedding, I who had been sacrificing to the gods, I for whom everything was going just as I wished only just now, I am no longer sure, by Athene, that I have not gone blind! No, I walk onward with an irresistible pain suddenly afflicting me. See how incredible it is![21a] Am I sane or am I mad? Am I bringing on myself a great misfortune by acting without certain knowledge?' Then follows (219ff.) the account of what Demeas witnessed from the store-room of his house which is preserved in the Cairo manuscript. In many places the new evidence helps us to improve the text; but since these do not affect the general picture, I shall not go into them. Regrettably the lacuna after l. 33 of the Cairo text (248) is not filled by the new manuscript.

Next follows the scene in which Parmenon returns from the market and is questioned by Demeas, and after that the scene of Chrysis' expulsion from the house (283–398). Then Nikeratos enters with the sheep, and finds Chrysis standing outside the house

21a. See Turner, loc. cit. (n. 19), 353–4, for the reading in 216. What he says about 214–15 is more dubious.

of Demeas. She tells him how Demeas has expelled her and he replies, 'Demeas is off his head' (416, which is l. 201 of the old text). At that point the text of the Cairensis breaks off, a whole folio – containing, as we now learn, 131 lines – being lost. 'The Black Sea is not a healthy place', Nikeratos continues (418ff.), 'Come in with me to my wife! Cheer up! What do you expect? He will come off it once he has got over his fit of craziness, when he has come to realize what it is he is doing now.'

Here the third act ends, as is shown by the stage direction indicating that a choral *entracte* took place at this point. The fourth act begins (421) with Nikeratos coming out of his house, saying to his wife who is still inside. 'You will lay me flat, wife! Now I'm going to tackle him!' Then he continues, now in soliloquy: 'I wouldn't have had this happen at any price, in heaven's name! In the middle of the wedding a bad omen has occurred for us; someone has been thrown out and come to us with a child; tears are being shed, the women are in a panic, Demeas is being an obstinate fool;[22] by Poseidon and all the gods, he'll regret his folly!'

Now Moschion enters (428), with the words, 'Will the sun never set? What can I say? The night has forgotten itself. What a long afternoon! I'll go and wash myself for the third time; what else is there for me to do?' Now Nikeratos attracts his attention with, 'Moschion, good day!' 'Are we having the wedding now?' Moschion replies, 'Parmenon told me so when he met me just now in the market. Is there anything to stop me from going to fetch the bride now?' 'Don't you know the situation here?' Nikeratos answers. 'What situation?' 'What situation, do you ask? An extraordinary kind of unpleasantness has arisen.' 'By Heracles, what is this? I came in total ignorance.' 'Chrysis has been driven out of the house just now by your father.' 'What a thing you've told me!' 'It's the truth.' 'Why?' 'On account of the child.' 'So where is she now?' 'In our house.' 'What a shocking and astonishing story you've told me!' 'If you think it shocking…!'

Now Demeas enters (440), still talking to the women inside his house. 'If I once take a stick', he says, 'I'll see to it that these tears are beaten out of you. What's this nonsense? Won't you help the

22. Dr Dedoussi on her l. 205 rightly points out that σκατοφάγος can be used in comedy as a synonym for ἀναίσθητος. With this in mind I would now accept V. Martin's σκατοφάγως at *Dysc.* 488.

cook? Yes, indeed the matter deserves your tears; you've lost such a great blessing from the house; the facts prove that!' Now Demeas turns in prayer, as tragic characters sometimes do, to the statue of Apollo Agyieus that stands on the stage outside his house.[23] 'Dearest Apollo', he says, 'grant that the marriage which we are now about to celebrate may take place with good fortune for us all! For I am going to celebrate the marriage, gentlemen, swallowing my wrath', he adds for the benefit of the audience. Then he continues with his prayer: 'Protect me', he says, 'so that no one finds me out; force me to sing the wedding song...I now feel miserable;[24] but what of it? She can never return.' Then he turns to his son and says, 'You go up to him before me, Moschion.'[25]

'But tell me, father', says Moschion, 'why are you doing this?' (452) 'Doing what, Moschion?' 'Do you ask me what? Why has Chrysis gone away? Tell me!' 'This is an embassy to me', says Demeas aside, 'shocking!' Then to Moschion: 'This isn't your affair, by Apollo; it's altogether mine!' Then again aside: 'What's this nonsense! This is becoming scandalous! He is in the plot against me?' 'What are you saying?' asks Moschion. Demeas goes on aside. 'It is clear; why else does he come to me to plead for her? That must be so, surely.' 'Father', says Moschion, 'what do you think your friends will say when they hear of it?' '(Don't talk about)[26] my friends, Moschion! Leave me alone!' 'It would be disgraceful if I didn't try to stop you.' 'What, are you going to try?' 'Yes!' 'This is really going too far! That was bad enough, but this is worse!' 'No, one shouldn't give way to anger in everything.' Then Nikeratos puts in, 'Demeas, he's right' (463). 'Let me alone, Moschion! Let me alone, for the third time! I know the whole story.' 'What do you mean, the whole story?' 'Don't talk to me!' 'But I must, father.' 'You must? Haven't I the right to control my own affairs?' 'Grant me this request as a favour!' 'What do you mean, a favour? Are you asking me to clear out of the house and leave the two of you in it? Let me celebrate the marriage! Let me celebrate the marriage, if you have any sense!' 'Why, I'm not

23. See Eduard Fraenkel, *Aeschylus, Agamemnon*, III, 491; for the prayer intended for the god's ear only (447ff.) cf. Sophocles, *Electra*, 637ff.
24. In l. 450 I conjecture ἐγὼ ⟨κακ⟩ῶς ἔχω νῦν; cf. *Dysc.* 730.
25. In l. 451, keep μου; see Austin, *ZPE*, loc. cit., 168.
26. Reading e.g. [μὴ λέγῃς] at 459. I prefer this to an infinitive; cf. 465. (But Austin draws attention to 471.)

preventing you! Only I would like Chrysis to be with us.'[27] '*Chrysis?*' 'It's on your account that I'm so eager.' 'Isn't this obvious, isn't it certain?' Then he turns again to the statue of Apollo: 'Be my witness, Loxias! Some one is in league with my enemies! Ah, I shall burst with fury!'

'What do you mean?' asks Moschion, completely puzzled. 'Do you want me to tell you?' 'Indeed I do.' 'Come here!' 'Well, tell me!' 'I will! The child is yours! I know it, I've heard it from the one who knows the secret, Parmenon. So don't make game of me!' 'Well, what harm has Chrysis done you, supposing the child is mine?' 'But who is it who...? You...' 'What has she done wrong?' 'What are you saying? Have you and she nothing on your minds?'[28] 'Why are you shouting?' 'Why am I shouting, scum? Do you ask me that? Are you taking the blame on yourself, I'd like to know? Do you dare to look me in the face and tell me that? Have you perhaps written me off completely?' 'Written you off?' 'Why? Do you think fit to ask me that?' 'Why, the thing isn't so very shocking; any number of people have done the same, father!' 'Zeus, what insolence! I put the question to you in front of witnesses: who is the mother of this child of yours? Tell Nikeratos, if you don't think this shocking!' 'Well, it becomes shocking if I have to tell this to him. He'll be angry when he knows.'

Now Nikeratos returns to the conversation: 'You are the world's greatest villain! Why, I begin at last to suspect what happened and what sacrilege you have committed.' 'Then I'm finished!' exclaims Moschion. 'Now do you realize, Nikeratos?' says Demeas. 'Indeed I do!' replies his friend, 'What a monstrous action! You make Tereus' rape, Oedipus' incest, Thyestes' adultery[29] and every other such act we have heard of seem trivial!' 'Do you mean me?' 'Did you have the impudence, the

27. Austin's ἡμῖν, Arnott complains ((1), p. 19), 'makes B's omission unaccountable', and he substitutes a neat palaeographical conjecture. He may be right; but does he think that omissions are always accountable?

28. ΔΗ. τί φής; οὐδὲν ἐνθυμεῖσθε; see Handley, 'Menander's *Aspis* and *Samia*', p. 105, Sandbach *ap.* Austin, *ZPE* 168.

29. Tereus raped his wife's sister, a story told in Sophocles' famous play *Tereus* (see Pearson, *Fragments of Sophocles* ii, 221f.); Thyestes' seduction of his brother's wife Aerope, like the parricide and incest of Oedipus, was familiar to the public from many tragedies, including Sophocles' *Atreus* and Euripides' *Thyestes*. On the use of such allusions in Menander, see Eduard Fraenkel, *Elementi Plautini in Plauto*, p. 11.

effrontery to do this thing? Now, Demeas, you ought to be as angry as Amyntor[30] and put his eyes out!' 'You have brought all this to light', says Demeas. 'What would you stop at?' says Nikeratos. 'What crime would you not commit? And then am I going to let you marry my daughter? Before I'd allow that – and at the very thought I spit into my lap to propitiate Nemesis – I'd take Diomnestos as my son-in-law[31] and court obvious disaster.' 'The wrong you did me has quickly brought you down, Moschion', says Demeas. 'You are a slave, Demeas!' Nikeratos continues, 'If it had been *my* bed you dishonoured, you would not have gone on to outrage any other person, neither would your partner in guilt. I would have sold my mistress the next day, as soon as possible, and at the same time disinherited my son, so that every barber's shop and every portico would have been crowded, and from early morning people would have sat there talking about me and saying, "Nikeratos is a real man! He took a just revenge for the murder!"' 'Murder?' 'I regard outrages against another such as this as murder.' 'I've gone dry, I'm paralysed by distress, by all the gods', says Moschion. 'And on top of everything I took the author of the atrocity into my house!' exclaims Nikeratos. 'Nikeratos', says Demeas, 'I beg you to turn her out! Be a friend, and treat the crime against me as one against you!'

Nikeratos starts to return to his own house to eject Chrysis. 'I shall burst with fury at the thought of what I've lived to see! Do you look me in the face, you barbarian, you proper Thracian? Won't you let me pass?' With that he disappears into his house. 'Father', says Moschion, 'do listen!' 'I won't listen to a thing', says Demeas. 'Not even if none of the things you suppose is true?'[32]

30. The story of how Phoenix seduced the mistress of his father Amyntor is told in the *Iliad* IX. 447ff.) but the blinding first appears in tragedy. Sophocles wrote a *Phoenix* (see Pearson, loc. cit. (n. 28), II, 320ff.), but the most celebrated *Phoenix* was that of Euripides (see Nauck, *TGF*, 2nd edn, pp. 621ff.).

31. On the practice of spitting to propitiate Adrasteia, or Nemesis, see Gow on Theocritus VI. 39; R. Muth, *Träger der Lebenskraft* (1954), pp. 42ff. has a detailed discussion. Nothing seems to be known of Diomnestos, but the context clearly implies that he is a proverbial evil-doer, like Eurybates or Phrynondas. Perhaps it is worth calling attention to Aristophanes, *Eq.* 1287, where Πολυ-μνήστεια ποιῶν seems to imply disgraceful behaviour, and is not likely to refer to the Colophonian musician Polymnestos, as the writer of a scholion *ad loc.* supposes. Was there confusion between Polymnestos and Diomnestos? (See Dedoussi, *Entretiens*, pp. 167–8 for a possible explanation.)

32. 521–2: see Arnott (1), p. 20 for an excellent treatment of these lines.

says Moschion, 'I've only just understood.' 'What do you mean, none of them?' 'Chrysis is not the mother of the child she's now looking after; she pretended it was hers as a favour to me.' 'What are you telling me?' 'The truth!' 'And why is she doing you this favour?' 'I don't want to tell, only I'm admitting a lesser charge to clear myself of a greater, if you understand the facts correctly!' 'I'll be dead before you get it out!' 'It's the child of Nikeratos' daughter by me! I didn't want this known.' 'What do you mean?' 'The truth!' 'Take care you're not trying to make a fool of me!' 'The thing can be established.' 'What good will that do me?'[33] 'None; but someone's at the door.'

Now Nikeratos comes rushing out of his house, even more distressed than he was earlier, and using tragic language. 'Ah me, ah me! What a sight have I seen that sends me rushing through the door, demented, my heart smitten by a sudden pang!' 'What's he going to tell us?' says Demeas. 'I've just found my daughter in the house giving suck to the child!' 'There you are!' says Moschion, 'do you hear, father?' 'You have done me no wrong, Moschion', replies his father, 'and yet I did you wrong, when I suspected you of such an act!'[34] 'I'm coming to you, Demeas', says Nikeratos. 'I shall get out of the way!' Moschion exclaims. 'Never mind', Demeas says. 'I'm dead as I look at him', replies his son, as he slips off.

'What is the matter?' Demeas asks Nikeratos. 'I've just found my daughter in the house giving suck to the child', Nikeratos repeats. 'Perhaps she was pretending.' 'She wasn't pretending, because when she saw me come in she suddenly collapsed.' 'Perhaps you only thought she did.' 'You'll lay me flat if you keep saying "perhaps"', replies Nikeratos. 'Is it my fault?' says Demeas. 'What are you saying?' 'What you say seems to me incredible.' 'I tell you, I saw it!' 'You're drivelling!' 'It's not mere talk! I'll go back and...' Here we have arrived at the point where the Cairo text resumes (545 = 202). After the half-demented Nikeratos has chased Chrysis out of his house and back again yelling blue murder, Demeas finally manages to calm him down and to accept his assurance that the marriage shall take place after all.

The information contained in the Cairo codex had of course enabled scholars to guess that the large gap in Act IV contained a scene in which Moschion tried to intervene on behalf of Chrysis,

33. See Austin, *ZPE* 169.   34. See Austin, loc. cit.

and so provoked Demeas to accuse him directly of having had an affair with her, with the result that Moschion was forced to tell Demeas the truth; but not surprisingly they could not predict the details. The scene starts dramatically with Demeas' rebuke to the servants who are lamenting the fate of Chrysis, followed by his prayer to Apollo to help him celebrate the wedding without betraying his grief. Then Moschion makes his intervention. It had been supposed that when Demeas learned the true facts about the child's paternity, he at once told Nikeratos; no one had imagined that Nikeratos was present on stage throughout the long scene between Demeas and Moschion. Moschion's plea for Chrysis infuriates his father, who first charges him with being the father of the child (475ff.); when Moschion admits this, but asks what wrong Chrysis has done (479), Demeas not unnaturally becomes even angrier. Many people, Moschion pleads, have done the same thing (486), and Demeas takes this as the extreme of impudence, and now insists (489) that Moschion should tell the facts not to himself, but to Nikeratos. This alarms Moschion, who has been dreading the moment when Nikeratos learns that he has seduced his daughter (490–4). Nikeratos becomes even more indignant than Demeas at the supposed crime, invoking tragic parallels and using tragic language. Had he been Demeas, he says, he would have sold his concubine and disinherited his son (507ff.) for an offence which he describes as murder (513–14). When Moschion finally manages to get out the truth (528ff.), Demeas will not believe him, till Nikeratos, who has returned to his own house (519–20) apparently to cancel the arrangements for the wedding (note 516–18), rushes back, having seen his own daughter giving the child suck. The misunderstanding has been kept in being up to the last moment, and the scene is so contrived that its comic possibilities are exploited to the full by means of the presence of Nikeratos. He does not reveal the serious side of his nature in the same way as Demeas; the delusion from which he suffers is purely comic, and his anger, expressed as it is in exaggerated language, richly farcical.

The fifth act begins, it will be remembered, with Moschion anxious to extract an apology from his father and prepared to threaten to depart and serve as a mercenary in order to do so. After he has forced Parmenon by violent means to go and fetch his equipment, a doubt strikes him (683ff. = 337ff.): will his father after all simply allow him to depart?

At this point the new material continues the text. 'Look, here is the cloak and sword!' says Parmenon (687), 'Take them!' 'Give them to me!' says Moschion, 'Did none of the people in the house see you?' 'No one.' 'No one at all?' 'No.' 'What do you mean?' says Moschion, 'may Zeus destroy you!' 'Go wherever you are going to!' replies Parmenon, 'You're being a fool!'

He is interrupted by Demeas who comes out of his house saying, 'Then where is he, pray? Ah, what's this?' 'Go faster!' says Parmenon to Moschion. 'What does this costume mean?' says Demeas, 'What's the matter? Are you leaving, Moschion?' 'As you see', says Parmenon, 'he's already going, is on the way, and is preventing me from saluting the company inside. I'm going now!' With that he vanishes into the house leaving Demeas to address Moschion in a brief but weighty speech.

'Moschion', he says, 'I love you for being angry. I don't blame you, because if you have suffered pain undeservedly, it is my fault. But all the same consider this: who is it that you're angry with? I'm your father; I took you over and brought you up. If you have a pleasant (haven?) for your life,[35] it is I who have given it you; because of this you must put up with my actions, even if they cause you pain, and tolerate what I do like a son. I made an unjust accusation against you; I was ignorant, I was mistaken, I was mad. Only consider this! Though I did wrong to others, I showed consideration for you, and kept to myself that piece of what I then took for knowledge.[36] I didn't make it public, to give joy to our enemies; but you are now publishing my mistake and are calling people to bear witness to my foolishness against me. I don't approve of this, Moschion! Don't remember the one day of my life on which I slipped up and forget what went before! I could say a great deal, but I will not; it's a shame to obey your father grudgingly, I tell you; you should do so willingly.'

Now Nikeratos enters, still talking to someone inside his own

35. In l. 699 Austin tentatively suggests εἴ σοι [λιμήν τι]ς; see *ZPE*, loc. cit., 169, 11.

36. See *ZPE*, loc. cit., 170. St Luke ii. 19 ἡ δὲ Μαρία πάντα συνετήρει τὰ ῥήματα ταῦτα συμβάλλουσα ἐν τῇ καρδίᾳ αὐτῆς. Cf. Polybius xxx. 30. 5 and LXX Si. ii. 15; this is one of St Luke's characteristic Greek idioms.

house. 'Don't bother me', he begins, 'Everything is ready, the bathwater, the sacrifice before, the wedding, so that *if* the bridegroom ever comes, he can take away the bride.' Then he sees Moschion: 'Oh! What's this!' 'I have no idea' says Demeas, embarrassed. 'What, you have no idea?' roars the once more infuriated Nikeratos, 'A military cloak! This fellow must be planning to take himself off!' 'That's what he says', says Demeas. 'He does, does he?' replies Nikeratos, 'But who's going to let him go, when he's been caught in a seduction and admits his guilt?' Then he says to Moschion, 'I'll tie you up young man this very minute!' 'Tie him up, I beg you!' says Demeas. 'You're still talking nonsense to me!' Nikeratos replies, 'won't you drop that sword at once?' 'Do drop it, Moschion!' says Demeas, 'In heaven's name, don't exasperate him!' 'Let it go!' says Moschion grandly, 'You have won me over by your entreaties.' 'Entreaties!' says Nikeratos, 'Come here!' 'Are you going to tie me up?' says Moschion. 'Don't do that!' says Demeas, 'Bring the bride out here!' 'Do you think I should?' says Nikeratos. 'Certainly!' 'If you'd done that at once', says Moschion, 'you wouldn't have had the trouble, father, of talking all that philosophy just now.' 'Come along!' says Nikeratos, 'In the presence of witnesses I give you this woman to be yours for the procreation of legitimate children; as dowry I give you all my property when I die (only I hope I never do, I hope I live for ever!).' 'I have her, I take her, I love her.' 'Now we only need to fetch the bathwater', says Demeas. 'Chrysis, send the women, the water-carrier and the flute-girl. Let someone bring us out a torch and garlands, so that we can join in the procession!' 'Here's this fellow bringing them', says Moschion. 'Cover your head and get yourself ready', says his father. 'But I...', Moschion begins, but Demeas interrupts him with a tetrameter variant of the usual concluding formulas: 'My pretty boys, young men, old men, men all together with all your strength send up to Bacchus the applause expressive of approval that he loves; and let the immortal goddess who is present at the noblest contests, Victory, always attend my choruses in kindly mood!'

Van Leeuwen's guess that Chrysis turned out to be Moschion's long-lost sister, so that Demeas could marry her,[37] turns out to be erroneous. Chrysis has, it would appear from 21ff., been an

37. Loc. cit., 100.

hetaira,[38] and if one has once practised this profession, one cannot turn out to be a citizen; if one is destined for marriage with an Athenian, one's virginity is preserved even in the most unpromising circumstances.

Wilamowitz, whose certainty about many details of the plot has proved so mistaken, saw and stated the central fact about the *Samia*;[39] from the start all the characters are eager for the marriage between Moschion and Plangon to take place, only by bad luck and bad management they themselves contrive to place one obstacle after another in its way. When the Cairo manuscript was discovered, a public whose notion of Menander had been based on the adaptations of Terence was suprised to learn how comparatively strong an element of farce had survived into the New Comedy; Menander was the ancestor not only of Molière, but also of Feydeau.[40] In the *Samia* this element is particularly strong. The notion that Menander made much of a contrast in character between the two fathers[41] is not borne out by the new material. There is no evidence that Demeas is urban but Nikeratos rustic; nor that their characters are opposed; each in turn is calm when all seems to be going well for him, but angry when his cherished plans seem to have collapsed. They are of course different, and Demeas has a serious side such as Nikeratos does not reveal.

Attempts to make the wife and daughter into speaking characters are shown to have been misguided; the world of New Comedy is in the main a man's world. Even the character of Chrysis – though she may have had more to do during the plotting scene than now appears – cannot have been developed in depth. The person after whom a play is named is not necessarily the leading figure, any more than a chorus which gives its name to the play is a chorus that is specially important in the action; and Chrysis, though perhaps a precursor of Habrotonon in the *Epitrepontes* as a good-hearted hetaira, cannot have had so long a part. Parmenon's assumed innocence in the fifth act has not surprisingly turned out to be a fraud, for he was the main contriver of the plot to pass off

38. Some scholars have denied this; they seem to have been mistaken.

39. Loc. cit., 71 = 421. Cf. Gomme, *Essays in Greek History and Literature*, p. 288.

40. Arnott (2), 10 has made the same point.

41. This seems to go back to Leo, *Hermes* 43 (1908), 163; cf. Jensen, *Menandri Reliquiae in papyris et membranis servatae* (1929), p. xliv; Webster (p. 47) rightly contradicts it.

Plangon's child as that of Chrysis. He is an intriguing slave of the familiar type, encouraged during the early scenes by his young master's timidity to be even more impertinent than such slaves usually are. He is paid out, after having congratulated himself prematurely, by the unexpected violence of Moschion during the fifth act.

The two characters who matter most are Demeas and Moschion.[42] Each is devoted to the other, and the devotion of each triumphantly surmounts every test to which it is exposed by the farcical concatenation of events. Before the action begins, Demeas is prepared to sacrifice his own love-affair rather than upset Moschion; and later, when he thinks Moschion has had a liaison with his own mistress, he cannot believe that the young man deserves the major share of blame. Moschion has unselfishly urged his father to take Chrysis to live with him, and in the prologue shows touching gratitude for Demeas' kindness; later he is deeply wounded to think that Demeas has thought him capable of an affair with Chrysis.

Demeas is a dominating character, to whom Nikeratos, irascible as he too is, plays second fiddle, as we see clearly in the delightful scene of the return from the Black Sea; he likes to shape other people's lives, and is impatient of opposition to his plans. Why has he never married? I suspect that if we had the whole of Moschion's prologue speech, we should know Demeas to have been a confirmed bachelor, deeply disapproving of the women of his own class with their gossip, their extravagances and their success in getting their own way. He probably approves of Plangon as a daughter-in-law for reasons not unlike those which are said to recommend the daughter of Knemon.[43] When he thinks Moschion has betrayed him, he is deeply stirred; but after the first shock he is able to reflect and find mitigating circumstances in his son's case.

Deeply fond though he is of his adoptive father, Moschion is also much in awe of him, as he is of Nikeratos. The prospect of having to persuade Demeas to get Nikeratos to allow the wedding

42. Cf. Treu, 'Humane Handlungsmotive', pp. 249ff. I do not find the conception of a son exemplified by Moschion or the conception of a father exemplified by Demeas as revolutionary as Mette, loc. cit. (n. 7), 439 supposes.

43. *Dysc.* 384f. For a confirmed bachelor who adopts a son, compare Micio in the *Adelphi* of Terence.

to take place at once fills him with alarm, and so does that of
having to persuade him to allow the supposed child of Chrysis to
be reared. Parmenon mocks him for his cowardice, remarkable in
one who commands his tribe's cavalry and thinks of pretending to
enlist in mercenary service. Demeas matters so much to him that
even when the way is clear for him to marry the mother of his child,
of whom he is genuinely fond, he wants first to make his father
express regret for not having trusted him. He supposes that either
Demeas will fall on his neck and implore forgiveness or else he
will allow him to depart; but not surprisingly neither of these
things happens.[44] Instead, Demeas explains to him that he ought
to show as much tolerance for his father's failings as his father has
shown for his.

A competent performance is certain to reveal that the serious
element, important as it is, is always kept subordinate to the
general comic effect. That serious element lies almost entirely in
the sympathetic study of the relation between adoptive father and
adopted son. In that it is far from unique among Menander's
works; we think above all of the Terentian adaptations, of the
relation of Simo and Pamphilus in the *Andria*, of Menedemus and
Clinia in the *Hauton Timoroumenos* and above all of Micio and
Aeschinus in the *Adelphi*. The *Samia* was probably a comparatively
early play,[45] yet seems to foreshadow several features of the late
Menandrian masterpiece which lies behind Terence's *Adelphi*.[46]
But above all things it is a brilliant, fast-moving light comedy, not
without a decided element of farce.[47]

44. Van Leeuwen (p. 100) intelligently guessed this.

45. On the date see K.–T. 1, xlf. The view of Stoessl, 'Die neue Menanderpublikationen', p. 208, that the *Samia* is 'a bitter and sarcastic play' seems to
be absurd.

46. Cf. Treu, 'Humane Handlungsmotive', pp. 244f.

47. I am greatly indebted to Dr Austin and Professor Jean-Marie Jacques
without whose generous collaboration this article could hardly have been
written. Dr Austin has read it and effected many improvements.

The choral odes of the
Bacchae of Euripides

MARYLIN ARTHUR

IN THE *Bacchae*, the last work of his old age, Euripides reverted to a more archaic, more conventional, more Aeschylean type of drama.[1] The conventional treatment of the chorus in this play is particularly remarkable; for the Euripidean choral odes had shown a tendency to become detached from the main concerns of the drama, to verge on becoming the ἐμβόλιμα associated with the successors of Sophocles and Euripides.[2] But in the *Bacchae*, the structure as a whole is more coherent than in other late plays, and the chorus plays an unusually important and integral part in the drama.

It is well to examine, however, the nature of the relevance of the chorus in this play, and its involvement in the action of the play. We can note at the outset that we must distinguish between the chorus as participants in the dramatic action, and the use of choral odes to treat important themes in the play. The chorus of the *Bacchae* participates directly in the action of the play at only two points: 604ff., and 1024ff. Otherwise the chorus sings its odes and utters, at 263–5, 328–9, and 775–7, remonstrances or warnings derived from the vast store of Greek traditional wisdom which the chorus characteristically propounds.[3] We can, therefore, contrast

1. This idea, now commonly accepted, seems to have originated with Gilbert Murray, in *Euripides and his Age* (London 1913), pp. 19, 182.

2. Aristotle, *Poetics* 140a. The remarks of ancient editors indicate that such a view was held of Euripides' choral odes in antiquity; cf. the scholiast on Aristophanes, *Ach.* 442: [Εὐριπίδης] εἰσάγει τοὺς χοροὺς οὐ τὰ ἀκόλουθα φθεγγομένους τῇ ὑποθέσει, ἀλλ᾽ ἱστορίας τινὰς ἀπαγγέλλοντας, ὡς ἐν ταῖς Φοινίσσαις. Some modern scholars have challenged this traditional view, and have pointed to the narrowness of the ancient (and modern) definition of 'relevance'. See especially the work of Hugh Parry, *The Choral Odes of Euripides: Problems of Structure and Dramatic Relevance*, diss., University of California, Berkeley, 1963 (University Microfilms, Ann Arbor 1963), and that of A. E. Phoutrides, 'The Chorus of Euripides', *HSCP* 27 (1916), 77–170.

3. The remarks at 263–4 and 328–9 are like those which characteristically interrupt a heated exchange of *rheseis*. We can compare *Al.* 673–4 and 756–7

the chorus in the *Bacchae* with that in, for example, the *Ion*, where the intense devotion of the chorus to their mistress leads them to disregard Xuthus' injunction of silence, and to reveal his plan to Creusa. In several other plays the chorus engages in long and often excited dialogue with characters in the drama.

It will be my contention that Euripides achieves, in this late play, a successful integration of chorus with plot-action precisely because he follows his already developed inclination to treat the chorus as a separate entity, and not only as another actor in the play. In this I take issue with E. R. Dodds' treatment of the chorus in his edition of the *Bacchae*,[4] who mistakenly, I think, emphasizes the *function* of each choral ode in the drama. That is, Dodds notes the thematic relation of the choral ode to events which have just transpired or are just about to, and asserts that this relation 're-inforces...the emotional effect of the preceding scene and leads up to the following one'.[5] Such a treatment of the chorus concentrates on the mood set rather than the ideas presented, because it assumes that the choral odes are related to the rest of the play only insofar as they provide some kind of commentary on the action which has preceded or which will follow, or insofar as they enlarge upon ideas already presented or anticipate those to come.[6] My own emphasis will be on certain ideas and themes developed by the chorus which are independent of, although not unrelated to, the dramatic action of the play. That is to say, I would contend that the stasima of the *Bacchae* do not operate as a kind of *basso continuo*, supporting already articulated themes and ideas, but rather that the dramatic action of the play and the choral odes work like two melodies in counterpoint, complementing each other to be sure, but having each an existence and a thrust independent of the other.

It will be helpful to begin our analysis with some kind of over-view of the chorus' character and development. The Bacchants

where similar sentiments are expressed in an analogous situation. *IA* 505–6 parallels *Ba.* 328–9 in both thought and language.

4. Oxford 1960[2]; hereafter referred to as Dodds.

5. Dodds, p. 142. See also his comments on the other choral odes, where he makes similar remarks: pp. 117, 182–3, 198, 219.

6. This 'echo theory' is applied freely by many critics besides Dodds, of course. G. M. A. Grube remarks, about the first antistrophe of the first stasimon: 'The whole stanza is a natural comment on the previous scene...The chorus, as choruses will do, echo Teiresias' disapproval of their enemy [Pentheus]' (*The Drama of Euripides* (London 1941), p. 406).

are, of course, devotees of the god Dionysos and, as such, both participate in and represent the Eastern Dionysian religion. E. R. Dodds[7] and others have discussed in detail points in the choral odes and in the play as a whole where we can discern reflections of actual cult practice. In the first choral ode (the *parodos*) in particular, we find references to the form and instruments of worship.[8] But it is the spirit of Dionysian worship which has fascinated most critics of the play and students of religion. For it is by the power of Dionysos that wine, dancing, or religious inspiration brings a heightened consciousness, an ecstasy in the literal sense, and a full experiencing of what it means to be an alive, sentient being. But a concomitant aspect of the god's character is an utter disregard for any of the natural and social bonds that unite men in families and cities, and a horrible carelessness of individual human lives. The extremes and contradictions of the Dionysian religion, and its general anti-rational character, have been held to parallel the irrational, bestial element in the natures of men. Therefore, when the *Bacchae* presents a confrontation with the god Dionysos, it emerges also as the drama of man in struggle with the darker, irrational elements in his own nature. Most modern literary critics of this play, for all the peculiarities of their individual interpretations, have focused ultimately on the struggle between two forces (whether on the personal or cosmic level) as the unifying element, and have defined the message of the play in terms similar to those of Albin Lesky: 'The poet's intention was not to make a rational protest. What made him write this tragedy was a profound experience of Dionysiac religion with its mysterious polarity of compulsion and liberation, its calm return to nature and vital surging of the secret forces of life, its highest rapture and deepest anguish.'[9]

The concentration on the religious aspect of both the chorus and the play has led, I believe, to an unfortunate lack of attention to the totality of the chorus' characterization. For the chorus operates also, throughout the play, as an apologist for bourgeois morality. We encounter again and again in the course of the drama, injunctions

7. In the introduction to his edition, especially in II, 'Traditional Elements in the *Bacchae*', where he refers also to the pioneering work in discovering the form and nature of the Dionysian ritual.

8. Dodds discusses them in detail in his commentary on the *parodos*.

9. Albin Lesky, *Greek Tragedy* (London 1965), p. 200.

to moderation and to knowing one's limits in the spirit of the Delphic precept μηδὲν ἄγαν. Such a posture of the chorus has been difficult for critics to understand for two reasons: the moral views of the chorus, being 'as characteristically Greek as anything in Pindar or Sophocles',[10] seem incongruous in the mouths of Asian maenads; second, the doctrine of moderation is at odds with the extremism of both the spirit of Dionysos and the principle of violent revenge which the chorus also adopts. This side of the chorus' character has been either ignored,[11] assimilated to one pole of the Dionysian contradiction,[12] or treated as a purely formal device.[13] Such treatment has largely ignored the content and form of large sections of the chorus, and has been content merely to point to the fact that such sentiments exist. I believe that the moral views of the chorus can sustain close analysis, and that such analysis will reveal that Euripides has focused in the play, not on the Dionysiac element itself, but rather on how the *polis* incorporates elements (such as the Dionysian) which are hostile to it and on how it sustains (or does not sustain) itself against its own contradictions. I shall follow a procedure of treating each choral ode (except the *parodos*) individually and sequentially.

The long *parodos* celebrates Dionysos as the god of ecstasy and his worship as sweet and joyous. A complete discussion of it is best

10. James Adam, *The Religious Teachers of Greece* (Edinburgh 1908), p. 313.

11. As by Lesky, *Greek Tragedy*, and *History of Greek Literature* (London 1966), trans. Willis and de Heer.

12. R. P. Winnington-Ingram comments as follows on the moralizing first stasimon: 'The function of this ode is to present and to render attractive with the grace of lyric poetry one aspect of Dionysiac religion, namely, its joyous peace...There is another side to his worship...In the present ode it is suppressed or concealed, and for obvious dramatic ends' (*Euripides and Dionysos* (Cambridge 1948), p. 66).

13. T. G. Rosenmeyer, commenting on the first antistrophe of the first stasimon, writes as follows: 'Why, then, does Euripides put the pious precept into the mouth of a chorus whose primary artistic function is to communicate precisely what it is condemning, the spirit of unbridled mouths and lawless extravagance? It may be noted that such injunctions in Greek tragedy are often illusory. Setting off as they do a heroic imbalance or a cosmic disturbance, they underscore the poignancy of the action. But in this particular instance the use of the Delphic motto is even more startling than usual. The direction of the metaphysical impact is rudely deflected and the opacity of the poem enhanced by this conventional reminder of irrelevant quietist values' (*The Masks of Tragedy* (University of Texas Press 1963), pp. 137–8).

reserved for those interested in the cult itself, but we can note that throughout the *parodos*, the wilder, more feral aspects of the worship are played down in favor of its joy-bringing character.[14] This is especially clear in the epode:

> Sweet it is in the mountains, whenever he rushes out of
> the running band and falls to the ground,   136
> wearing the holy fawnskin, hunting the
> blood of the slain goat, delight of eating raw flesh,
> rushing to the Phrygian, to the Lydian, peaks –   140
> and the leader is Bromios, euoi.
> The plain flows with milk, flows with wine, flows with
> the nectar of bees.
> Then the Bacchic one, raising high
> the fiery flame of pine,   145
> like the smoke of Syrian incense
> streams it from the narthex
> as he runs and dances,
> rousing the stragglers
> and spurring them with shouts,
> and tossing his luxurious hair into the wind.   150
> In answer to their cries he roars out:
> Oh, run Bacchants,
>   run, Bacchants,
> glitter of the golden-flowing Tmolus,
> hymn with your deep-resounding drums   155
> Dionysos,
> joyfully delighting the Evian god
> with Phrygian shouts and cries,
> whenever the sacred, sweet-sounding flute   160
> shouts its holy gaiety, in accompaniment
> to those who rush to the mountain, to the mountain.   165
> And then, like a colt beside its grazing mother,
> the Bacchant runs and gambols for joy.[15]

14. J. de Romilly remarks about this *parodos*: 'La strophe entière décrit, en fait, un bonheur particulier, tout entier fait d'exaltation religieuse et même mystique. Le "programme" des bacchantes, c'est un bonheur sacré' ('Le Thème du Bonheur dans les *Bacchantes*', *REG* 76 (1963), 362).

15. The text I quote throughout is that of Gilbert Murray (Oxford 1913); a note just following the body of the article lists a few departures from this text.

Lines 137–8 are the only references in the *parodos* to the *ōmophagia*, and the emphasis on rushing and shouting, as well as the increasing excitement and irregularity of the meter, mark this epode as the emotional as well as literal climax of the *parodos*. Yet any sense of savagery or brutality is absent. Instead the sweetness (135, 165) and beauty of the celebration are prominent, and the concluding image of the colt's leap is that of a sudden and exciting moment of fragile loveliness.

The first stasimon

Reverence, mistress among gods,   370
Reverence, who over earth
hold your golden wing,
do you see how Pentheus acts?
Do you see his unholy
insolence toward Bromios, the   375
son of Semele, who of the blessed ones
is first at the lovely-crowned
time of rejoicing? whose cares are these:
to gather people together in the dance,
to laugh with the flute, and   380
to cut short worries,
whenever the gleam of the grape-cluster
is present at the feast of the gods,
and the mixing-bowl casts sleep
over ivy-crowned men at the feasts.   385

Of unbridled mouths
and disobedient foolishness
the end is affliction.
But the life of quiet pleasure
and ordinary thoughts remain unshaken   390
and hold together families.
For still, the heavenly ones
who live far away in the sky
oversee the affairs of men.
What is wise is not wisdom.   395
And to think unmortal thoughts
spells a short life. And in this case

who would pursue great aims and
miss what is near at hand?
In my view, these are the ways   400
of mad
and ill-counseled men.
Would that I could go to Cyprus,
the island of Aphrodite,
where dwell the Loves, enchanters of
mortal hearts,   405
and to Paphos, made fertile by the
rainless, hundred-mouthed stream
of the foreign river;
or where Pieria is,
the beautiful haunt of the Muses,   410
and the holy slope of Olympus.
Bromios, Bromios, lead me there,
joyful god who leads the Bacchants!
There are the Graces;
there is Desire; there it is lawful
to celebrate the Bacchic rite.   415

The god who is the son of Zeus
delights in the banquet.
But he also loves Eirene, the
child-nurturing goddess of peace.   420
And his gift of the griefless delight of wine
he grants equally to the rich
and to the poor.
But he hates the man who does not
care to lead the pleasant life   425
throughout the day and pleasant night;
it is wise to keep one's heart and mind
away from intemperate men.
Whatever ordinary people think   430
right and proper,
this I too would accept.

In this stasimon is our first encounter with the doctrine of
moderation mentioned above. The chorus sing of the moderate

happiness of the life of quiet pleasure, rather than the extremes of joy which membership in the *thiasos* brings. They magnify the simple life and the small pleasures to be derived from the acceptance of things as they are; they reject excess in every form; they demonstrate the traditional mistrust for the man of ambition and high thoughts. In short, they are the representatives of a bourgeois morality peculiar to and necessary for civilized life as the Greeks knew it. Historically, the development of such moral views corresponds with the rise of the *polis* and of Greek democracy;[16] and we can readily see how, in a hierarchical political system, only the willing acceptance by each group of its particular economic and social limitations can produce εὐνομία.

The form in which the chorus express their moral views is important also, for their use of a series of contrasts reveals an important characteristic of the attitude they adopt: their celebration of quietism involves a simultaneous non-quietistic hostility toward unbelievers. We see that in 386–8 the chorus is distrustful of the life without restraint in proportion as they exalt (in 389–92) the life of quiet pleasure. In line 395 one kind of wisdom is rejected in proportion as another is accepted. Lines 395–6 contrast the man who 'thinks mortal thoughts' and concentrates on τὰ πρὸς ποδός with the man whose aspirations are higher than is proper for mortals. (We can note here also that the chorus' belief in a divinity which oversees human action is an essential accompaniment to a commitment to the quiet virtues.)[17]

The Dionysos of this ode is also associated with the *polis*. He is now celebrated as 'the genial wine-god whom the Athenian δῆμος knew'.[18] He is still, as he was in the *parodos*, a god of joy, but now the joy he brings is the pleasant, quiet laughter of the feast, rather than the ecstatic, wild joy of his Eastern rites. The assignment to Dionysos of certain areas of influence (378–85, 417–24)

16. The urbanization of Greece, during the eighth and seventh centuries, and the period of colonization of the eighth, seventh and sixth centuries, was also the period of the codification of the law, and the time when the *polis* 'found its spiritual basis in the ideas of justice and good order (*dikē, eunomiā*)' (V. Ehrenberg, *From Solon to Socrates* (London 1968), p. 15). Such ideas form a major theme in the preserved writings of Hesiod, Solon, Tyrtaeus and others.

17. A. W. Adkins, in *Merit and Responsibility* (London 1960), discusses the commitment to moderation and stability under the rubric of the 'quiet morality', and finds that 'an inevitable divine justice, dispensed in this life, is [its] essential foundation' (p. 164).   18. Dodds, p. 117.

was a way of incorporating him into an existing mythological system, and of canalizing the wilder aspects of his nature. His Hellenization was further accomplished by assigning him an Olympian lineage as the son of Zeus,[19] the father of all the Greek deities. Euripides' treatment of Dionysos in this ode, then, accords well with what we know of the way in which the god was, in fact, introduced and integrated into the Greek religion.[20] And the social services[21] which Dionysos renders as wine-god are just those which Plato found indispensable for the city in the first book of the *Laws*.[22]

This god of a now civilized and tempered joy is an appropriate complement to the emphasis on moderation in the chorus' views. The very structure of the ode suggests such a parallelism: the first antistrophe exalting the life of quiet pleasure responds to a strophe which celebrates the god of the shining wine; antistrophe β is similarly divided between the love of Dionysos for the peace and joy of the feasts, and his hatred of the ἀνὴρ περισσός. And in the light of the chorus' divided concern we can see that their opening invocation to Ὁσία is doubly appropriate: the application of ὅσιος[23] in the spheres of both formal religion and everyday morality makes it an appropriate watchword for a chorus whose concerns are similarly divided. And the typical connotation of ὅσιος, that of moderation and restraint in one's dealing with both supernatural and human forces, makes Ὁσία the ideal representative of the spirit of the whole ode.

19. Throughout the play, both Dionysos' divine birth and his connection with Thebes are heavily emphasized; he is specifically referred to as the child of Zeus eleven times (1, 27, 42, 84, 243, 366, 417, 466, 550, 581, 603) in the first 600 lines of the play, and nine times (3, 28, 41, 91, 181, 278, 375, 468, 581) as the child of Semele. Furthermore, the circumstances of his birth and rebirth are developed at length in the prologue, in the first antistrophe of the *parodos*, and in the strophe of the second stasimon. And although both Pentheus and Teiresias refer to Dionysos as τὸν νεωστὶ δαίμονα (219–20, 272), the exact nature of his foreignness is more complex, since the emphasis on Dionysos as the child of Zeus and Semele, born beside the river Dirce and washed in its waters, is an insistence upon Dionysos as a Greek and a Theban.

20. W. K. C. Guthrie, *The Greeks and their Gods* (Boston 1955), ch. 6.

21. The emphasis is on the relief which he brings (381) and on the democratic distribution of his gifts (421–2); it is just these benefits (among others) of Athenian democracy that are singled out for comment in the funeral speech of Pericles (Thuc. *History* II. 36–8).   22. 649 D–E.

23. Van der Valk, in his study of this word ('Zum Worte Ὅσιος', *Mnemosyne* III, X (1942), 113–40), defines the range of its application.

We have yet to discover the chorus' attitude toward the values which they reject. We noted above that they must be hostile to a competing system of values, but it is the form and nature of this hostility which determines the extent to which the contradictions inherent in their moral system become destructive of it. In this stasimon, the chorus' attitude toward the life without restraint is less aggressive opposition than fearful shrinking away. This is made clear in the final lines of the stasimon, where the emphasis is on keeping away (σοφὰ δ' ἀπέχειν – 427) from those dangerous individuals (φῶτες περισσοί – 428), and embracing the more proper, more common ideal (τὸ φαυλότερον – 431). Furthermore, the use of the interrogative form, which becomes more frequent in later choral odes, operates as a formal analogy to the chorus' lack of assertiveness and general unsureness. Even when it is used to express righteous indignation, as in the first half of strophe α, the question implies a certain element of astonishment and confused disbelief.

The emphasis on an attitude of non-involvement is expressed most dramatically in strophe β of this ode: the escape-prayer. The strophe itself is rather plain and is mainly geographical. It lacks the ornamentation or the richness of mythological allusion of some of Euripides' other escape-odes.[24] However, it is interesting to note the switch from the optative (ἱκοίμαν – 403) which expresses yearning desire, to imperatives at the end of the strophe (412–16) and the sudden intervention of iambics (in 412–14) in an otherwise normal Aeolic scheme. At the same time, there is a reversion to the language and cries of the *parodos* (412–13) and the introduction of short, staccato sentences (414–16). Unlike the rest of the strophe, in which a mood of dream-like yearning predominates, the escape-ode closes with a sudden rise to a frenzied, excited pitch. The strong and imperative note in these lines belies in part the chorus' otherwise quiet acquiescence and peaceful willingness to put up with things as they are, and anticipates the time (977ff.) when the same cry (ἴτ' εἰς ὄρος) calls for the quick, deadly leap of the hunter, rather than for peace-bringing escape.

We have observed in this stasimon a complex integration of the notion of a tempered, Athenian Dionysos with the moral founda-

24. Other escape-odes are at *Helen* 1479ff., *IT* 1137ff., *Phoen.* 226ff., *Orestes* 983ff., and *Hipp.* 732ff.

tions of political stability. And we shall therefore be suspicious of an exclusive concentration on the ecstatic, orgiastic, and foreign form of worship of Dionysos. For the drama of the *Bacchae* presents what is in some sense a crisis of internal subversion, rather than the less complex, less ambiguous, and certainly less interesting problem of naked foreign aggression.

The episode intervening between the first and second stasima presents the first confrontation between Dionysos and Pentheus; Pentheus is, for the moment, victorious, but the sense of a mysterious power which Dionysos' strange threats[25] suggest still hangs in the air. In such an atmosphere the chorus sing the second stasimon, a lyrical presentation of the confrontation between Dionysos and Pentheus: the strophe deals with the birth of Dionysos, the antistrophe with the ancestry of Pentheus.

> O daughter of Achelous,
> lovely virgin mistress Dirce,   520
> for you once received in your streams
> the baby of Zeus,
> when its parent Zeus snatched
> it from the deathless fire
> into his thigh, crying aloud: 525
> 'Come, Dithyramb, enter
> my male womb.
> I show you forth to Thebes
> as "the Bacchic one".'
> But now, oh blessed Dirce,   530
> you thrust me away when
> I seek to celebrate my ivy-crowned rites on your banks.
> Why do you deny me? why do you flee me?
> Yet still, I swear by the clustered delight
> of Dionysos' wine,   535
> still, you will come to have a care for Bromios.

> What a rage, what a rage

25. At 508:   ΔΙ. ἐνδυστυχῆσαι τοὔνομ' ἐπιτήδειος εἶ,
and 515f.:   ΔΙ. στείχοιμ' ἄν· ὃ τι γὰρ μὴ χρεών, οὔτοι χρεὼν
              παθεῖν. ἀτάρ τοι τῶνδ' ἄποιν' ὑβρισμάτων
              μέτεισι Διόνυσός σ', ὃν οὐκ εἶναι λέγεις·
              ἡμᾶς γὰρ ἀδικῶν κεῖνον εἰς δεσμοὺς ἄγεις.

does the earthborn race display,
dragon-born Pentheus,
whom earthborn Echion fathered,   540
an animal-like monster,
no mortal human,
but like the deadly giant
that opposed the gods.
He intends to capture me, me   545
Bromios' follower, in ropes,
and he already holds my fellow-reveler
within his house, hidden
in dark bonds.
Do you see this, oh Dionysos,   550
child of Zeus, your followers
in the bonds of necessity?
Come, shaking your golden thyrsus,
down from Olympus,
and restrain the insolence of this murderous man.   555

Whereabouts on beast-nurturing Nysa
are you leading
your bands of worshipers,
or where on the Corycian peaks?
but perhaps you are in the leafy recesses   560
of Olympus,
where once Orpheus summoned together the
trees with his lyre and songs,
and called together wild beasts.
Oh blessed Pieria,   565
the Evian one will honor you,
and he will come to lead the dance
with his revelries;
he will lead his whirling Maenads
across the swiftly flowing Axios,   570
and father Lydias,
the river which brings blessings to mortals,
and which, as I have heard,
makes rich the land of horses
with its lovely waters.   575

Dirce, the river of Thebes, is invoked throughout the strophe, but in two different contexts. She is first addressed as the river beside whose banks Dionysos was born and in whose waters he was first washed. There follows the story of Dionysos' divine second birth, which is familiar from the prologue and *parodos*. The chorus then call upon the Dirce which, in contrast with its treatment of the infant Dionysos, now thrusts away his followers. The Lydian, Bacchic character of the chorus begins to re-emerge even here; we noted that throughout the first stasimon they were treated, except in a brief outburst at 412–16, as representatives of an ordinary and everyday Greek morality. Now, in proportion as they proclaim their eastern character, they begin to insist upon their rights and abandon the policy of quiet submission which they had counseled so strongly in the first stasimon. Their questions addressed to Dirce in 533 are, however, pleading, not angry; they are frightened at the threats made against them by Pentheus in 511ff.;[26] and lines 545–6 show that they take him seriously. They identify themselves with Dionysos, and his hereditary rights in Thebes they proclaim as their own.

The god of this choral ode is still primarily the Greek, civilized god of the first stasimon. But his wilder, more eastern aspects, like those of the chorus, begin to emerge throughout this stasimon. We can observe, for example, in the closing lines of the strophe, that the chorus swears by the god of the shining wine, but they then swear that Thebes will come to know and have a care for the god *Bromios*, the thundering, raging god.

Pentheus' ancestry, which receives extensive treatment in the play, and is the major subject of the antistrophe of this stasimon, is of special importance in understanding his characterization and his place in the drama, and I have therefore treated it fully in an appendix to this article. For our present purposes we need only note that although many critics apologize for Pentheus and seek to mitigate the more brutal aspects of his character, the chorus regard him always as the φόνιος ἀνήρ of l. 555. Their presentation of him as a δράκων initiates an emphasis on the imagery of

26. 511ff.:   ἐκεῖ χόρευε· τάσδε δ' ἃς ἄγων πάρει
              κακῶν συνεργοὺς ἢ διεμπολήσομεν
              ἢ χεῖρα δούπου τοῦδε καὶ βύρσης κτύπου
              παύσας, ἐφ' ἱστοῖς δμωίδας κεκτήσομαι.

violence which increases in the following odes. And their characterization of him in this ode as a threatening and dangerous force
is an important justification for the increasing violence of their
own attitude toward him.

In the second half of the antistrophe the chorus reflect on their
own situation, as they did in the second half of the strophe. The
interrogative form is here used effectively again. The chorus' own
growing sense of affliction and anxiety is a function of the increasing manifestation of Pentheus' oppressive, violent nature, and
of the increasing realization of their own rights. However, their
call is, typically, for restraint of the threatening force (555).

In the epode, the question is used again, as the chorus lists the
places where the god may be found. This epode has affinities with
the escape-hymn of the previous stasimon: the chorus' tender
addresses to Dionysos' haunts suggest a longing to escape to those
places. It may be significant that they enumerate the geographical
points in roughly the sequence that they would follow in leaving
Greece and returning east;[27] perhaps they here accomplish in
song what they cannot accomplish in reality. Although the chorus
invoke the wild, remote mountain-glens, their language emphasizes
the benign, peaceful aspects of nature;[28] similarly, the image of
Orpheus leading in song and dance the trees and, especially, the
wild beasts, is a picture of control over wild and potentially
destructive natural forces. The attitude of the chorus in this epode
is then still predominantly one of frightened and confused amaze-
ment at Pentheus; their instinct is still to withdraw from a situation which they find unpleasant.

Just following this epode is the palace-miracle scene. There are
many difficulties of interpretation connected with this scene, difficulties which take their start from Gilbert Norwood's 'rationalized'
view of the miracle, which claims that it does not actually take
place.[29] For our purposes, it is sufficient that the chorus believe
that the palace-miracle actually happened, which they un-

27. Nysa is probably indefinite (see Dodds *ad loc.*), then the Corycian peaks
of Mount Parnassus, Mount Olympus and finally two rivers of Macedonia, the
Axios and Lydias.

28. θηροτρόφου, πολυδένδρεσσιν, ὀλβοδόταν, εὔιππον, καλλίστοισι.

29. In *The Riddle of the 'Bacchae'* (Manchester 1908). His interpretation of
the palace-miracle scene was the only part of his theory which he did not
recant, in *Essays on Euripidean Drama* (London 1954).

questionably do. They throw themselves to the ground[30] in fright and horror. Shrinking back in terror or rushing forward to help are the usual ways for the chorus to engage in the dramatic situation.[31] It is a particularly striking scene in this play because the chorus' direct participation has otherwise been restricted. And Norwood was certainly right in attaching (for whatever reason) a great deal of importance to this scene. It is the first manifestation of Dionysos' power and therefore represents for the chorus the first indication that their own situation is not as hopeless as it had seemed.[32]

In the scenes that now follow, the first messenger's speech, and the tempting of Pentheus, the fact and the nature of Dionysos' power become more and more evident. As the chorus had identified themselves with Dionysos in his rejection by Thebes,[33] so now they come to realize that they share in his power. And the new power which they feel is theirs effects an enormous change in their attitude, as the next choral ode makes clear.[34]

> Shall I ever, as I
> whirl about in the night-long dances,
> set down my white foot,
> throwing up my neck into the dewy air,   865
> like a fawn who romps
> in the green delight of the meadows,
> when it has fled its snare
> and the fearful chase,
> over the well-woven nets,   870
> and the hunter cries out, spurring
> his hounds on in the chase.
> And with efforts of swift running and pantings
> she leaps into the plain beside the river

30. 600f.: δίκετε πεδόσε τρομερὰ σώματα
δίκετε, Μαινάδες;

604f.: βάρβαροι γυναῖκες, οὕτως ἐκπεπληγμέναι φόβῳ
πρὸς πέδῳ πεπτώκατ';

31. See Décharme, *Euripides and the Spirit of his Dramas* (New York 1906), trans. James Loeb, pp. 289f.

32. 612 makes it clear that they had believed themselves completely deserted and helpless.

33. In the antistrophe of the second stasimon; see above.

34. 775-7 are a transitional combination of fear (ταρβῶ) and aggressiveness (ἀλλ' ὅμως εἰρήσεται).

and delights in the freedom from humans   875
and the shoots of dark-leaved branches.

What is wisdom? or what more beautiful prize
do the gods grant to mortals
than to hold the hand in strength above the head
of one's enemies?   880
What is lovely is always dear.

It is slow to start, but nevertheless
the strength of the gods can be counted on.
It straightens out those mortals
who honor foolishness   885
and, in their insane thinking,
fail to revere the gods.
But the gods cleverly hide
the long foot of time and
they hunt down the ungodly one.   890
For one must not think or act
above the law.
Since it costs little to realize
that this principle holds strong:
the divine, whatever it is,
the lawful, sanctioned by time, and   895
what is by nature.

What is wisdom? or what more beautiful prize
do the gods grant to mortals
than to hold the hand in strength above the head
of one's enemies.   900
What is lovely is always dear.

Happy is the one who has fled
the wintry sea-storm and reaches the harbor;
happy the one who comes out on top of his
troubles. Everyone achieves some happiness   905
at some time, in some way.
And yet there are a thousand people
with a thousand hopes.
Some hopes end up in happiness

for mortals, some vanish away.
But the man who is happy   910
day by day, him I call blessed.

At the beginning of the third stasimon, the escape-theme of the
first and second stasima appears. But there are important differences; although the chorus begin with a questioning, plaintive
longing to escape, that escape is soon accomplished in the lyrics,
and the mood at the end of the strophe and in the epode is exaltation in new-found freedom. The image of the fawn–bacchant
leaping into the air recalls the joyful abandon of the colt at the end
of the epode of the *parodos*. But the leap into the air is no longer
the spontaneous expression of joy (165 – ἡδομένα) that we encountered in that epode; there the colt was left suspended in mid-
air, in the middle of a transport of joy. Here the happiness (874 –
ἡδομένα) is the exultation of escape – from the hunter who braces
his hounds not far behind the fleeing fawn. Her foot comes
down in freedom, in the cool green shade of the trees (874–6), but
now the hunted becomes the hunter. For the escape of the fawn
has its counterpart in the revenge exacted from her oppressor: the
foot of the fawn which comes down in freedom has its complement
in the long foot of time which hunts down the unholy man (889–
90).

Although in the course of this third stasimon the longing for
escape disappears, and the revenge-theme rises into prominence,
the imagery remains the same: only the chorus now clearly
identify themselves with the pursuer rather than the pursued. The
two desires (for escape and for revenge) are closely linked in this
play,[35] and we must inquire what notion of the relationship between them led Euripides to link them in such a way. The third
episode, as we noted above, brings about a considerable change in
the position of the chorus. Throughout it there is one after another
manifestation of the terrible and versatile power of Dionysos; the
chorus, as his votaries, and as protected by his priest, share in this
power. It is this new-found power, we must believe, that now
causes the alteration in the chorus' attitude: the energy which goes

35. See the studies of R. R. Dyer ('Image and Symbol: The Link between
the two Worlds of the *Bacchae*', *AUMLA* no. 21 (1964), 15–26) and Winnington-
Ingram (above, n. 12), *passim*.

into self-restraint, into ever holding back, is never expended but waits to be transformed into aggression and assertiveness with the advent of power.

As the chorus begin to assert in earnest the revenge-theme, there are reminiscences of the revenge-songs of the Furies in the *Eumenides* of Aeschylus. In particular, the second stasimon (307–96) of that play has certain suggestive affinities with this antistrophe. The most striking parallelism is in the 'foot-images':

> μάλα γὰρ οὖν ἁλομένα
> ἀνέκαθεν βαρυπετῆ
> καταφέρω ποδὸς ἀκμάν,
> σφαλερὰ <καὶ> τανυδρόμοις
>   κῶλα, δύσφορον ἄταν (372–6 Murray).

For I give a high leap
and bring down from above
the heavy fall of my foot –
even swift runners' legs
buckle, a wretched doom.

Both songs are dominated by a sense of enormous power, inexorable and inescapable, and by a consciousness of impending ruin. The Bacchants, in this and the next two choruses, become, in their bloodthirsty delight in vengeance, more and more like the Erinyes. This is not to say, of course, that there is any historical justification for equating the power of Dionysos with that of the Furies, but there are certain points of contact between these powers that Euripides has chosen to exploit. They are both associated with the instinctual, with sources of power that originate from within the human being. The Erinyes, it is also true, were by no means solely instruments of vengeance,[36] but it is in the *Eumenides* of Aeschylus that this aspect of their power receives its fullest expression.

Not only, then, is the idea of vengeance a prominent one in this stasimon, but it is expressed, in this and the following stasimon, in terms of the moral vocabulary which has been prominent throughout the play and was developed most fully in the first stasimon. According to Winnington-Ingram, 'wisdom in the second choral ode and wisdom here [in the antistrophe of the third stasimon] have the same roots in the unthinking acceptance of popular, of

36. E. R. Dodds, *The Greeks and the Irrational* (Boston 1957), pp. 7ff.

natural standards'.[37] It is true that there is a similarity in the attitudes of the chorus in both stanzas, in that both make an appeal to the virtues of bourgeois morality: they praise conduct which reflects the established norms of behavior and which is pious. But there are important differences between them also, differences which do not lie only in the fact that 'what seemed in the earlier passage to issue solely in peace and quietness is now seen to lead equally to violence and cruelty'.[38] Euripides has given us some clues about how such a transformation can take place. For, although the ἀγνωμοσύναν τιμῶντας καὶ μὴ τὰ θεῶν αὔξοντας of lines 885–7 are very like the μαινόμενοι καὶ κακόβουλοι φῶτες of 399–401, the concern is now not with avoiding such persons (as before; see lines 427–8), but with disciplining or chastising them (ἀπευθύνει – 884). The sanction for the chorus' attitude in the earlier stanza was merely whatever is most commonly held valid (430ff.); now they appeal to the laws (νόμοι) which not only reflect common practice, but have the force of authority (either divine or human) behind them.[39]

The strophe and the antistrophe of this stasimon are alike in that they both discuss the same act – pursuit – from different points of view. However, the language of the strophe is almost entirely metaphorical, while the antistrophe is made up of a series of γνῶμαι, the customary form for the traditional wisdom so common in this play. A further difference between the strophe and antistrophe is in the tempo of either stanza. Despite the sameness in metrical pattern, the strophe describes a swift, rushing motion, and the sweep of the description itself is broken by only one major pause (at the end of 872). The antistrophe is made up of a series of short sentences, and it is slowness and sureness of movement which is emphasized: ὁρμᾶται (882), δαρὸν χρόνου πόδα (889), ἐν χρόνῳ μακρῷ (895), ἀεὶ φύσει πεφυκός (896). We can contrast the descriptive language of the strophe, which emphasizes rapidity and suddenness of motion: φύγῃ (868), θωΰσσων (871), συντείνῃ δράμημα (872), ὠκυδρόμοις τ' ἀέλλαις (873), θρῴσκει (874).

The use of γνῶμαι, then, and the emphasis on slow, but strong and sure movement, in the stanza concerned with revenge, operate as a vehicle for the revenge-theme itself. The bloody and brutal

37. Op. cit. (n. 12), p. 113. 38. Ibid.
39. See especially σθένος (884), κρεῖσσον (891), and ἰσχύν (893).

aspects of revenge are ignored in this choral ode, for Euripides' concern here is rather to link this desire with the established, accepted norm of behavior, and with the doctrine of moderation. The conjoining of these two seemingly contradictory ideals is seen most clearly and most strikingly in the refrain of this stasimon.

The exaltation of revenge in this refrain has always seemed disturbingly out of tune with the quietism of the epode, and Dodds deals in his note on the passage with some of the attempts to interpret the refrain. Most of the discussion has centered around the meaning of the first question (τί τὸ σοφόν;), and I have reserved for an appendix a detailed treatment of this point. But in view of the general lines of interpretation which I have followed, we shall not be so disturbed as most by the conjunction of an appeal to popular, quietistic morality with a call to revenge. The chorus of the *Bacchae* are concerned that their thoughts and actions be wise. It is the quality of the wisdom that changes, not their attitude toward it. There is a wisdom, they say at first, in keeping away (427) from the man of excess (and it is his excess of cleverness which is contrasted with prudence in 395). Now (in the refrain of stasimon three) the chorus find not only wisdom, but a beautiful honor, divinely sanctioned, in triumph over one's enemies. The revenge-theme articulated here is identified not with inhuman cruelty, but with loveliness, wisdom, and the gods' benignant smile. This is the same idea and the same tone which we found in the antistrophe of the stasimon, and we noted that the poet's concern throughout had been to present the desire for revenge in as favorable and respectable a light as possible, and to associate it with the joy of escape and freedom.

We shall not, then, be surprised to find that the epode of this stasimon emphasizes these more positive, more joyous, and quieter ideals of the chorus. The thought and language of the epode recall the earliest parts of the play: we can compare 910–11 with 389–90 and 425–6; and 907–9 with 397–9. And εὐδαίμων, μακαρίζω were prominent words in the beginning of the play and appear in striking contexts at the end.[40] But the epode, with its γνῶμαι, its moral quietism, its delight in escape, and its references to happiness and blessedness, is preceded by the refrain which

40. In the scene of Agave's triumphant entrance; see Winnington-Ingram's treatment of this scene, and de Romilly's (above, n. 14) remarks.

extols the joys of revenge, and is followed by the entrance of Pentheus dressed as a maenad. In such a context, the peaceful joy of the epode is startling; but we are just beginning to see how readily the language and ideals of bourgeois morality can be accommodated to an opposite system of values.

The fourth stasimon

Run, swift hounds of Lyssa, run to the mountains,
where the daughters of Cadmus are celebrating in a band,
goad them on
against the frenzied one, who has come in women's
     clothes   980
to spy on the maenads.
First his mother will catch sight of him, as
he spies from some rock or pinnacle,
and she will cry out to the maenads,
'Oh Bacchants, who is this mountain-roaming tracker,   985
who has come to the mountain, to the mountain?
Who ever gave him birth?
For he was not born from a woman's blood,
but from some lioness
or one of the Libyan gorgons.'   990

Let justice show herself clearly, let her carry a sword
and thrust it through the throat
of the godless, lawless, unjust   995
earthborn child of Echion.

For he has come with unjust intention and lawless rage
against your rites, Bacchus, and those of your mother;
in his frenzy
and delirium he has come
to conquer by force the invincible.   1000
Death will correct his intentions; but to
be unquestioning in divine matters,
and to live as is proper for mortals, spells a griefless
life. I rejoice in the unhesitating pursuit of wisdom   1005
and in those other great and outstanding quests;
for it leads life toward the beautiful

when one is holy and reverent throughout the night and
    day,
and having cast aside lawless matters,
honors the gods.   1010

Let justice show herself clearly, let her carry a sword
and thrust it through the throat
of the godless, lawless, unjust   1015
earthborn child of Echion.

Let us behold you as a bull, or a many-headed dragon,
or a fiery lion.
Run, oh Bacchic one, and   1020
with a smile on your face cast the deadly noose
about the neck of the hunter of the Bacchants
who falls beneath the herd of maenads.

The fourth stasimon is separated from the third by only sixty-
five lines, and is close to it in structure as well as in dramatic time.
Both choral odes are about the same length, and both include a
refrain and an epode. The strophes of both stasima are highly
metaphorical; in both the antistrophe is composed of a series of
γνῶμαι. The strophe of the third stasimon is dominated by the
image of the triumphant escape of the fawn; the strophe of the
fourth stasimon calls on the hounds of Lyssa, and presents a picture
of Agave rousing her Theban maenads against Pentheus. The
associations with the Erinyes which we noted in connection with
stasimon three become more explicit as the chorus invoke Lyssa,
a figure 'akin to the Erinyes'.[41] The pack of hounds with which
she runs provides an easy point at which to effect her transition
into the existing metaphorical structure of the play.

    We noted in connection with the second stasimon that the more
assertive of their rights the chorus became, the more they re-
assumed their character as maenads which had been obscured in
the first stasimon. And it is certainly true that, in this and the
following stasimon, all the chorus' hostility toward Pentheus finds
expression in the ritual language of the *parodos*, and in an invocation of the Bacchic god and the sacred objects of the Dionysian
religion. The ἴτ' εἰς ὄρος (977) and ἐς ὄρος ἐς ὄρος (986) are the

41. Dodds, p. 199.

joyful cries of the epode of the *parodos*, and the longing for escape into peace of the escape-hymns, translated into the cry of the hunter. Animal imagery is prominent not only in the invocation of the hounds of Lyssa, but in Agave's hysterical question of lines 985–90. The question, a form which we had come to associate with the wondering, astonished, and sometimes indignant attitude of the chorus, is here invested with a new and cruel sarcasm. Further, as both we and the chorus are aware, when Agave calls Pentheus a lion cub, she implies her own symbolic identification with a lioness.

The refrain of the chorus, like that of the previous stasimon, unites the ideas of justice, rightness, and wisdom with vengeance. Here the chorus invoke δίκα, the personification of an idea which, even before it evolved into a moral value, represented stability – a lack of unbalance, things and persons in their proper places.[42] The chorus call upon δίκα to inflict upon Pentheus the ultimate punishment. Like the binding song of the Furies, which it obviously resembles, the refrain has a chanting effect, the result in part of the single-minded, simple command which it has to communicate, and partly of the anaphora in line 991 and the parechesis in 995.

The antistrophe of this stasimon, like that of stasimon three, is a series of moralizing reflections. Now there is no holding back about the kind of misfortune that awaits the lawless man. Pentheus is described, in lines 997–1001, by terms which we had associated with him from the first stasimon on;[43] the chorus' concern is no longer to draw away from such περισσοὶ φῶτες (as in the first stasimon) nor are they now content to call for the chastisement or straightening out of such as Pentheus (as in the third stasimon). Now they call for death as a suitable and just revenge.[44]

The chorus now turn once again to the general principles which it has been their wont to expound. Lines 1005–6 are discussed in the appendix on τὸ σοφόν; but lines 1006–9 are so

42. Guthrie (above, n. 20), pp. 123f.
43. See lines 387ff., 396ff., 427ff., 544, 555, and 881ff.
44. We cannot be exactly sure of the reading here. Dodds' suggestion for 1002ff. seems quite good; but whether or not his arrangement of the clauses is exactly correct, the parallels he cites for θάνατος as σωφρόνισμα make it unthinkable to eliminate θάνατος (as other editors have done), and make it seem very likely indeed that σωφρόνισμα is the correct reading.

thoroughly corrupt that it is impossible to restore them with any degree of certainty. Fortunately we are in no doubt as to their general meaning; it is clear that the chorus here return to their exaltation of the quiet virtues, and of the day-by-day happiness which they bring.[45] But now they adopt a much more aggressive attitude toward the pattern of life which does not correspond with their own.

The epode of this stasimon, unlike that of the last which seemed so different in tone from the rest of the stasimon, reinforces the brutality of the whole ode. The substitution of Dionysos in his animal forms for δίκα, as the subject of the chorus' invocation, makes clear once again their identification of justice with the revengeful inflicting of death. Here the theme is resumed in the animal and hunting imagery whose prominence in the play has already been noted. In the epode, all the major figures on Mount Cithaeron are assimilated to animals: Pentheus is the prey of the animal god and the herd (ἀγέλαν) of maenads. The savage delight which the chorus feel withstands the shocked disapproval of the messenger in the scene which immediately follows this ode; the murder of Pentheus brings for them escape from the power of Thebes (1035 and 1037f.) and a reassertion of their eastern character (1034).

> Let us dance to the Bacchic one,
> Let us celebrate with shouting the disaster
> of Pentheus, the child of the dragon.   1155
> He put on the woman's dress
> and he took up the narthex, a promise of death,
> the lovely thyrsus;
> he had a bull to lead him to disaster.
> Cadmean Bacchants,   1160
> you have turned a lovely, bright victory-hymn
> into one of groans and tears.
> A lovely victory – to embrace one's child
> in a hand dripping with its blood.

The final choral ode is a victory song, in which the chorus celebrate the terrible death of Pentheus with undisguised delight. The reminiscences of the joyful *parodos* become more explicit as the

45. See lines 910f. and 389ff.

language and instruments of the ecstatic cult are applied freely to Pentheus' death: the thyrsus, now εὔθυρσος, has become a wand of death (πιστὸν Ἅιδα). They call καλός the tragedies of Pentheus and Agave, with a full sense of the cruel irony which is implied (as the phrases in 1162 and their taunting of Agave in the next scene demonstrate [see esp. 1192ff.]). Animal imagery is still prominent (1155, 1159) and is only abandoned in the final sad word of this song, with which the return to the human world, of human cares and loves, is sudden and shocking: τέκνῳ.

Aeschylus had shown, in the *Oresteia*, in reference to that revenge associated with bloodguilt, the necessity of finding indirect ways of dealing with the law of revenge. The transformation of the moaning, black, foul-smelling creatures of the first scene of the *Eumenides*, into the saffron-robed daughters of night, guardians of the peace and justice of the city, is a glorification of the legal and political structure of the *polis*, and of the power of Athenian law to encompass and contain the destructive and chaotic forces of the world. The solemn beauty of the torchlight procession which ends the trilogy and which was renewed every year at Athens was the visual symbol of the faith in the effectiveness of the political structure of the *polis*, and in the possibility for justice.

The *Bacchae* treats the reverse of this process. Instinctual forces and primitive drives surge up through the overlay of legal and social structure to bring about the fall of the *polis*. But this primal drive does not suddenly rush forth in a destructive frenzy any more than one decision over one case occasioned the birth of legal justice in Greece. What Euripides treats through the chorus in the *Bacchae* is a process of transformation. The *polis*, as Euripides seems to have seen it, depended upon a fragile compact between several parties whose basic interests conflicted, but who entered into an unspoken and even unconscious agreement to accept curtailments of their own drives and rights in the interests of a democratic city-state. However, once the *polis* is no longer able to function so as to grant a minimum satisfaction to each of the elements and interests which compose it, the covenant is broken, and the preservation of order then depends upon the ruthless exercise of authority. The contradiction inherent in the structure of the *polis* is reproduced in the system of values in its service: the bourgeois morality of con-

stancy, stability, and moderation which the chorus preach involves
a self-denial and repression which engenders an immoderate
hostility toward rival value-systems. Changes in the language, in
the thought, and in the form of expression of the ideals of the
chorus indicate a change in attitude from quiet submission to
violent opposition. Nevertheless, the chorus remain dedicated
throughout the play to the principles of justice, wisdom, order and
piety.

We recall that it is the desire for revenge which operates for
Thucydides, in his paradigmatic treatment of the Corcyrean
revolution (III. 70–83), as one of the chief causes of the revolution
and the breakdown in morals and society.[46] And in the *Bacchae*,
the extent of the destruction wrought is apparent in that the final
scene of the play represents the end of the house of Cadmus,
legendary founder of Thebes, and ancestor of its nobility (1302ff.).
He, for reasons which are not entirely clear, due to the mutilated
state of the last scene of the play, was exiled from his country, and
Agave and her sisters were likewise expelled (probably because of
the pollution incurred by Agave in killing her son).[47]

Finally, Thucydides' example of the extremes of violence (III.
81. 5: καὶ γὰρ πατὴρ παῖδα ἀπέκτεινε) and the subordination of
family ties to those of party (III. 82. 6: καὶ μὴν καὶ τὸ ξυγγενὲς τοῦ
ἑταιρικοῦ ἀλλοτριώτερον ἐγένετο) has its gruesome parallel in the
inability of Agave, no longer a mother, but one of a herd (1130) of
maenads, to recognize her own son:

> Ἐγώ τοι, μῆτερ, εἰμί, παῖς σέθεν
> Πενθεύς, ὃν ἔτεκες ἐν δόμοις Ἐχίονος·
> οἴκτιρε δ' ὦ μῆτέρ με, μηδὲ ταῖς ἐμαῖς
> ἁμαρτίαισι παῖδα σὸν κατακτάνῃς (1118–21).

---

46. See III. 82. 3: πολὺ ἐπέφερε τὴν ὑπερβολὴν τοῦ καινοῦσθαι τὰς διανοίας
τῶν τ' ἐπιχειρήσεων περιτεχνήσει καὶ τῶν τιμωριῶν ἀτοπίᾳ. III. 82. 7: ἀντι-
τιμωρήσασθαί τέ τινα περὶ πλείονος ἦν ἢ αὐτὸν μὴ προπαθεῖν. III.82.8: ἐτόλμησάν
τε τὰ δεινότατα ἐπεξῇσάν τε τὰς τιμωρίας ἔτι μείζους.

47. See the *Christus Patiens* of Pseudo-Gregorius, lines 1674ff.

NOTES ON THE TEXT

Following is a list of my departures from Murray's text, with an indication of where to find a discussion of the reading I have adopted. In every case but one I have simply chosen among authorities, on the basis of the arguments they present, and in most cases I have followed either the choice or the suggestion of Dodds.

135 ἡδύ γ' for ἡδύς; J. de Romilly, 'Le Thème du Bonheur dans les *Bacchantes*', *REG* 76 (1963), 364, n. 3.

154 χλιδά for χλιδᾷ; Wilamowitz: see Dodds *ad loc.*

395 add period at end of line; see Dodds *ad loc.*, who follows the Aldine and other editions.

396 omit period at end of line; see Dodds *ad loc.*

399 substitute question mark for period; Tyrwhitt and Hcadlam: see Dodds *ad loc.*

427 σοφά δ' for σοφὰν δ'; Dindorf: see Dodds *ad loc.*

1002–4 major alteration; I have quoted Dodds' version presented and discussed *ad loc.*

1005–6 οὐ φθόνῳ χαίρω for οὐ φθονῶ· χαίρω; see my discussion of these lines in Appendix B.

1006 τά θ' for τά δ'; my emendation, an insignificant one from a paleographical point of view, but one which is necessary to give the sense of continuity between lines 1005–10 which my interpretation requires.

1007 see Dodds *ad loc.* for a discussion of his reading, which I here adopt.

1157 ῎Αιδα for ῎Αιδαν; Dodds *ad loc.*

1162 γόον for στόνον; Canter: see Dodds *ad loc.*

1164 τέκνῳ (i.e. τέκνωι) for τέκνου; see Dodds *ad loc.*; I adopt a reading discussed, but not preferred by him.

APPENDIX A: THE ANCESTRY OF PENTHEUS

Pentheus is the son of Agave and Echion. The line of his descent, through Cadmus the founder of Thebes on the maternal side, and through the dragon from whose teeth Echion sprang, receives prominent notice in this play: at lines 213, 250, 254, 264–5, 507, 537–44, 995, 1015, 1030, 1155, 1274–6, 1305–15, and 1358–9. The most extensive development of Pentheus' dragon nature is in the antistrophe of the second stasimon. This stasimon has certain suggestive affinities with another Euripidean ode, *Phoenissae* 638–96, and a comparison of the two odes, written about the same city and within a few years of one another,[48] reveals some interesting points of contact:

> Tyrian Cadmus came to this land;
> for him the uncompelled fall
> of the four-legged calf   640
> was the destined sign
> that there the oracle
> directed him to settle
> the wheat-bearing plains,
> where the lovely-flowing stream   645
> of water runs over the farmland,
> the green and deeply fertile
> lands of Dirce.
> There the mother gave birth
> to Bromios, fathered by Zeus.   650
> Right away the twining tendrils
> of ivy covered the baby,
> blessing him
> with its dark-green shoots –
> and there is the Bacchic dance   655
> for Theban maidens and women crying euoi.
>
> There was the murderous dragon
> of Ares, a savage watchman
> keeping guard with the
> far-stretching glances of his eyes   660
> over the watery streams
> and green rivers.
> Cadmus washed himself pure
> and then killed the dragon with a marble rock,
> having struck the beast's bloody head   665
> with his death-dealing arm.   666
> Then, according to the counsel of Pallas,   669

48. It is generally agreed that the *Phoenissae* is to be dated about 411/10.

the unmothered daughter of Zeus,   668
he cast its teeth down into the deeply fertile earth.   667
From there the earth sent up over the surface   670
of the land a fully armed display.
But an iron-hearted slaughter sent them
down into their native earth.
This killing wet the earth with blood, the earth
which had shown them forth to the sunny breaths of wind.

                                                                                    675

The most obvious parallelism between the two stasima is the similarity of mood and theme: the strophes concentrate on a productive, joyful, and natural Thebes. The river Dirce, as a fertilizing, peace-nurturing stream, is prominent in both stanzas. In both Dirce initially received and nurtured the baby Dionysos. The joy of his birth and the presenting of him to Thebes is prominent in the *Bacchae* strophe, the joy of the founding of the city of Thebes is central in the strophe of the *Phoenissae* ode. The mood in the strophe of the *Bacchae*, where the joyful invocation of Dirce yields to expressions of plaintive confusion (530ff.) is more ambiguous than that in the *Phoenissae* strophe, where the sense of fruitfulness and joyful celebration is unqualified.

In the antistrophes of both stasima the δράκων is the dominant figure. In the *Phoenissae* the details of the dragon's connection with Thebes are made clear, while in the *Bacchae* it stands in the background as Pentheus' ancestor. The predominant mood in both stanzas is dark, threatening, and violent. The dragon, like Ares his protector, like Pentheus and his army, is a manifestation of external force or authority. In this respect he is to be contrasted with Dionysos who, like Aphrodite, represents internal force or potency. The power of Ares is essentially destructive, that of Dionysos basically productive.[49]

49. Ares and Dionysos are connected at the beginning of the third stasimon of the *Phoenissae* in such a way as to suggest this contrast:

ὦ πολύμοχθος Ἄρης, τί ποθ' αἵματι
καὶ θανάτῳ κατέχῃ Βρομίου παράμουσος ἑορταῖς;

                                                                (784–5 Murray).

And George Bernard Shaw seems to have held a similar view on the nature of the forces involved and of their conflict, when, in *Major Barbara*, he pits Andrew Undershaft, 'a maker of cannons', against his daughter, the title figure and an officer of the Salvation Army. They both, as Undershaft remarks,

In the *Phoenissae* the δράκων is a present and important element in the founding of the city of Thebes. Before Cadmus can establish the foundations of his city he struggles with and conquers the dragon and the armed band that springs up from its teeth. Cadmus thereby appropriates to himself the external power or authority symbolized by the dragon over which he has been victorious. In his ode on the founding of Thebes, I think Euripides has intended to make clear the nature of the foundation on which the city-state rests. That is, the authority which the ruler of the city holds is guaranteed by his ability to call into service at any time the forces of bloody death and destruction. The order and the productive forces of civilization can only be guaranteed by the rulers' control over these forces of chaos and disorder. These are important points to understand in connection with the characterization of Pentheus in the *Bacchae*. Like his ancestor the dragon he represents martial power, the power of Ares.[50] Some critical attitudes seek to mitigate the more brutal aspect of Pentheus' character. Winnington-Ingram and others have identified Pentheus' dragon quality as a symbolic representation of Pentheus' own similarity and consequent susceptibility to the Dionysiac element; for the dragon (or snake) 'is an avatar of Dionysos, in whose honour they [the chorus] wear snakes in their hair and as girdles; later they will pray that he may appear in the form of a snake'.[51] Although this may be a secondary aspect of Pentheus' dragon nature, surely we must regard as primary the explicit connection of Pentheus with the bloody dragon of Ares. E. M. Blaiklock[52] and others claim that Pentheus is a misguided and confused but essentially responsible

preach Blood and Fire. Shaw's play was written shortly after the publication of Gilbert Murray's English version of the *Bacchae* (from which Shaw quotes), and *Major Barbara*, as Shaw himself remarks, 'stands indebted to him [Gilbert Murray] in more ways than one'.

50. See especially ll. 780–5:

στεῖχ' ἐπ' 'Ηλέκτρας ἰὼν
πύλας· κέλευε πάντας ἀσπιδηφόρους
ἵππων τ' ἀπαντᾶν ταχυπόδων ἐπεμβάτας
πέλτας θ' ὅσοι πάλλουσι καὶ τόξων χερὶ
ψάλλουσι νευράς, ὡς ἐπιστρατεύσομεν
βάκχαισιν.

51. Op. cit. (above, n. 12), p. 80.

52. *The Male Characters of Euripides* (Wellington, New Zealand, 1952), chapter 11.

ruler. However, in approaching the characterization of Pentheus
in the *Bacchae* it is doubly important to abandon the common but
unwarranted assumption that poets write only propaganda –
write, that is, to champion or oppose one or another cause or
character. A less simplistic approach to the question of Euripides'
attitude toward Pentheus will admit that Euripides does not seek
to condemn or praise Pentheus, but to reveal the nature of his
position as ruler of Thebes. We shall then encounter no difficulty
in assimilating Pentheus' more gentle and human side to our
general picture. For like Cadmus, from whom he is also descended,
he was the preserver of order and justice, and a guarantee for the
continuance of the race and the city:

> Pentheus to whom the house looked up – you, oh
> child, who sustained my ruling house, child of
> my child; and you were a terror to the city.   1310
> No one dared insult the old man when you were about.
> For you would exact justice from him.
> But now I am cast out in dishonor from my house,
> Cadmus the great, who sowed the Theban race,
> and reaped a most beautiful harvest.   1315
> Oh, dearest of men – for, child, although dead you
> shall be counted among those dearest to me –
> no longer will you touch my chin with your hand,
> kissing me, calling me 'father of your mother',
> and asking, 'Who wrongs you, old man, who dishonors   1320
> you? Who is grievous to you and disturbs your heart?
> Tell me, so that I may punish the one who
> molests you, oh father.'

It is clear that even in this passage, Pentheus is first and last the
policeman, inspiring fear (1310), chastising wrongdoers (1312),
and prohibiting transgression (1322). And it is through this
characterization of Pentheus that we can perceive Euripides'
concept of the city-state as a temporary alliance for order and
progress, whose continued existence is sanctioned only by the
repressive forces which it ultimately controls.

APPENDIX B: τὸ σοφόν

The problem of τὸ σοφόν in the *Bacchae* is primarily one of establishing for the chorus an attitude toward this idea which remains consistent throughout the play. Since the chorus invoke τὸ σοφόν in contexts which seem to imply different attitudes, one or another passage has usually had to be twisted in order to yield the desired consistency of viewpoint. Otherwise, critics have had to fall back on a kind of 'situation ethics' approach in which τὸ σοφόν is acknowledged to be a good or bad value in accordance with the context in which it appears.

The starting-point for all discussion of this question is the famous line 395: τὸ σοφὸν δ᾽ οὐ σοφία. Editors and translators alike have always assumed that the chorus here reject τὸ σοφόν as false wisdom and adopt σοφία as true wisdom. Then, in the third and fourth stasima, where the chorus seem to approve τὸ σοφόν, critics attempt to make adjustments. However, it seems to me that there is no compelling reason to assume that τὸ σοφόν is rejected in line 395. The main reason for doing so has been Teiresias' words in line 203, where he invokes an unquestioning faith in received tradition as the surest standard by which to judge:

πατρίους παραδοχάς, ἅς θ᾽ ὁμήλικας χρόνῳ
κεκτήμεθ᾽, οὐδεὶς αὐτὰ καταβαλεῖ λόγος,
οὐδ᾽ εἰ δι᾽ ἄκρων τὸ σοφὸν ηὕρηται φρενῶν.

No argument will overthrow the ancestral
traditions, old as time, which we have received,
not even if sharp wits have discovered what is wise.

Teiresias' position in this play is far from unambiguous, and the attitudes that he assumes are difficult to define with any clarity or consistency. In the above-quoted passage, for example, he seems to advise the acceptance of a *new* god on grounds of the inviolability of *age-old* tradition; and if line 203 refers to the practice of rationalizing about the gods, then Teiresias' speech to Pentheus in lines 272ff. is a superb example of it.

Even if Teiresias' position were not so far from clear, we should still be better advised to define the chorus' attitude toward the wise from what they themselves say about it, and not to make the questionable assumption of continuity of their vocabulary with

Teiresias, particularly when line 395 points up a linguistic paradox. An examination of the moral doctrine of the chorus, which is first presented in the stasimon in which line 395 appears, demonstrates that they remain throughout exponents of a bourgeois moral code. And an adherence to a wisdom which is probably better called prudence and a concurrent rejection of an immoderate intellectualism is thoroughly appropriate to a commitment to bourgeois values. Just such a contrast is suggested by line 395. However, although the elements of the paradox which the chorus suggest are clear, it is not at all clear which element is to be associated with which half of the paradox. We can see the same linguistic ambiguity in the English translation which I have suggested for the line: what is wise is not wisdom.[53] And so, when the line comes up in the tragedy, clearly the dominant idea is the paradox which it suggests, and we have no way to associate a particular attitude with either τὸ σοφόν or σοφία. However, when we have considered the other uses of τὸ σοφόν in the play and examine the lines in retrospect, it will then be clear that σοφία is rejected here as false or excessive wisdom, and τὸ σοφόν is accepted as prudence.

The next appearance of the idea of prudence is later in the first stasimon, at line 427, where the chorus make more explicit the content of their attitude toward the wise: σοφὰ δ᾽ ἀπέχειν πραπίδα φρένα τε περισσῶν παρὰ φωτῶν. τὸ σοφόν itself occurs next in the refrain of the third stasimon, and has recently been discussed in an article by R. P. Winnington-Ingram.[54] His argument that the chorus here reject the false wisdom which τὸ σοφόν represents to them receives its impetus from the traditional interpretation of line 395 (the rejection of τὸ σοφόν). He suggests that we read the whole passage as Murray had printed it,[55] and understand τί τὸ σοφόν; as a formula of 'contemptuous rejection'. The false wisdom (τὸ σοφόν) which the chorus reject is, according to Winnington-Ingram's argument, that intellectual cleverness of the late fifth century which called wrong the age-old precept of revenging your-

53. This can mean: (*a*) whatever it is that is wise, it is certainly not 'wisdom', or (*b*) 'it is not wisdom merely to be wise' (in the words of Santayana).

54. 'Euripides, *Bacchae* 877–881 = 897–901', *BICS* no. 13 (1966), 34–7.

55. Winnington-Ingram cites A. M. Dale's metrical analysis of the passage against Dodds' suggestion that we omit the second τό in 877 (= 897).

self on your enemies. Two objections suggest themselves at once: the lack of parallels for the formula of contemptuous rejection,[56] and the fact that in Euripides, at any rate, the finer or more sensitive view of retaliation as sub-human is by no means restricted to the more clever, more inquiring minds.[57] However, Winnington-Ingram's discussion of the doctrine of retaliation upon one's enemy and the moral views of the chorus leads him to conclude that the chorus will in fact identify an unexpressed true wisdom and the 'traditional valuation of revenge'.[58] The usual interpretation of these lines, when it is innocent of any attempt to evolve a consistent attitude toward τὸ σοφόν, assumes that it is just such a doctrine which the chorus is celebrating, but that the wisdom of revenge is in fact expressed in the question τί τὸ σοφόν; For, since ἢ τί τὸ κάλλιον κτλ. is an alternative way of formulating τί τὸ σοφόν;,[59] χεῖρ' ὑπὲρ κορυφᾶς κτλ. is an answer to both questions. It is only the preconceived notion that τὸ σοφόν must be rejected that prevents Winnington-Ingram from seeing in the refrain the chorus' expression of what is, by his own admission, the expected and logical attitude.

The final example of τὸ σοφόν is a particularly troublesome one, since it occurs in a corrupt passage: the antistrophe of the fourth stasimon. Both Dodds and Winnington-Ingram, following Dodds, read in lines 1005–6 τὸ σοφὸν οὐ φθονῶ· χαίρω θηρεύουσα τάδ' ἕτερα, 'The wise can have their wisdom: my joy is in pursuing these other aims' (p. 204). But the manuscript (we have only the evidence of P after line 775 of this play) reads φθόνω [*sic*], the Aldine edition of 1503 (which used P and a copy of L) and many older editions (as Dodds notes) read φθόνῳ. Here again, the assumed meaning of line 395 dictates Dodds' interpretation. His primary reason for rejecting φθόνῳ and writing φθονῶ is that the chorus 'cannot say here that they rejoice to pursue τὸ σοφόν', when they have, in his view, previously rejected it. But if we look with un-

56. Soph. *OC* 598 is certainly not a formula of rejection, nor does Winnington-Ingram claim it as such; but it is open to legitimate doubt whether it is even 'scornful or sceptical', as he claims.

57. The messenger's sentiments, at 1032f. and 1038f., mark him as a man of humane character.

58. Op. cit. (above, n. 12), p. 36.

59. For this use of ἢ see Smyth, *Greek Grammar* §2860, and Kühner–Gerth, vol. 2 part 1, p. 297.

prejudiced eyes upon this passage and the previously discussed refrain, it will be clear that the chorus exalt τὸ σοφόν throughout the play and that the rejected value in line 395 must therefore be σοφία.[60]

60. σοφία has just this meaning in a choral passage at *Heracl.* 608–17, where the moral outlook is basically the same as that of the *Bacchae*.

Stylistic characterization in Thucydides: Nicias and Alcibiades

DANIEL P. TOMPKINS

THAT characters exist in Thucydides, and that their distinctive traits influence historical action, cannot be disputed. Themistocles' wit and effectiveness are first displayed (I. 90–3, I. 135–8) and then described (I. 138. 2–3). The traits that made Pericles a great statesman are affirmed, as are the personal qualities that determined Cleon's influence (II. 65, III. 38. 6, V. 16. 1). We are also given an explicit statement that Alcibiades' character proved harmful to Athens by alienating public trust (VI. 15. 1), while later passages imply that Nicias' personal stubbornness hurt the expedition in Sicily (VII. 48. 3, VII. 50. 4).

The general outlines of the roles of Nicias and Alcibiades in Thucydides are clear, and, while differences of opinion exist as to the precise motives of these men, the importance of their characters is undeniable.[1] It is also undeniable that the speeches are a major source of information about these men. In Nicias' speeches, for instance, we are given strong arguments for hesitation and conservative ἀπραγμοσύνη, while Alcibiades' exhortation to the Athenians urges action and defends the speaker's competitiveness.

Despite the general admission that characters are important in Thucydides, and the agreement that their speeches provide insight into them, modern scholars insist that these speeches show no individuality of language. Thus Friedrich Blass says: 'spricht nun der Athener wie der Lakedaimonier, Perikles wie Kleon und Brasidas, was die Form der Rede und den Ausdruck anbelangt'.[2] Another great figure of nineteenth-century rhetorical scholarship, Richard Jebb, was equally unyielding:

1. On Nicias, see in particular A. B. West, 'Pericles' Political Heirs', *CP* 19 (1924), 124–46, 201–28; H. D. Westlake, 'Nicias in Thucydides', *CQ* 35 (1941), 58–65; and Mary Morse Fuqua, *A Study of Character Portrayal in the History of Thucydides* (Dissertation, Cornell University 1965).

2. Friedrich Blass, *Die attische Beredsamkeit*, I (Leipzig 1868), pp. 229–30, cf. p. 238.

Thucydides has given us distinct portraits of the chief actors
in the Peloponnesian War, but these portraits are to be found
in the clearly narrated actions of the men; the words ascribed
to them rarely do more than mark the stronger lines of the
character; they seldom reveal new traits of a subtler kind.
The tendency of Thucydides was less to analyse individual
character than to study human nature in its general or
typical phenomena...The dramatic truth, so far as it goes,
is in the matter, not in the form. He may sometimes indicate
such broad characteristics as the curt bluntness of the ephor
Sthenelaidas or the insolent vehemence of Alcibiades. But, as
a rule, there is little discrimination of style. In all that concerns expression, the speeches are essentially the oratorical
essays of the historian himself.[3]

The denial of characteristic language has been echoed by nearly
every scholar who has seriously concerned himself with Thucydides.[4] In it we can see the effect of several attitudes widely held
by classicists. First of these is a widespread reluctance to consider
character important in Greek literature, and a consequent failure
to observe characteristic language.[5] Another is the traditional view

---

3. R. C. Jebb, 'The Speeches of Thucydides', in *Essays and Addresses*
(Cambridge 1907), pp. 404, 419–20.

4. Cf. John H. Finley, Jr, in *Three Essays on Thucydides* (Cambridge, Mass.
1967): 'Preface' (1966), p. x; 'Euripides and Thucydides' (1938), pp. 4–6, 52;
'The Origins of Thucydides' Style' (1939), p. 116; and *Thucydides* (Cambridge,
Mass. 1941), p. 275; K. J. Dover, ed., *Thucydides. Book VI* (Oxford 1965), p. xi;
Otto Regenbogen, *Thukydides: Politische Reden* (Leipzig 1949), pp. 16–17;
C. N. Cochrane, *Thucydides and the Science of History* (Oxford 1929), p. 26;
David Grene, *Man in his Pride* (Chicago 1950), pp. 220–2; Werner Jaeger,
Paideia. The Ideals of Greek Culture, trans. Gilbert Highet (New York 1945), I, 397;
A. W. Gomme, 'The Speeches of Thucydides', in *Essays on Greek History and
Literature* (Oxford 1937), pp. 165–6; Wilhelm Schmid, in Schmid–Staehlin,
Geschichte der griechischen Literatur I, 5 (Munich 1948), p. 171; John Edmund
Ziolkowski, *Thucydides and the Tradition of Funeral Speeches at Athens* (Diss.,
University of North Carolina 1963), pp. 2–3; Karl Reinhardt, 'Herodots
Persergeschichten', and 'Thukydides und Machiavelli', in *Vermächtnis der
Antike*, 2nd ed., ed. Carl Becker (Göttingen 1966), pp. 173–4, 193.

5. A reluctance recently exemplified in various ways by John Jones, *On
Aristotle and Greek Tragedy* (London 1962), and by Hugh Lloyd-Jones: 'The
"Supplices" of Aeschylus: The New Date and Old Problems', *AC* 33 (1964),
370–1; 'The Guilt of Agamemnon', *CQ* 12 (1962), 187. See too his reviews of
Jones, *RES* Ser. 2, 15 (1964), 221–4, and of Kurt von Fritz, *Antike und moderne
Tragödie* (Berlin 1962), *Gnomon* 34 (1962), 740–1. For other examples of this

that Thucydides was primarily a political scientist and his speeches political analyses of past and future events.[6] A third is the classicist's hesitancy, widespread though not universal, to study stylistic elements other than those sanctioned by tradition.

This essay is aimed only indirectly at these assumptions, and more directly at the argument based on them, but discussion of the one inevitably affects our view of the other. If it can be shown that Thucydidean speakers do vary significantly in their manners of speaking, and moreover that there is a particular aptness of styles to speakers, the canonical denial of differentiated styles must be challenged; if the distinguishing traits of these styles are ones not usually studied, the limited nature of conventional classical stylistics may become evident; if the speeches reveal emotional qualities as well as political theory, we must widen our view of Thucydides' characters, and become skeptical of the claim that characterization is absent from fifth-century Greek literature.

The two studies that follow, on the language of Nicias and Alcibiades, are provisional attempts to gather evidence for stylistic characterization. The method is simple: a search for the dominant stylistic elements in a work or passage, followed by an attempt to interpret these and relate them to other stylistic traits and thus illuminate the work's tone and meaning.[7] This basically inductive method is the opposite of more encyclopedic approaches, like that of Holger Thesleff's recent *Studies in the Styles of Plato*.[8] While Thesleff finds traits that aid in establishing general classification of

attitude, cf. Tycho von Wilamowitz-Moellendorff, *Die dramatische Technik des Sophokles*, Philologische Untersuchungen 22 (1917); A. J. A. Waldock, *Sophocles the Dramatist* (Cambridge 1951); Walter Zuercher, *Die Darstellung des Menschen im Drama des Euripides* (Basel 1947); R. D. Dawe, 'Inconsistency of Plot and Character in Aeschylus', *PCPS* 9 (1963), 21–62. More moderate views are expressed by C. Garton, 'Characterization in Greek Tragedy', *JHS* 77 (1957), 247–54, and G. H. Gellie, 'Character in Greek Tragedy', *AUMLA* 20 (1963), 241–55.

6. So Reinhardt, 'Thukydides und Machiavelli', p. 193, 'Herodots Persergeschichten', p. 173, Blass, pp. 229–30, and Jaeger, p. 388.

7. Readers will recognize the derivation of this method from that of Leo Spitzer. Spitzer's method is outlined in the first chapter of his book, *Linguistics and Literary History* (Princeton 1948), pp. 1–39. Unfortunately, many English-speaking scholars know of Spitzer only from the somewhat inaccurate discussion in the handbook, *Theory of Literature*, by René Wellek and Austin Warren (2nd ed., New York 1956), pp. 172–3. Wellek has admitted the shortcomings of these comments in his necrology, 'Leo Spitzer (1887–1960)', *Comparative Literature* 12 (1960), 310–34. 8. Helsinki 1967.

style (colloquial, rhetorical, intellectual, etc.), our aim is to recognize precisely those stylistic idiosyncrasies that reveal distinctions among passages in the same classification,[9] thus demonstrating the subtlety and flexibility of Thucydides' prose.[10]

I. SENTENCE COMPLICATION IN THE SPEECHES OF NICIAS

Ἡ μὲν ἐκκλησία περὶ παρασκευῆς τῆς ἡμετέρας ἥδε ξυνελέγη, καθ' ὅτι χρὴ ἐς Σικελίαν ἐκπλεῖν· ἐμοὶ μέντοι δοκεῖ καὶ περὶ αὐτοῦ τούτου ἔτι χρῆναι σκέψασθαι, εἰ ἄμεινόν ἐστιν ἐκπέμπειν τὰς ναῦς, καὶ μὴ οὕτω βραχείᾳ βουλῇ περὶ μεγάλων πραγμάτων ἀνδράσιν ἀλλοφύλοις πειθομένους πόλεμον οὐ προσήκοντα ἄρασθαι. [2] καίτοι ἔγωγε καὶ τιμῶμαι ἐκ τοῦ τοιούτου καὶ ἧσσον ἑτέρων περὶ τῷ ἐμαυτοῦ σώματι ὀρρωδῶ, νομίζων ὁμοίως ἀγαθὸν πολίτην εἶναι ὃς ἂν καὶ τοῦ σώματός τι καὶ τῆς οὐσίας προνοῆται· μάλιστα γὰρ ἂν ὁ τοιοῦτος καὶ τὰ τῆς πόλεως δι' ἑαυτὸν βούλοιτο ὀρθοῦσθαι. ὅμως δὲ οὔτε ἐν τῷ πρότερον χρόνῳ διὰ τὸ προτιμᾶσθαι εἶπον παρὰ γνώμην οὔτε νῦν, ἀλλὰ ᾗ ἂν γιγνώσκω βέλτιστα, ἐρῶ. [3] καὶ πρὸς μὲν τοὺς τρόπους τοὺς ὑμετέρους ἀσθενὴς ἄν μου ὁ λόγος εἴη, εἰ τά τε ὑπάρχοντα σῴζειν παραινοίην καὶ μὴ τοῖς ἑτοίμοις περὶ τῶν ἀφανῶν καὶ μελλόντων κινδυνεύειν· ὡς δὲ οὔτε ἐν καιρῷ σπεύδετε οὔτε ῥᾴδιά ἐστι κατασχεῖν ἐφ' ἃ ὥρμησθε, ταῦτα διδάξω. (VI. 9)

The vocabulary of this passage resembles that of other speeches by Nicias, and points to underlying concerns that seem constant in his speeches.[11] μὴ οὕτω βραχείᾳ βουλῇ reminds us strongly of εὐβουλία (cf. VI. 23. 3), a conservative and Dorian catchword in Thucydides and elsewhere.[12] The aversion to κινδυνεύειν (VI. 9. 3) finds echoes elsewhere in Nicias' speeches and in narrative

---

9. This is not at all to denigrate Thesleff's work, from which I have profited, but to show that it is different from my own.

10. I am indebted to Professors Adam M. Parry and C. M. Dawson for considerable help in writing this paper.

11. This and other quotations are from Jones' Oxford text.

12. Cf. Ar. *Birds* 1539, *Ach.* 1008, Pindar, *Ol.* 13. 6, cited in Robert Alexander Neil's edition of Aristophanes, *Knights* (Cambridge 1901), 'Appendix II: Political Use of Moral Terms'.

descriptions of him,[13] and seems more appropriate to a Spartan than an Athenian.[14] σῴзειν, although lodged in a conditional clause, nevertheless recalls the fact that Nicias uses or is referred to by words like σῴзειν and σωτηρία eleven times in Thucydides. All these words put Nicias in a conservative light.

The syntax, too, appears to be characteristic. The potential optative construction (VI. 9. 2, 9. 3) is typical of Nicias.[15] Another syntactic feature of the paragraph is perhaps best indicated by an outline of the transitions and shifts of directions it contains:

> We are here to discuss provisions...*But* it seems imperative to consider whether we really should sail...*yet* I am honored and fearless, *although* I think a man could be fearful and still remain an ἀγαθὸς πολίτης....*Still*, I have never spoken against my γνώμη, nor will I now; I will say what I must, weak though it might be if I should call for a secure policy...*But* I'll show that your policy is difficult and wrong-headed.

As the italicized words show, this paragraph is packed with concessions and reversals. These cause a constant subordination of one thought to another. Thus in VI. 9. 1a, the main verb is ξυνελέγη. Subordinate to the main clause is a clause containing χρή, which is in turn completed by the infinitive ἐκπλεῖν, a further step in subordination.[16] Slightly adapting the terminology of T. B. L. Webster, we can say that this sentence contains two levels, or degrees, of subordination, or complexity.[17] The next sentence is yet more complex, and can be diagrammed as follows according to its stages of subordination:

13. Cf. VI. 10. 5, VI. 12. 1, VI. 12. 2, VI. 13. 1, VI. 47, VII. 77. 2.

14. Cf. I. 73. 2, 74. 2, 74. 3, II. 39. 1, 40. 3, 42. 4, 43. 4, 61. 1 for the Athenian willingness to take risks, and II. 11. 3, IV. 18. 5, 87. 2, 126. 5, V. 9. 2, VIII. 24. 5, and VIII. 64. 4 for the opposed sentiments of Spartans and conservatives.

15. He uses it more than any other speaker in Thucydides except Hermocrates.

16. Although subordinate clauses can be governed by nouns, they all contain verbs, and for convenience of notation I will refer to them by the verbs they contain.

17. I use with slight modification the system of classifying sentences proposed by T. B. L. Webster in 'The Architecture of Sentences', in *Studies in French Language and Medieval Literature Presented to Professor Mildred Pope* (Manchester 1939), pp. 381–2, and 'A Study of Greek Sentence Construction', *AJPh* 62 (1941), 385–415.

δοκεῖ   (main verb)
  χρῆναι   (first level of subordination)
    σκέψασθαι   (second level)
     ἐστιν   (third level)
    ἐκπέμπειν   (second level)
    ἄρασθαι   (second level)
     πειθομένους   (third level)
     προσήκοντα   (third level)[18]

In VI. 9. 2a, προνοῆται depends on εἶναι, which leads to νομίζων, which in turn qualifies ὀρρωδῶ, thus producing a sentence that is complex to the third level. The next two sentences reach only the first degree of subordination, while the two that follow again reach the third degree.

Analysis of the seven sentences in VI. 9 could thus be summarized in chart form:

level of complexity	number of sentences reaching each level
I	2
2	I
3	4

On investigation, the chart turns out to be typical not only of this paragraph but of all the speeches of Nicias. The distinguishing characteristic of these speeches is their consistently high level of complexity. Four of the seven sentences in the paragraph are complex to at least the third degree, which means that they contain at least three clauses subordinate to one another. In the speech as a whole, seventeen of the thirty-six sentences reach this level, and the level is maintained in Nicias' other speeches and harangues.[19]

Comparison with the speeches of other characters shows that

18. This scheme follows the commentaries of Steup and Dover (in *Thucydides. Book VI*. Ed. K. J. Dover (Oxford 1965)). If we were to view ἐκπέμπειν and ἄρασθαι as dependent on ἐστιν, the sentence would be yet more complex. The difficulty in determining the order of subordination is indicated by de Romilly's translation, which seems to allow either choice.

19. I follow the punctuation of the Oxford Classical Text. De Romilly and Classen–Steup seem rather consistently to mark fewer sentences than Jones, while Bekker (1821) marks more. For further comments on punctuation and sentence-length, see below, n. 20.

Nicias' level of complexity is extraordinarily high. That the level is maintained over the course of two books, in six speeches short and long, is yet more remarkable.

Proportion of sentences with three or more levels of complexity in Thucydidean speeches (in descending order)

Speaker and passage	Proportion of sentences complicated to third level
Spartans, IV. 17–20	0·615
Corinthians, I. 37–43	0·555
Nicias, VI. 20–3	0·533
Nicias, VI. 68	0·500
Nicias, VII. 61–4	0·500
Syracusans, VI. 66–8	0·500
Nicias, VI. 9–14	0·472
Nicias, VII. 11–15	0·464
Brasidas, V. 9	0·455
Hermocrates, VI. 76–80	0·438
Brasidas, IV. 85–7	0·409
Nicias, VII. 77	0·357
Euphemus, VI. 82–7	0·351
Athenians, I. 73–8	0·333
Pericles, II. 60–4	0·333
Hermocrates, IV. 59–64	0·325
Cleon, III. 37–40	0·318
Athenagoras, VI. 36–40	0·313
Pagondas, IV. 92	0·308
Corcyraeans, I. 32–6	0·303
Alcibiades, VI. 16–18	0·297
Hermocrates, VI. 33–4	0·296
Thebans, III. 61–7	0·291
Corinthians, I. 120–4	0·289
Plataeans, III. 53–9	0·288
Corinthians, I. 68–71	0·283
Diodotus, III. 42–7	0·268
Archidamus, II. 11	0·267
Alcibiades, VI. 89–92	0·262
Pericles, I. 140–4	0·236

Pericles, II. 35–46	0·228
Mytileneans, III. 9–14	0·166
Brasidas, IV. 126	0·154
Sthenelaidas, I. 86	0·125
Archidamus, I. 80–4	0·111
Phormio, II. 89	0·095
Spartans, II. 87	0·067

Nicias uses subordination more consistently than any other speaker. About half of all his sentences are complex to the third degree, as compared with one-fourth of Pericles' and one-third of Cleon's.[20]

Several stylistic tendencies cause subordination and thus contribute to Nicias' high level of complexity. I will discuss in particular the use of abstract nouns and adjectives, and impersonal constructions, that take a dependent infinitive, and then consider the motives behind sentence-complication, of which at least two can be singled out with some certainty: Nicias' constant concern with himself, and his habit of making concessions and admissions of inadequacy.

20. This insistence on subordination, as might be expected, can affect sentence-length. Thus two of Nicias' speeches have far and away more 'long' sentences (over thirty words) than other speeches in Thucydides: in VII. 61–4, 0·563 of the sentences are 'long' by this standard, and in VI. 20–3, 0·533 are long. No other speech by any character goes beyond 0·440. But other speeches by Nicias are not abnormal in this regard: in VI. 9–14, 0·278 of the sentences are long; in VI. 68, 0·250; in VII. 11–15, 0·258; and in VII. 77, 0·286. There is, therefore, no necessary correlation between sentence-length and degree of subordination. (With most recent students of Greek sentence-length, I count as sentences clauses ending in half stops. Cf. William C. Wake, 'Sentence-Length Distributions of Greek Authors', *Journal of the Royal Statistical Society*, A, 120 (1957), 334; A. Q. Morton and John McLeman, *Paul, The Man and the Myth* (N.Y. 1966), p. 54; and Tore Janson, 'The Problems of Measuring Sentence-Length in Classical Texts', *Studia Linguistica* 18 (1964), 28–30. Wake has a useful discussion of ancient ideas on punctuation. Texts of Thucydides vary considerably in marking sentences, but the distinction between full and half stop seems, on the basis of checks of over two hundred sentences in four editions, to be unimportant.)

A. SOME SYNTACTIC SOURCES OF SENTENCE-COMPLICATION: IMPERSONAL VERBS AND ABSTRACT NOUNS

Impersonal verbs are frequent in Nicias' speeches. So are a number of abstract terms, both nouns and neuter adjectives, which, with the verb 'to be' expressed or understood, take the infinitive. Both these classes have roughly the same force, as we shall see below. Nicias uses these words consistently, and in a manner that reveals a good deal about the way he thinks. The following table, based on five major speakers in Thucydides, helps to document this argument.

Impersonal verbs and abstract terms causing subordination
in five speakers in Thucydides

	Nicias	Alcibiades	Pericles	Cleon	Hermocrates
1. Abstract terms					
ἔργον	0	0	0	0	1
δῆλον	0	0	0	1	0
ῥᾴδιον	1	0	0	0	0
αἰσχρόν	1	0	3	0	0
δίκαιον	1	0	2	0	1
καλόν	0	0	1	0	1
οἷον	1	0	1	0	1
ἀδύνατον	0	0	0	0	1
ἀνέλπιστον	0	0	0	0	1
πρέπον	0	0	1	0	0
ἀναγκαῖον	1	1	1	0	0
ἀνάγκη	1	3	1	0	0
δεινόν	1	0	1	1	2
ἀνόητον	1	0	0	0	0
χαλεπόν	1	0	1	0	1
εὔλογον	0	0	0	0	1

	Nicias	Alcibiades	Pericles	Cleon	Hermocrates
εἰκός	3	2	3	1	4
καιρός	1	0	0	0	0
ξυγγνώμη	0	0	0	0	1
ἄπορον	1	0	0	0	0
δυνατόν	1	0	0	0	0
Total	15	6	15	3	15

2. Impersonal Verbs[21]

	Nicias	Alcibiades	Pericles	Cleon	Hermocrates
ἔστι	1	0	0	0	1
δοκεῖ	4	0	4	1	2
χρή	12	4	9	2	4
δεῖ	6	0	1	3	0
πρέπει	1	0	0	0	0
ξυμβαίνει	1	0	2	0	2
λέγεται	1	0	1	0	0
ἐνδέχεται	0	0	2	0	0
προσήκει	1	1	0	0	0
ξυμφέρει	0	0	1	0	0
μέλει	0	0	1	0	0
ὑπάρχει	1	0	0	0	0
ἀρκεῖ	0	0	1	0	0
μέτεστι	0	0	1	0	0
περιγίγνεται	0	0	1	0	0
Total impersonals	28	5	24	6	9
Total abstracts	15	6	15	3	15
Total of both classes	43	11	39	9	24

21. More properly 'quasi-impersonals' with 'proleptic *it*'. Cf. Schwyzer–Debrunner, 621–2.

	Nicias	Alcibiades	Pericles	Cleon	Hermocrates
Number of sentences in speeches	120	82	176	45	101
Average number of abstracts and impersonals per sentence[22]	0·358	0·134	0·222	0·200	0·238

The nine sentences in VI. 21–3 contain nine examples of the infinitive with abstract terms and impersonal verbs, as well as six infinitives in indirect discourse and still more in other dependent constructions:

[VI. 21. 1] Πρὸς οὖν τοιαύτην δύναμιν οὐ ναυτικῆς καὶ φαύλου στρατιᾶς μόνον δεῖ, ἀλλὰ καὶ πεζὸν πολὺν ξυμπλεῖν, εἴπερ βουλόμεθα ἄξιον τῆς διανοίας δρᾶν καὶ μὴ ὑπὸ ἱππέων πολλῶν εἴργεσθαι τῆς γῆς, ἄλλως τε καὶ εἰ ξυστῶσιν αἱ πόλεις φοβηθεῖσαι καὶ μὴ ἀντιπαράσχωσιν ἡμῖν φίλοι τινὲς γενόμενοι ἄλλοι ἢ Ἐγεσταῖοι ᾧ ἀμυνούμεθα ἱππικόν [2] (αἰσχρὸν δὲ βιασθέντας ἀπελθεῖν ἢ ὕστερον ἐπιμεταπέμπεσθαι, τὸ πρῶτον ἀσκέπτως βουλευσαμένους)· αὐτόθεν δὲ παρασκευῇ ἀξιόχρεῳ ἐπιέναι, γνόντας ὅτι πολύ τε ἀπὸ τῆς ἡμετέρας αὐτῶν μέλλομεν πλεῖν καὶ οὐκ ἐν τῷ ὁμοίῳ στρατευσόμενοι καὶ ὅτε ἐν τοῖς τῇδε ὑπηκόοις ξύμμαχοι ἤλθετε ἐπί τινα, ὅθεν ῥᾴδιαι αἱ κομιδαὶ ἐκ τῆς φιλίας ὧν προσέδει, ἀλλ' ἐς ἀλλοτρίαν πᾶσαν ἀπαρτήσοντες, ἐξ ἧς μηνῶν οὐδὲ τεσσάρων τῶν χειμερινῶν ἄγγελον ῥᾴδιον ἐλθεῖν. [22.1] ὁπλίτας τε οὖν πολλούς μοι δοκεῖ χρῆναι ἡμᾶς ἄγειν καὶ ἡμῶν αὐτῶν καὶ τῶν ξυμμάχων, τῶν τε ὑπηκόων καὶ ἤν τινα ἐκ Πελοποννήσου δυνώμεθα ἢ πεῖσαι ἢ μισθῷ προσαγαγέσθαι, καὶ τοξότας πολλοὺς καὶ σφενδονήτας, ὅπως πρὸς τὸ ἐκείνων ἱππικὸν ἀντέχωσι, ναυσί τε καὶ πολὺ περιεῖναι, ἵνα καὶ τὰ ἐπιτήδεια ῥᾷον ἐσκομιζώμεθα, τὸν δὲ καὶ αὐτόθεν σῖτον ἐν ὁλκάσι,

22. Nicias also uses these words more often than others in comparison with the total number of words he uses, if we care to count in that way. But since we are looking at the function of the words counted in sentence-building, this method of calculating appears to be best.

πυροὺς καὶ πεφρυγμένας κριθάς, ἄγειν, καὶ σιτοποιοὺς ἐκ τῶν μυλώνων πρὸς μέρος ἠναγκασμένους ἐμμίσθους, ἵνα, ἤν που ὑπὸ ἀπλοίας ἀπολαμβανώμεθα, ἔχῃ ἡ στρατιὰ τὰ ἐπιτήδεια (πολλὴ γὰρ οὖσα οὐ πάσης ἔσται πόλεως ὑποδέξασθαι), τά τε ἄλλα ὅσον δυνατὸν ἑτοιμάσασθαι, καὶ μὴ ἐπὶ ἑτέροις γίγνεσθαι, μάλιστα δὲ χρήματα αὐτόθεν ὡς πλεῖστα ἔχειν. τὰ δὲ παρ' Ἐγεσταίων, ἃ λέγεται ἐκεῖ ἑτοῖμα, νομίσατε καὶ λόγῳ ἂν μάλιστα ἑτοῖμα εἶναι. [23.1] ἢν γὰρ αὐτοὶ ἔλθωμεν ἐνθένδε μὴ ἀντίπαλον μόνον παρασκευασάμενοι, πλήν γε πρὸς τὸ μάχιμον αὐτῶν, τὸ ὁπλιτικόν, ἀλλὰ καὶ ὑπερβάλλοντες τοῖς πᾶσι, μόλις οὕτως οἷοί τε ἐσόμεθα τῶν μὲν κρατεῖν, τὰ δὲ καὶ διασῶσαι. [2] πόλιν τε νομίσαι χρὴ ἐν ἀλλοφύλοις καὶ πολεμίοις οἰκοῦντας ἰέναι, οὓς πρέπει τῇ πρώτῃ ἡμέρᾳ ᾗ ἂν κατάσχωσιν εὐθὺς κρατεῖν τῆς γῆς, ἢ εἰδέναι ὅτι, ἢν σφάλλωνται, πάντα πολέμια ἕξουσιν. [3] ὅπερ ἐγὼ φοβούμενος, καὶ εἰδὼς πολλὰ μὲν ἡμᾶς δέον εὖ βουλεύσασθαι, ἔτι δὲ πλείω εὐτυχῆσαι (χαλεπὸν δὲ ἀνθρώπους ὄντας), ὅτι ἐλά- χιστα τῇ τύχῃ παραδοὺς ἐμαυτὸν βούλομαι ἐκπλεῖν, παρασκευῇ δὲ ἀπὸ τῶν εἰκότων ἀσφαλὴς ἐκπλεῦσαι. ταῦτα γὰρ τῇ τε ξυμ- πάσῃ πόλει βεβαιότατα ἡγοῦμαι καὶ ἡμῖν τοῖς στρατευσομένοις σωτήρια. εἰ δέ τῳ ἄλλως δοκεῖ, παρίημι αὐτῷ τὴν ἀρχήν.

First we have a statement of necessity: 'It is necessary (δεῖ) for a large infantry force to sail' (as well as a fleet). At the end of this sentence comes a qualifying parenthesis introduced by αἰσχρόν with ἐστί understood, 'It is shameful to be forced to return or call for reinforcements, because we planned without care'. vi. 21 ends with an impersonal expression with ῥᾴδιον. A little later we find a double impersonal assertion, 'It seems to be necessary (δοκεῖ χρῆναι) for us to bring many hoplites', and a little below this, 'bring as much as is possible' (δυνατόν). Then, 'It is necessary (χρή) to consider that we are going to found a city among foreign and hostile men, and it is fitting (πρέπει) for us, on the first day that we are there, to conquer, or to know that, if we are tripped up, everyone will oppose us'. In following sentences we find δέον, χαλεπόν, and δοκεῖ. Thus the nine sentences of this section contain nine instances of abstract terms or impersonal verbs with the in- finitive (and two without it).[23]

23. Similar passages exist in Nicias' other speeches: cf. vi. 11. 1–6, vi. 68. 1–3, vii. 14. 2–vii. 15, vii. 62. 3–vii. 63. 2, and vii. 77.

These words contribute to circumlocution and to complexity. Each verb engenders a dependent expression, thus deepening the level of subordination. The contributions made to a sentence are affective rather than factual, and it is possible to classify them under four headings, as follows:

subjective reasoning	moral judgement	eventuality, like- lihood, possibility	necessity
ἀνόητον	αἰσχρόν, δεινόν	ἀδύνατον, ἀνέλπιστον	χρή
δῆλον	δίκαιον, καλόν	ἄπορον, εἰκός	δεῖ
δοκεῖ	πρέπει, πρέπον	ἔξεστι, ἔστι	ἀναγκαῖον
εὔλογον	προσήκει, ξυγγνώμη	δυνατόν, ἐνδέχεται	ἀνάγκη
		οἷον, ῥᾴδιον	ἔργον
		ὑπάρχει, χαλεπόν	

The headings give an idea of how these terms are employed. They all betray adherence to *a priori* concepts. To say 'it seems good', δοκεῖ, requires a prior belief in what is good; the ability to invoke statements like 'it is possible', 'it is fitting', 'it is necessary', or to say a thing is pardonable, hard, or easy, rests on similar antecedent commitments.

Students are commonly told of Thucydides' penchant for abstraction.[24] It has not, however, generally been noticed that within the text of Thucydides abstract expressions of the type discussed here vary considerably from speaker to speaker, and that Nicias' dependence on these words reveals two characteristic thought-patterns: a tendency to view life in abstractions, and a reliance on vague moral concepts like fitness, necessity, and justice. These patterns, exceptional among Thucydidean characters, contrast especially with the attitude of Thucydides himself, who more than any other fifth-century writer noted and regretted the emptiness of both the concepts and the terms.[25]

24. Cf. as an example Finley, *Thucydides*, p. 261.

25. Thus the *Archeology*, the demonstration of what forces are operative in history, contains over fifty words for 'power' and very few for morality. This is not to say, with Paul Shorey ('Implicit Ethics and Psychology of Thucydides', *TAPA* 24 (1893), 66–88), that Thucydides was amoral or even dispassionate: I. 23, II. 48–53, III. 82, VII. 29, and VII. 86, among other passages, refute that view.

B. THE MOTIVATION FOR SENTENCE COMPLICATION

The grammatical sources of complexity so far discussed are related to two habits of Nicias: his insistence on talking about himself, and his tendency to admit concessions that weaken his argument. Each of these merits separate discussion.

1. *Personal considerations in the speeches of Nicias*

In four passages in his speeches Nicias refers to himself, usually in an attempt to justify his policies. This is not in itself unusual: *ad hominem* attacks and defenses are frequent in Thucydidean oratory. Pericles had defended himself and his policies in II. 61, and Alcibiades in VI. 16. 1–2, to take two notable examples. Yet these defenses differ in important ways from those of Nicias.

Pericles' defense has a vivid and energetic tone. Two sentences open strongly with καί (II. 61. 1a, II. 61. 2a), and both are stylistically simple.[26] Each of these short sentences is followed by a longer one of greater involvement, but the involvement springs from Pericles' strongly antithetical and gnomic manner of expression. Thus II. 61. 1a has an antithetical statement of the consequences of irresolute behavior, and ends with a gnomic utterance: ὁ φυγὼν τὸν κίνδυνον τοῦ ὑποστάντος μεμπτότερος. The next long sentence is complicated to the fifth degree, but again less through personal considerations than by another gnomic antithesis on the effects of misfortune: τὸ μὲν λυποῦν ἔχει ἤδη τὴν αἴσθησιν ἑκάστῳ, τῆς δὲ ὠφελίας ἄπεστιν ἔτι ἡ δήλωσις ἅπασι (II. 61. 2b). The next sentence, simple and gnomic again in its structure, moves the subject away from Pericles' personal character to the nature of war in general: δουλοῖ γὰρ φρόνημα τὸ αἰφνίδιον καὶ ἀπροσδόκητον καὶ τὸ πλείστῳ παραλόγῳ ξυμβαῖνον (II. 61. 3a). Pericles thus justifies himself by turning the discussion toward general points and by sharply contrasting alternate courses to his own, without long discussion of his own motives and abilities.

Alcibiades' self-defense is vigorous: the speech begins with καί; only one of the first six sentences is complex (VI. 16. 1a). Most sentences in which Alcibiades speaks of himself remain at the first level or lower. The effort to link his own acts to the city's benefit

26. By this I mean that they remain at or below the second level of subordination; by 'complex', that they attain at least the third level.

is constant: we get not only τιμή, he says, but an impression too of δύναμις (VI. 16. 2b); there is envy for me, but foreigners think us strong (VI. 16. 3a); my 'folly' is useful to the *polis* (VI. 16. 3b). The next two sentences are complicated by gnomic antitheses. After a long and complex statement again emphasizing his aid to the city (VI. 16. 5) comes a less complex imperative sentence, two still less subordinated assertions of civic usefulness and action against Sparta (VI. 16. 6), and then two simple transitional sentences leading to a defense of the invasion (VI. 17. 1–2).[27]

It is precisely Nicias' references to himself, unlike those of Pericles and Alcibiades, that seem to cause complication. In the first speech, for instance, Nicias' opening statements concern himself. He turns the discussion in this direction abruptly with μέντοι (VI. 9. 1), shifts course again for the same reason (καίτοι, VI. 9. 2), and yet again to explain his motives (with concessive νομίζων: 'although I consider...'). The next reference to himself is introduced by ὅμως δέ, another reversal of the line of thought, and VI. 9. 3 finally expands the subject of the speech but only with an antithetical reference to himself, ὑμετέρους: μου. VI. 9. 1a is carried to the fifth level of complexity, partly by ἐμοὶ δοκεῖ, an emphatic reference to the speaker's person. In VI. 9. 2, the sentence is perfectly straightforward and uncomplicated up to ὀρρωδῶ whereupon a parenthetical explanation with νομίζων, 'although I think...', brings on a string of subordinate clauses.

Nicias' discussion of his motives in the second speech is briefer but again interesting. At VI. 23. 3 he says, essentially, that 'We should sail protected as well as possible from τύχη':

ὅπερ ἐγὼ φοβούμενος, καὶ εἰδὼς πολλὰ μὲν ἡμᾶς δέον εὖ βουλεύσασθαι, ἔτι δὲ πλείω εὐτυχῆσαι (χαλεπὸν δὲ ἀνθρώπους ὄντας), ὅτι ἐλάχιστα τῇ τύχῃ παραδοὺς ἐμαυτὸν βούλομαι ἐκπλεῖν, παρασκευῇ δὲ ἀπὸ τῶν εἰκότων ἀσφαλὴς ἐκπλεῦσαι.

It is not until near the end of this sentence that we reach the main verb, βούλομαι ἐκπλεῖν; the whole opening of the sentence is occupied by the long parenthetical expression ὅπερ ἐγὼ φοβούμενος, καὶ εἰδὼς... which in turn produces three levels of subordi-

27. Alcibiades is again concerned with defending himself in his last speech, VI. 89–92, but again the style is uncomplicated and the passages of self-justification (VI. 89, VI. 92) show a similar capacity to generalize rather than to dwell on oneself.

nate clauses. The only other place at which the sentence reaches the second level of subordination is with the participle παραδούς, which again refers to Nicias and is followed emphatically by ἐμαυτόν. If we were to diagram the increasing subordination of verbs in this sentence, we would get a pattern like this:

βούλομαι (first degree)
   ἐκπλεῖν (second degree)
      παραδούς (third degree)
   ἐκπλεῦσαι (second degree)
   φοβούμενος (second degree)
   εἰδώς (second degree)
      δέον (third degree)
         βουλεύσασθαι (fourth degree)
         εὐτυχῆσαι (fourth degree)
           ὄντας (fifth degree)

Thus we have one subordinate clause at the fourth degree of complication and two at the third, all used to describe Nicias' fears and feelings, and filled with his contradictory thoughts (we must have good τύχη, yet not commit ourselves to τύχη). Nicias seems compelled to speak in the first person singular, to stress the personal nature of his concerns. At the very start of the expedition we thus see a tendency in Nicias to use himself as his constant point of reference, and to neglect other points of view. Later in the same paragraph we see the tendency once again, although not, this time, resulting in subordination: εἰ δέ τῳ ἄλλως δοκεῖ, παρίημι αὐτῷ τὴν ἀρχήν (VI. 23. 3c). The same self-centered attitude that we see here had led Nicias to offer Cleon the command at Pylos (IV. 28. 1) and to refuse to leave Sicily even at the cost of disaster (VII. 48. 4).

When Nicias sends his letter home, in the start of the seventh book, his self-concern has grown with the hopelessness of the expedition. Toward the end of the letter, he complains: τούτων δὲ πάντων ἀπορώτατον τό τε μὴ οἷόν τε εἶναι ταῦτα ἐμοὶ κωλῦσαι τῷ στρατηγῷ (χαλεπαὶ γὰρ αἱ ὑμέτεραι φύσεις ἄρξαι) (VII. 14. 2).

'The most difficult thing is that I am unable to prevent any of these difficulties even though I am general (emphatic: ἐμοὶ...τῷ στρατηγῷ).' Immediately on turning to himself, Nicias adds a parenthetical explanation that has little to do with the situation: 'For your natures are difficult to control.' As Dover says: 'this appears to have no bearing on the difficulties of the situation as Nikias has described them... It is, however, a theme prominent in Nikias' mind... and it was perhaps his habit to suggest that he could have dealt with all difficulties if only he could have relied more on his troops.'[28] The parenthesis also contributes to the high degree of subordination. Although the sentence takes on even greater complexity later, the parenthetical justification of Nicias' ineffectiveness plays a role in heightening the complication.[29]

The line of thought in Nicias' last speech (VII. 77) is complex, partly as a result of personal reflections. This is especially true of the first four sentences:

> [1] Καὶ ἐκ τῶν παρόντων, ὦ ᾿Αθηναῖοι καὶ ξύμμαχοι, ἐλπίδα χρὴ ἔχειν (ἤδη τινὲς καὶ ἐκ δεινοτέρων ἢ τοιῶνδε ἐσώθησαν), μηδὲ καταμέμφεσθαι ὑμᾶς ἄγαν αὐτοὺς μήτε ταῖς ξυμφοραῖς μήτε ταῖς παρὰ τὴν ἀξίαν νῦν κακοπαθίαις. [2] κἀγώ τοι οὐδενὸς ὑμῶν οὔτε ῥώμῃ προφέρων (ἀλλ᾿ ὁρᾶτε δὴ ὡς διάκειμαι ὑπὸ τῆς νόσου) οὔτ᾿ εὐτυχίᾳ δοκῶν που ὕστερός του εἶναι κατά τε τὸν ἴδιον βίον καὶ ἐς τὰ ἄλλα, νῦν ἐν τῷ αὐτῷ κινδύνῳ τοῖς φαυλοτάτοις αἰωροῦμαι· καίτοι πολλὰ μὲν ἐς θεοὺς νόμιμα δεδιήτημαι, πολλὰ δὲ ἐς ἀνθρώπους δίκαια καὶ ἀνεπίφθονα. [3] ἀνθ᾿ ὧν ἡ μὲν ἐλπὶς ὅμως θρασεῖα τοῦ μέλλοντος, αἱ δὲ ξυμφοραὶ οὐ κατ᾿ ἀξίαν δὴ φοβοῦσιν.

Nicias seems to be trying to say something like this:

1. 'We must have hope and not blame ourselves for our misfortunes.'
2. 'Look at me: I have been good on both human and divine terms.'
3. 'Therefore I have hope.'[30]

This would fit Nicias' ideas on divine rewards and punishments. But it is not in fact what he says, for it omits the crucial first sentence of VII. 77. 2 entirely, and passes over other indications that the tone and structure of the speech are at odds with its explicit claims.

28. In A. W. Gomme, A. Andrewes, and K. J. Dover, *A Historical Commentary on Thucydides*, IV (Oxford 1970). Dover's 1965 notes make the same point.

29. In VII. 15. 1 Nicias' complaint about his illness is simple and natural, but does complicate the sentence by two degrees.

30. Classen's interpretation runs along these lines (see his note on VI. 77. 3b), as does that of Otto Luschnat, *Die Feldherrnreden im Geschichtswerk des Thukydides*, *Philologus* Supp. 34. 2 (1942), 102–3.

Perhaps it is the particles that best show the importance of the omitted sentence. Three particles in that sentence, first of all, are strongly pathetic: τοι, δή, and που. (The last is rare, occurring only three times in Thucydides.) 'τοι is an appeal for human sympathy, as που is a resigned submission to the merciless *rerum natura*', says B. L. Gildersleeve in a noteworthy comment on Thucydidean language.[31] The emotional and personal tone of τοι is natural in Nicias' discussion of himself (note as well the emphatic ἐγώ); που with the negative, as here, indicates simultaneous resignation and protest.[32] The third particle, δή, adds pathos to the verb ὁρᾶτε. Denniston remarks of one use of δή with verbs:

> In the austerer style of Thucydides and the orators this usage is hardly to be found. The emphasis conveyed by δή is for the most part pathetic in tone, and it is particularly at home in the great crises of drama, above all at moments when death or ruin is present or imminent... an emotional factor of great importance.[33]

Although Denniston in fact goes on to claim that the usage under discussion really has 'less emotional force... a purely intellectual emphasis', basing this claim on the connection with ὁρᾶν (p. 216), I cannot accept this classification. δή occurs with verbs in Thucydides only eight times.[34] It comes here at a moment of crisis and pathos, and can hardly be said to have 'purely intellectual emphasis'. Denniston's convictions about Thucydidean austerity have perhaps led him to ignore the vital role of emotional factors in Thucydides' style.

These three 'pathetic' and largely poetic particles lend a sense of deep personal urgency to the sentence that contains them. Other words are also important. The sentence begins with καί, as does the opening sentence of the speech. Such an opening in itself tends

---

31. 'Brief Mention', *AJPh* 33 (1912), 239–40.

32. Gildersleeve well compares Zeus' tender utterance on human woe at *Iliad* XVII. 446–7: οὐ μὲν γάρ τί πού ἐστιν ὀϊζυρώτερον ἀνδρὸς
πάντων ὅσσα τε γαῖαν ἔπι πνείει τε καὶ ἕρπει.

33. J. D. Denniston, *The Greek Particles*[2] (Oxford 1959), p. 214.

34. I. 39. 1, II. 64. 5, IV. 59. 5, VI. 61. 2, VII. 77. 2, VIII. 9. 1, VIII. 48. 5, VIII. 87. 1.

to be vigorous in tone, as I will argue below. But after the forceful opening of this sentence comes a parenthesis, introduced by ἀλλά, 'But see! See how ravaged I am by disease' – given the δή we must interpret the clause this strongly. Then comes the adversative καίτοι opening the second sentence of VII. 77. 2: 'Yet I have been pious toward the gods in many ways and my human associations have been just and above reproach.'[35] Upon this sentence depends the conclusion, 'Therefore I am hopeful and unafraid'. Adversative καίτοι indicates that Nicias is strongly opposing the first half of VII. 77. 2 to the second, and that in that first sentence, with its three pathetic particles, he has so well described the pathos of his situation that he must reaffirm his faith forcefully. As with many of the examples from drama and elsewhere cited by Denniston (p. 557), Nicias is noticing that his emotions are too much in control, and adopting a new resolution. A Euripidean character might have said here, 'We are perishing undeservingly: the gods, were they really gods and really good, would not do this'. Nicias puts equal stress on his suffering, but then, rather than protesting, reaffirms his merit and restates his confidence that this will save him. It is as if he had gone on too long in the first sentence, and then had sharply to point out that 'all the same' (ὅμως as in LSJ III), according to his religious beliefs, salvation is sure. But the emotion of VII. 77. 2a may by this point have undermined our confidence in his religious beliefs.

From the same emotional source comes the constant urge to explain and subordinate: the antithesis, 'to our taste excessive',[36] between his health and his fortune, and the further elaboration on his sickness, so that the sentence is structured as follows:

αἰωροῦμαι
προφέρων
ὁρᾶτε
διάκειμαι
δοκῶν
εἶναι

---

35. Cf. καίτοι in VI. 9. 2 and Denniston, p. 557. καίτοι might be understood as conforming rather to Denniston's 'syllogistic' class (p. 561), the two sentences in VII. 77. 2 being viewed as a pair of premises. But the premises remain so opposed, the tone so desperate, and the salvation so remote and provisional, as to pull the 'syllogism' into an open statement of contradiction.

36. So Marchant *ad loc.*

We recognize the familiar pattern of subordination introduced by personal considerations. While the personal references of Pericles and Alcibiades, as we saw, tended to be forthright and uncomplicated, exactly the opposite occurs here, and the sentence moves out of the logical framework projected for it.

2. *Concessive elements as a complicating factor*

An important complicating factor in Nicias' sentences is his tendency to confuse lines of thought by interjecting concessions and reversals. Identification of such passages is often open to dispute, as the semantic and syntactic indicators are varied and complex, and indeed the very term 'concessive' is vague: any sort of conditional statement might logically be termed 'concessive'. In this section I will use the term of clauses and phrases that seem to require 'even if', 'even though', and 'although' in translation, and to exclude limitative and adversative passages.

There are, by my count, fifteen true concessions in the speeches of Nicias, compared with eight in those of Pericles, seven for Alcibiades, five for Hermocrates, and four for Cleon.[37] This is a provisional set of figures, but it does reveal Nicias' predilection for this form. Nicias' concessive clauses are mostly highly concentrated in his first speech in Book Six and his last two speeches in Book Seven. VI. 20–3 has none, VI. 68 one, and VII. 11–15 three. This should not be surprising. Nicias' second speech against Alcibiades is an attempt to speak forcefully, and for this reason it also has fewer potential optatives than the first speech.[38] VI. 68 is a harangue before a battle and follows a traditionally more straightforward form; VII. 11–15, despite its rhetorical elements, still represents a letter (it appears to have no gnomic expressions, uniquely among the speeches in Thucydides). The three speeches with high concentrations are those where Nicias is at his most emotional. A survey of the more interesting examples shows that Nicias' habit of conceding points is especially apparent in these speeches:

> καίτοι ἔγωγε καὶ τιμῶμαι ἐκ τοῦ τοιούτου καὶ ἦσσον ἑτέρων περὶ τῷ ἐμαυτοῦ σώματι ὀρρωδῶ, νομίζων ὁμοίως ἀγαθὸν πολί-την εἶνα ιὃς ἂν καὶ τοῦ σώματός τι καὶ τῆς οὐσίας προνοῆται (VI. 9. 2).

37. Nicias of course has the highest proportion as well as the highest absolute number.   38. There are ten in the first and two in the second.

'Yet[39] I am honored by this post and I fear for my own well-being less than others, although I consider him similarly a good citizen, who is prudent both about his body and his possessions.' νομίζων is concessive (cf. Dover *ad loc.*), and fosters the impression that Nicias feels he must backtrack and try to explain more precisely what he means.

καὶ οἴεσθε ἴσως τὰς γενομένας ὑμῖν σπονδὰς ἔχειν τι βέβαιον, αἳ ἡσυχαζόντων μὲν ὑμῶν ὀνόματι σπονδαὶ ἔσονται (οὕτω γὰρ ἐνθένδε τε ἄνδρες ἔπραξαν αὐτὰ καὶ ἐκ τῶν ἐναντίων) (VI. 10. 2).

'And perhaps you think that the present peace is somehow secure, which will be a peace in name only even if you remain peaceful (for thus men from here and from the enemy have arranged these things).'

ἡσυχαζόντων has been variously interpreted: 'even though you remain peaceful', or 'as long as you remain peaceful'. But Dover, observing that the parenthesis replies to the implication, 'in name only', in ὀνόματι, has given a strong reason for adopting the concessive interpretation.

καὶ γὰρ τοξόται πολλοὶ καὶ ἀκοντισταὶ ἐπιβήσονται καὶ ὄχλος, ᾧ ναυμαχίαν μὲν ποιούμενοι ἐν πελάγει οὐκ ἂν ἐχρώμεθα διὰ τὸ βλάπτειν ἂν τὸ τῆς ἐπιστήμης τῇ βαρύτητι τῶν νεῶν, ἐν δὲ τῇ ἐνθάδε ἠναγκασμένῃ ἀπὸ τῶν νεῶν πεζομαχίᾳ πρόσφορα ἔσται (VII. 62. 2).

Nicias now admits that the circumstances are serious. The Athenians are forced, he says, to fight a land battle in the harbor (ἠναγκασμένῃ...πεζομαχίᾳ). He says that his preparations are πρόσφορα, but his simultaneous admission that the situation is one of passivity (ἀνάγκη), along with our recollection of the low quality of earlier πεζομαχίαι ἀπὸ τῶν νεῶν, does not augur well.[40] Neither does the concessive, contrary-to-fact statement: 'Although we would not otherwise have used footsoldiers, for fear of reducing the role skill plays...' Nicias has no hope, it appears, that skill will play a role now.

39. Cf. καίτοι in VII. 77. 2.
40. For other examples of this sort of battle in Thucydides cf. I. 49. 3 and II. 89. 8.

καὶ Σικελιωτῶν, ὧν οὐδ' ἀντιστῆναι οὐδεὶς ἕως ἤκμαζε τὸ ναυτικὸν ἡμῖν ἠξίωσεν, ἀμύνασθε αὐτούς, καὶ δείξατε ὅτι καὶ μετ' ἀσθενείας καὶ ξυμφορῶν ἡ ἡμετέρα ἐπιστήμη κρείσσων ἐστὶν ἑτέρας εὐτυχούσης ῥώμης (VII. 63. 4).

'None of the Sicilians dared to oppose us while our fleet was at its peak. Show them that even while weak and stricken by disaster your skill is stronger than the strength of another, even though he is fortunate.'

Nicias has admitted that Athenian ἐπιστήμη would be injured by having an ὄχλος on board under normal conditions (VII. 62. 1), and he has not produced a new ἐπιστήμη to buttress his forces now. As in VII. 62. 2, we recall the last πεζομαχία ἀπὸ τῶν νεῶν. Then, a Spartan had claimed that military ἐπιστήμη was transferable from land to sea (II. 87. 4) and the result was disaster. The double concession that closes this sentence could hardly bolster the fleet's confidence, pointing first to their own weakness and then to a lack of τύχη, which Nicias had in other passages deemed essential.[41]

καὶ ἐκ τῶν παρόντων, ὦ Ἀθηναῖοι καὶ ξύμμαχοι, ἐλπίδα χρὴ ἔχειν (ἤδη τινὲς καὶ ἐκ δεινοτέρων ἢ τοιῶνδε ἐσώθησαν), μηδὲ καταμέμφεσθαι ὑμᾶς ἄγαν αὐτούς (VII. 77. 1).

'Even in such circumstances, Athenians and allies, you must have hope (already some have been saved from plights yet worse), and not blame yourselves too much.'

In his last speech as in VII. 61–4 Nicias tries to strengthen his men's courage, but can do so only to a limited degree. Once again, few signs remain that success is possible. Nicias uses the same ominous phrase as in 62. 1: ἐκ τῶν παρόντων. If 'circumstances' were dismal in the last speech they are far worse now, and to hear the same old line is not encouraging, especially with the parenthesis that follows: '*some* people have survived worse plights.' Some, perhaps: but not all.

κἀγώ τοι οὐδενὸς ὑμῶν οὔτε ῥώμῃ προφέρων (ἀλλ' ὁρᾶτε δὴ ὡς διάκειμαι ὑπὸ τῆς νόσου) οὔτ' εὐτυχίᾳ δοκῶν που ὕστερός του εἶναι κατά τε τὸν ἴδιον βίον καὶ ἐς τὰ ἄλλα, νῦν ἐν τῷ αὐτῷ κινδύνῳ τοῖς φαυλοτάτοις αἰωροῦμαι (VII. 77. 2).

41. Cf. v. 16. 1, VI. 23. 3, VII. 61. 3, VII. 77. 2, VII. 77. 3.

'And I, though superior to none of you in strength (see how I am laid low), and although I think I am no one's inferior in good fortune both in my private life and in other regards, am now caught up in the same danger with the weakest of you.' As I have said above, it is hard to make this sentence harmonize completely with VII. 77. I and VII. 77. 3.[42] Rather, it is more reasonable to view it as a personal digression, showing Nicias thinking about what matters most to him (his own fate) in a characteristic manner (with two concessive participles).

τό τε ξύμπαν γνῶτε, ὦ ἄνδρες στρατιῶται, ἀναγκαῖόν τε ὂν ὑμῖν ἀνδράσιν ἀγαθοῖς γίγνεσθαι ὡς μὴ ὄντος χωρίου ἐγγὺς ὅποι ἂν μαλακισθέντες σωθείητε καί, ἢν νῦν διαφύγητε τοὺς πολεμίους, οἵ τε ἄλλοι τευξόμενοι ὧν ἐπιθυμεῖτέ που ἐπιδεῖν καὶ οἱ Ἀθηναῖοι τὴν μεγάλην δύναμιν τῆς πόλεως καίπερ πεπτωκυῖαν ἐπανορθώσοντες (VII. 77. 7).

Even at the close of his speech Nicias invokes a concessive clause: 'Save the great power of your city, even though it has collapsed.' As I have suggested, Nicias' emotions in this speech often get the better of his intentions. The result in the present passage is a contradiction that implies that ruin (πεπτωκυῖαν)[43] and recovery are somehow not exclusive. The very hint of the fallen city strikes deeper than Nicias might wish. He had himself argued, at the start of the expedition, that the force resembled a city being founded (VI. 23. 2), and the image has returned to haunt him: 'They resembled nothing other than a city forced to surrender', Thucydides had said at VII. 75. 5. Nicias tries to use the image: αὐτοί τε πόλις εὐθύς ἐστε ὅποι ἂν καθέζησθε (VII. 77. 4); ἄνδρες γὰρ πόλις, καὶ οὐ τείχη οὐδὲ νῆες ἀνδρῶν κεναί (VII. 77. 7). He is right: the men are a city, but the resemblance fatally undercuts the gnomic sentence just cited, for by Nicias' own admission the 'city' built on these men is now a shambles.[44]

42. Dover attempts to do so in his 1965 notes. His 1970 *Commentary* attributes more complexity to the passage.

43. Cf. LSJ on πίπτω, B. II. 2, esp. E. *Hec.* 5, also of a ruined city.

44. Nicias' language contradicts his proposals also in VII. 77. 4: intending to say that human error is remediable, Nicias uses too strong an expression, ἄλλοι τινὲς...ἀνθρώπεια δράσαντες ἀνεκτὰ ἔπαθον, echoing the Aeschylean δράσαντι παθεῖν and undercutting the hope for survival: for in Aeschylus the criminal 'suffers' by dying.

Nicias' character is largely responsible for his situation. Had he been more forceful or less self-concerned, he might have averted the disaster. The most important point to be made here is that his speeches, by mirroring the personal traits that proved to be historically important, become a form of historical and psychological description that affirm the role of personal and even irrational qualities in determining historical action.

II. THE PARATACTIC STYLE OF ALCIBIADES

Καὶ ταῦτα ἡ ἐμὴ νεότης καὶ ἄνοια παρὰ φύσιν δοκοῦσα εἶναι ἐς τὴν Πελοποννησίων δύναμιν λόγοις τε πρέπουσιν ὡμίλησε καὶ ὀργῇ πίστιν παρασχομένη ἔπεισεν. καὶ νῦν μὴ πεφόβησθε αὐτήν, ἀλλ' ἕως ἐγώ τε ἔτι ἀκμάζω μετ' αὐτῆς καὶ ὁ Νικίας εὐτυχὴς δοκεῖ εἶναι, ἀποχρήσασθε τῇ ἑκατέρου ἡμῶν ὠφελίᾳ. καὶ τὸν ἐς τὴν Σικελίαν πλοῦν μὴ μεταγιγνώσκετε ὡς ἐπὶ μεγάλην δύναμιν ἐσόμενον (VI. 17. 1–2).

Each of these sentences begins with καί. Such clustering of initial καί occurs in only one other speech in Thucydides, and that too is by Alcibiades (VI. 89–92). In Greek prose generally it is unusual to find initial καί in three successive sentences.[45] In both of Alcibiades' speeches this initial καί plays an important role.

Consider the argument in VI. 17. Alcibiades began his speech by contending that personal extravagance benefited the city (VI. 16. 1). Then he defended his actual abilities as a statesman (VI. 16. 6), a defense that is still in process in VI. 17. 1, where he is ironically replying to Nicias' attack on him. Then the subject changes and by VI. 17. 2 we realize that the refutation of Nicias' attack is over and the commendation of Alcibiades' own plan under way. The transition is clever, even when compared to those in other speeches in Thucydides. H. Kleist perceptively pointed this out in 1876, but did not comment on the verbal particulars of the transition.[46]

Alcibiades gradually passes from discussion of his own capacities

45. In the long passages from other authors mentioned later in this section, and in other passages I have surveyed, I find only three examples: Andocides, *Myst.* 15, Antiphon, *Herod.* 23, and Pl. *Charm.* 153b–c (dialogue).

46. H. Kleist, *Über den Bau der thukydideischen Reden* 1 (Dramburg 1876), p. 8.

to consideration of the expedition. By keeping the focus on himself, however, and letting the expedition appear as his own idea and responsibility, he conceals the shift from self-vindication to proposals, from *refutatio* to *confirmatio*. The fulcrum of the transition is αὐτήν in the second sentence. Its antecedent is not immediately apparent, for it is in fact two words, νεότης and ἄνοια, which share a single article. Singular and plural are confused by the pronoun, and this confusion blurs our picture of what the antecedent has been. The next pronoun is just as indecisive as the last: it is αὐτῇ. The second sentence then closes with the word ὠφελία, indicating a shift from the negative quality νεότης καὶ ἄνοια (already qualified by δοκοῦσα) to the positive one, ὠφελία. All these words have the same gender and number. The large gap between antecedent and pronoun, and the emphasis given ὠφελία by its final position in the sentence and separation from the article, show that in Alcibiades' eyes the ἄνοια imputed to him is better described as ὠφελία, and is, therefore, good for Athens. Indeed, the same transition from supposed ἄνοια to real ὠφελία is found in vi. 16. 3.

Superficially, these sentences do not appear transitional. All three begin with καί, giving the impression that they are regular emphatic assertions aligned in clear parataxis, and so typical of Alcibiades' style. The difficulties in the sentence arise from the postponement of ὠφελία, not from extreme subordination or convolution of syntax. The formal parataxis seen here, with all its naïve and folkloric associations, is put to subtle use in Alcibiades' rhetoric.[47] As a first step in understanding Alcibiades' usage, we must note the rarity with which initial καί is used in classical Greek prose (see overleaf).

47. On the 'primitive' use of parataxis, see Alarik Rynell, *Parataxis and Hypotaxis as a Criterion of Syntax and Style, Especially in Old English Poetry* (Lund 1952), pp. 24–7, and Sophie Trenkner, *Le style καί dans le récit attique oral* (Assen 1960), pp. 74–8 (examples from a number of languages). Archibald Hill makes sensible qualifications of Rynell's thesis in *Language* 28 (1952), 534. On the varieties of Greek parataxis, which must be carefully distinguished, see Friedrich Zucker, 'Formen gesteigert affektischer Rede in Sprechversen der griechischen Tragödie', *IF* 42 (1955), 62–77; Jean Carrière, *Stylistique grecque* (Paris 1967), pp. 118, 132; Jean Humbert, *Syntaxe grecque* (Paris 1960), pp. 86–8, and Trenkner, *passim*.

Frequency of καί in initial position in
Greek prose passages

Author	Passage	No. of sentences in sample	No. of initial καί's	Proportion of initial καί's
Inscription	Tod 66	37	1	0·027
Herodotus	VII. 1–11	133	4	0·030
Herodotus	VIII. 49 = 64	83	2	0·024
Antiphon	*Herod.* 21–4[48]	18	5	0·278
Andocides	*Myst.* 11–18[49]	34	10	0.294
Xenophon	*Hellenica*:			
	I. 1. 14–26	31	3	0·096
	I. 4. 1 – 5. 21	72	4	0·056
	I. 6. 29–38	32	0	0·000
	II. 3. 24–34	27	4	0·148
	II. 35–49	38	0	0·000
Lysias	Oration 12	234	25	0·107
Plato	*Charmides* 153–6	97	17	0·124
Plato	*Republic* I	841	52	0·062
Demosthenes	*De Corona* 126–38, 160–80, 252–75	167	17	0·102

Compared to Thucydides, other authors use initial καί infrequently. But even within the text of Thucydides both speeches of Alcibiades stand out.

Narrative

	II. 1–8	57	7	0·123
	II. 95–103	72	9	0·125
	VII. 35–46	79	18	0·228

Speeches (in descending order)

Alcibiades	VI. 16–18	38	14	0·368
Alcibiades	VI. 89–92	44	14	0·318
Hermocrates	VI. 76–80	34	10	0·294
Corinthians	I. 68–71	46	12	0·261

48. Cited by Trenkner, p. 10, n. 2, as an example of the 'καί-style'. Note the small size of the sample.

49. Cited by Trenkner, p. 7, n. 1.

Frequency of καί in initial position in
Greek prose passages (*cont.*)

Passage		No. of sentences in sample	No. of initial καί's	Proportion of initial καί's
Speeches (in descending order)				
Nicias	VII. 61–4	16	4	0·250
Hermocrates	IV. 59–64	40	9	0·225
Corinthians	I. 37–41	36	8	0·222
Thebans	III. 61–7	55	12	0·218
Euphemus	VI. 82–7	37	8	0·216
Nicias	VII. 77	14	3	0·214
Archidamus	I. 80–4	45	9	0·200
Athenagoras	VI. 36–40	32	6	0·188
Corcyra	I. 32–6	33	6	0·182
Brasidas	V. 9	11	2	0·182
Athenians	I. 73–8	45	8	0·178
Plataeans	III. 53–9	52	9	0·173
Nicias	VI. 9–14	35	6	0·171
Nicias	VII. 11–15	31	5	0·161
Brasidas	IV. 126	13	2	0·154
Diodotus	III. 42–8	56	8	0·143
Pericles	II. 35–46	79	11	0·139
Pericles	I. 140–4	53	7	0·132
Sthenelaidas	I. 86	8	1	0·125
Nicias	VI. 68	8	1	0·125
Pericles	II. 60–4	42	5	0·119
Spartans	IV. 17–20	26	3	0·115
Mytileneans	III. 9–14	48	5	0·104
Brasidas	IV. 85–7	22	2	0·091
Corinthians	I. 120–4	39	3	0·077
Cleon	III. 37–40	45	3	0·067
Spartans	II. 87	15	1	0·067
Archidamus	II. 11	15	1	0·067
Nicias	VII. 11–15	18	1	0·056
Hermocrates	VI. 33–4	25	0	0·000
Phormio	II. 87	21	0	0·000
Pagondas	IV. 92	13	0	0·000
Nicias	VI. 20–3	15	0	0·000

The infrequency and consequent strong effect of initial καί have, as far as I know, never been pointed out.[50] Yet partly as a result of its frequency, initial καί can endow the comparatively few sentences in which it is employed with special vividness. The first example in Book VII of Herodotus has such a usage:

καὶ αὐτίκα μὲν ἐπηγγέλλετο πέμπων ἀγγέλους κατὰ πόλις ἑτοιμάζειν στρατιήν, πολλῷ πλέω ἐπιτάσσων ἑκάστοισι ἢ πρότερον παρεῖχον, καὶ νέας τε καὶ ἵππους καὶ σῖτον καὶ πλοῖα (VII. 1. 2).

'And straightway he ordered a mobilization', with καί underlining αὐτίκα. There are no more initial καί's until VII. 9. 2, where Mardonius stresses a paradox:

καὶ γὰρ δεινὸν ἂν εἴη πρῆγμα, εἰ Σάκας μὲν καὶ 'Ινδοὺς καὶ Αἰθίοπάς τε καὶ 'Ασσυρίους ἄλλα τε ἔθνεα πολλὰ καὶ μεγάλα ἀδικήσαντα Πέρσας οὐδέν, ἀλλὰ δύναμιν προσκτᾶσθαι βουλόμενοι, καταστρεψάμενοι δούλους ἔχομεν, Ἕλληνας δὲ ὑπάρξαντας ἀδικίης οὐ τιμωρησόμεθα.

'It would *indeed* (καὶ γάρ: cf. Denniston, p. 108) be grave', if we should leave the Greeks, who have harmed us, after enslaving others, who have not.

The third initial καί emphasizes a point in Artabanus' speech (VII. 10. γ2), as does the fourth, a bit later (VII. 10. θ2). These are the only passages with initial καί in the first thirty-eight chapters of this book.

In Xenophon's *Hellenica*, the καί that opens sentences can be unemphatic, as in some narrative sections (cf. 1. 4. 21, 1. 5. 7, 1. 5. 10, 1. 5. 19), but in other narrative passages it serves to accentuate points (1. 1. 17, 1. 1. 21, 1. 1. 25) and in speeches it can be used emphatically, as in Critias' attack on Theramenes:

καὶ ἐάν τινα αἰσθανώμεθα ἐναντίον τῇ ὀλιγαρχίᾳ, ὅσον δυνάμεθα ἐκποδὼν ποιούμεθα (II. 3. 26).

50. There are good but brief comments on the 'steigernde Kraft' of καί in Kuehner–Gerth (II. 246–8), though the particle's emphatic initial position is only noticed in interrogative sentences. Liddell and Scott remark that καί can open questions and demands (A. II), and at times has the force of καίτοι (A. II. 2). Denniston's long section on καί only tells us that when used copulatively it can come first in a sentence or clause (p. 325), with no comment on its force in this position. Denniston's discussion of emphatic καί contains a few examples of its use at the beginning of a sentence, but without comment. Trenkner does not discuss the subject, although many of her examples of the καί-style have the word in initial position.

καὶ γὰρ ὁ κόθορνος ἁρμόττειν μὲν τοῖς ποσὶν ἀμφοτέροις δοκεῖ, ἀποβλέπει δὲ ἀπ' ἀμφοτέρων· (ΙΙ. 3. 31)

καὶ εἰσὶ μὲν δήπου πᾶσαι μεταβολαὶ πολιτειῶν θανατηφόροι, σὺ δὲ διὰ τὸ εὐμετάβολος εἶναι πλείστοις μὲν μεταίτιος εἶ ἐξ ὀλιγαρχίας ὑπὸ τοῦ δήμου ἀπολωλέναι, πλείστοις δ' ἐκ δημοκρατίας ὑπὸ τῶν βελτιόνων (ΙΙ. 3. 32).

In the last two instances καί effects a rapid transition from one point to the next. Finally, the last sentence of Critias' speech is introduced by καί in a manner similar to that of the climactic usages of Alcibiades in epilogues (Thuc. VI. 18. 6, VI. 92. 5): καὶ ὑμεῖς οὖν, ἐὰν σωφρονῆτε, οὐ τούτου ἀλλ' ὑμῶν αὐτῶν φείσεσθε (ΙΙ. 3. 34).

Turning to Alcibiades, we find that in only two of the total number of twenty-eight sentences is this initial καί part of a καί...καί, 'both...and' construction. In the other twenty-six cases, initial καί is itself responsive, taking up the sequence of thought of the preceding sentence with nuances variously translatable as 'also', 'even', or 'actually'. In each case the sentence beginning with καί is closely bound to the preceding one, and its content appears to follow as a logical development of that sentence, with no need to explain the sequence by a subordinating conjunction, or to alter the train of thought by a limitative or adversative particle (ἀλλά, οὖν, δέ, γε). The ultimate effect of this practice is to give an impression of clarity and simplicity. Moreover, καί often functions so as to prevent antithesis. A sentence with two halves coordinated by καί...καί rather than μέν...δέ, οὐ μόνον...ἀλλὰ καί, etc., or a sentence opening with καί rather than δέ, δή or ἀλλά, for instance, has removed one opportunity for antithetical expression.[51]

The three sentences in VI. 17. 1–2 reach only the second level of subordination, the opportunity for complexity being reduced by the use of καί.[52] The concomitant lessening of antithesis (note that even Alcibiades and his opponent are linked by τε...καί in VI. 17. 1, rather than μέν...δέ) gives an impression more of harmony than contentiousness. The reader is led in a linear progression from one

51. Trenkner, pp. 32–4, does see an adversative potential in καί...καί.
52. The initial καί is one of many reasons for retaining VI. 17. 5 against Classen–Steup.

14

thought to the next, undisturbed by insistent rhetorical devices, antitheses, or subordinations. The unusual occurrence of initial καί in three consecutive sentences increases an effect of vividness and directness. Alcibiades sweeps the reader along as though there were no call for discussion of nuances and no need for subordination of thought. One idea follows directly on the last, while shifts of direction and emphasis occur below the surface structure. Initial καί is used elsewhere in Thucydides in moving from one section of a speech to the next, but in no other speech in Thucydides does a series of sentences produce so vigorous and direct a stylistic progression simultaneously with a conceptual and rhetorical transition.

καί produces an effect of swiftness and an emphatic tone elsewhere in this speech. vi. 16. 1 is one of four cases in Thucydides where the conjunction opens a speech, and all are emphatic.[53] Alcibiades uses it at vi. 16. 3 in defending his expenditures and proving he is useful (with the same progression from supposed ἄνοια to real ὠφελία as in vi. 17. 2). Later in the speech, sentences beginning with καί lead up to conclusions (vi. 17. 3–4, vi. 18. 3 (twice), vi. 18. 4), or introduce new proofs (vi. 17. 5, vi. 17. 8) in the same vigorous manner.

The penultimate sentence of Alcibiades' first speech is one of the best examples of his clever use of καί. The sentence (vi. 18. 6) is the keystone of the whole speech, and the preparation for it has been thorough. After defending himself and showing the weakness of τὰ ἐκεῖ Alcibiades had in vi. 17. 7 turned to affairs at home, τὰ ἐνθάδε. The key argument in that passage was that οἱ πατέρες, although they had the same foreign enemies as in Alcibiades' day, were able to establish τὴν ἀρχήν. οἱ πατέρες, more than simply introducing a stock τόπος,[54] picks up Nicias' exhortation to the πρεσβύτεροι not to be intimidated by the young followers of Alcibiades (vi. 13. 1). Alcibiades, as the deuteragonist, aims to refute the arguments of Nicias, and οἱ πατέρες are mentioned in

53. The others are: the last orations of Nicias and Pericles (vii. 77. 1, ii. 60. 1), and Archidamus' speech at Sparta (i. 80. 1). Krueger compares this last passage to Hdt. viii. 109, where καί opens a speech by Themistocles, one of the most vigorous and sophistic speakers in Herodotus. (Compare his techniques and language in viii. 83. 1 and viii. 111. 2–3.)

54. Cf. Karl Jost, *Das Beispiel und Vorbild der Vorfahren bei attischen Rednern bis Demosthenes* (Paderborn 1936), p. 55.

VI. 17. 7 partly for this reason.[55] Mention of the ancestors begins an extended comparison between the period following the Persian Wars and the present. ἀρχή is the key word in this comparison: not only is it what οἱ πατέρες got possession of in VI. 17. 7, but, from that passage on, it is repeated insistently:[56]

τήν τε ἀρχὴν οὕτως ἐκτησάμεθα καὶ ἡμεῖς καὶ ὅσοι δὴ ἄλλοι ἦρξαν (VI. 18. 2).

καὶ οὐκ ἔστιν ἡμῖν ταμιεύεσθαι ἐς ὅσον βουλόμεθα ἄρχειν, ἀλλ᾽ ἀνάγκη, ἐπειδήπερ ἐν τῷδε καθέσταμεν, τοῖς μὲν ἐπιβουλεύειν, τοὺς δὲ μὴ ἀνιέναι, διὰ τὸ ἀρχθῆναι ἂν ὑφ᾽ ἑτέρων αὐτοῖς κίνδυνον εἶναι, εἰ μὴ αὐτοὶ ἄλλων ἄρχοιμεν (VI. 18. 3).

καὶ ἅμα ἢ τῆς Ἑλλάδος τῶν ἐκεῖ προσγενομένων πάσης τῷ εἰκότι ἄρξομεν, ἢ κακώσομέν γε Συρακοσίους, ἐν ᾧ καὶ αὐτοὶ καὶ οἱ ξύμμαχοι ὠφελησόμεθα. (VI. 18. 4).

The repetition of ἀρχή points up the necessary connection between supremacy and survival for Athens, and the tension between these two concepts continues into VI. 18. 6:

καὶ μὴ ὑμᾶς ἡ Νικίου τῶν λόγων ἀπραγμοσύνη καὶ διάστασις τοῖς νέοις ἐς τοὺς πρεσβυτέρους ἀποτρέψῃ, τῷ δὲ εἰωθότι κόσμῳ, ὥσπερ καὶ οἱ πατέρες ἡμῶν ἅμα νέοι γεραιτέροις βουλεύοντες ἐς τάδε ἦραν αὐτά, καὶ νῦν τῷ αὐτῷ τρόπῳ πειρᾶσθε προαγαγεῖν τὴν πόλιν, καὶ νομίσατε νεότητα μὲν καὶ γῆρας ἄνευ ἀλλήλων μηδὲν δύνασθαι, ὁμοῦ δὲ τό τε φαῦλον καὶ τὸ μέσον καὶ τὸ πάνυ ἀκριβὲς ἂν ξυγκραθὲν μάλιστ᾽ ἂν ἰσχύειν, καὶ τὴν πόλιν, ἐὰν μὲν ἡσυχάζῃ, τρίψεσθαί τε αὐτὴν περὶ αὑτὴν ὥσπερ καὶ ἄλλο τι, καὶ πάντων τὴν ἐπιστήμην ἐγγηράσεσθαι, ἀγωνιζομένην δὲ αἰεὶ προσλήψεσθαί τε τὴν ἐμπειρίαν καὶ τὸ ἀμύνεσθαι οὐ λόγῳ ἀλλ᾽ ἔργῳ μᾶλλον ξύνηθες ἕξειν.

Without the eleven uses of καί and three of τε, this sentence, the second longest in a Thucydidean speech,[57] would easily have gone

55. The advantages of the deuteragonist were commonly acknowledged. Cf. Pl. *Ep.* VII 343ᴅ, Aristotle, *Rhet.* 1402a, and F. M. Cornford, *The Origin of Attic Comedy* (London 1914), p. 72.

56. Even the strange play of ἄρχειν, 'to command', against ἄρξασθαι, 'to begin', in VI. 16. 1 had the rhetorical function of planting the word and the concept behind it in our minds.

57. Five other sentences in Thucydidean speeches have a hundred words or more: II. 43. 1 (100), IV. 87. 2–3 (102), III. 59. 3–4 (102), and VI. 22a (109).

beyond the fourth level of complexity. καί not only opens the sentence but is the chief connective within it, so that the sentence appears to move clearly from point to point, just as in VI. 17. 1–2. Alcibiades counters Nicias' arguments by incorporating them into his own statement and showing that a variety of components cause Athens' greatness. οἱ πατέρες, Alcibiades had said in VI. 17. 7, founded the empire. Here that term is repeated, as though it had been held poised over the last page. But this is no simple rhetorical *Vorbild*, for Alcibiades has added the paradox that these forefathers were once young men themselves just as Alcibiades is now; then the further paradox, that as youths they got the empire by ἅμα νέοι γεραιτέροις βουλεύοντες, proving νεότητα μὲν καὶ γῆρας ἄνευ ἀλλήλων μηδὲν δύνασθαι. A shift from age to class differences then follows immediately, and is made to seem natural by the continuing parataxis: ὁμοῦ δὲ τό τε φαῦλον καὶ τὸ μέσον καὶ τὸ πάνυ ἀκριβὲς ἂν ξυγκραθὲν μάλιστ' ἂν ἰσχύειν.

The next clause is again introduced by καί, and might seem a corollary to what preceded, but in fact its content is new: ἡσυχία will cause the city to deteriorate and its skill to 'become decrepit' (ἐπιστήμην ἐγγηράσεσθαι). The metaphorical twist subtly disparages Nicias' view by hinting that decay and decline are typical of the elderly and that only co-operation with other age groups can prevent them.

The sentence in VI. 18. 6 is in Alcibiades' normal style, and this style, with its appearance of harmony, accords well with the picture he presents of decision-making at Athens. The use of καί permits Alcibiades to revise and elaborate on Nicias' simple antithesis of youth against age, and to show that the two groups must be mutually dependent.

The only other speech in Thucydides containing three consecutive sentences with initial καί is Alcibiades' appeal to the Spartans:

> καὶ διατελοῦντός μου προθύμου ὑμεῖς πρὸς Ἀθηναίους καταλ-
> λασσόμενοι τοῖς μὲν ἐμοῖς ἐχθροῖς δύναμιν δι' ἐκείνων πράξαντες,
> ἐμοὶ δὲ ἀτιμίαν περιέθετε. καὶ διὰ ταῦτα δικαίως ὑπ' ἐμοῦ πρός
> τε τὰ Μαντινέων καὶ Ἀργείων τραπομένου καὶ ὅσα ἄλλα
> ἐνηντιούμην ὑμῖν ἐβλάπτεσθε· καὶ νῦν, εἴ τις καὶ τότε ἐν τῷ
> πάσχειν οὐκ εἰκότως ὠργίζετό μοι, μετὰ τοῦ ἀληθοῦς σκοπῶν
> ἀναπειθέσθω (VI. 89. 2–3).

Alcibiades first succinctly relates his unrewarded benevolence to Sparta and his revenge when he was betrayed, and concludes by absolving himself of blame. Again the use of initial καί permits terse and emphatic argumentation as Alcibiades moves energetically from one point to the next. The other occurrences of initial καί in this speech resemble those in vi. 16–18: they introduce sentences that contain emphatic points (vi. 89. 6, vi. 90. 1, vi. 91. 3 (twice), vi. 91. 7) or move to new points in the argument (vi. 91. 1, vi. 91. 5, vi. 92. 2, vi. 92. 4, vi. 92. 5). καί opens sentences in the sophistic analysis of patriotism at vi. 92. 2–3, where Alcibiades defends his behavior. The first of these sentences is complex to the fourth degree, but the second, a direct statement on the nature of patriotism, reaches only one level of complexity. The tone established by καί is one of simple parataxis, of moving from point to point with no hint that these points are not logically connected:

καὶ χείρων οὐδενὶ ἀξιῶ δοκεῖν ὑμῶν εἶναι, εἰ τῇ ἐμαυτοῦ μετὰ τῶν πολεμιωτάτων φιλόπολίς ποτε δοκῶν εἶναι νῦν ἐγκρατῶς ἐπέρχομαι, οὐδὲ ὑποπτεύεσθαί μου ἐς τὴν φυγαδικὴν προθυμίαν τὸν λόγον (vi. 92. 2).

καὶ πολεμιώτεροι οὐχ οἱ τοὺς πολεμίους που βλάψαντες ὑμεῖς ἢ οἱ τοὺς φίλους ἀναγκάσαντες πολεμίους γενέσθαι (vi. 92. 3).

These sentences are followed by a long peroration of 63 words (vi. 92. 5b), the second longest sentence in the speech and the third longest in either speech of Alcibiades, and one that without the use of καί (seven times) and τε (four times) would be subordinated far beyond the fourth degree:

καὶ αὐτοὺς νῦν νομίσαντας περὶ μεγίστων δὴ τῶν διαφερόντων βουλεύεσθαι μὴ ἀποκνεῖν τὴν ἐς τὴν Σικελίαν τε καὶ ἐς τὴν Ἀττικὴν στρατείαν, ἵνα τά τε ἐκεῖ βραχεῖ μορίῳ ξυμπαραγενόμενοι μεγάλα σώσητε καὶ Ἀθηναίων τήν τε οὖσαν καὶ τὴν μέλλουσαν δύναμιν καθέλητε, καὶ μετὰ ταῦτα αὐτοί τε ἀσφαλῶς οἰκῆτε καὶ τῆς ἁπάσης Ἑλλάδος ἑκούσης καὶ οὐ βίᾳ, κατ' εὔνοιαν δὲ ἡγῆσθε (vi. 92. 5b).

The points, Alcibiades implies, are simple: attack now, in order to save Sicily and destroy Athens' army, and to live securely and rule Greece. Long though the sentence is, its low level of subordination makes it easy to interpret.

The above discussion is limited to two aspects of Alcibiades' language: his use of καί, especially to open sentences, and the consequent avoidance of complex subordination. There are other distinctive features in Alcibiades' speeches,[58] but these two suffice to show how clearly Thucydides characterizes the man by his style of speaking as well as by commentary and narrative.

III. CONCLUSION

These studies indicate that Thucydidean speakers are more individualized by their styles than has been thought. If this is true, several of the assumptions mentioned in the introduction must be revised. Thucydides now appears to be more dramatic than Jebb and Blass allowed. The designation of Lysias as the inventor of stylistic characterization must be qualified (and the meaning of ἠθοποιία reconsidered), as we learn more about fifth-century achievements in this regard. Finally, the frequent claims that Attic literature gives us only the ideal and general, and that no notion of 'personality' existed in this period, may under examination turn out to be rather the legacy of Neo-Classicism than a reasoned deduction from ancient evidence.

58. One thinks of the frequent ironic uses of the potential optative.

Scientific apparatus onstage in 423 B.C.

ROBERT S. BRUMBAUGH

THIS PAPER offers supporting evidence for the true, but un-stylish, thesis that Western science entered Athens in the mid-fifth century B.C. like a tinker's cart, hung about with jangling and gleaming hardware. That thesis, in turn, is a vital link in an inductive proof that Western science has never actually developed apart from close interaction with measures, models, and machines.

The traditional view, common to histories of science and philosophy and to more general interpretations of classical culture, made the use of models, observation, and apparatus the crucial difference between 'science' in its classical and in its modern form.[1] This did not quite match the actual documents and achievements of classical work from Archimedes through Ptolemy, and more detailed study led to a new and different consensus.[2]

1. In what follows, I am not arguing against the existence of a theory-building, speculative *emphasis* in classical science; for better or worse, that is there. But the myth of a total, perhaps deliberate, rejection of all mechanical models or empirical investigation (a myth already well under way by Plutarch's time; witness his 'Life of Marcellus') needs demolition. Standard histories of science – the most important of which was George Sarton's – make Plato the baneful spokesman for an anti-empiricism. (On this point, and the weaknesses of its presentation, see James Haden, 'The Challenge of the History of Science, Part 1', *Review of Metaphysics* VII (1953), 74–88.) But a similar view, without the negative evaluation, occurs in the work of A. N. Whitehead, himself both scientist and Platonist (e.g. in *Science and the Modern World* (New York 1925), chapter 1). And a similar overall appraisal opens S. Sambursky's excellent study, *The Physical World of the Greeks* (trans. M. Dagut, London 1956), pp. 2, 3.

2. Some works, particularly Heron of Alexandria's, suggest a radical change of interest and competence by the second century A.D., just as Sextus Empiricus represents a new theoretical stance favoring strict 'empiricism'. The conclusive piece of evidence that upsets the application of a 'no technology or apparatus' label to the Hellenistic period, however, is the 'Antikythera machine' (Derek J. Price, 'An Ancient Computer', *Scientific American* (June 1959), cover, pp. 60–7).

Since 1951, the empirical character of post-Aristotelian science has
been recognized, and explained as the result of a confluence of
Near Eastern computational, observational technique and a more
austere classical qualitative, speculative fondness for theory construction. The date of fusion is put at about 323 B.C., the death of
Alexander the Great.[3] On this recent view, apart from an inci-
dental early coincidence, science in Greece before 323 would still
have been the austere, anti-empirical enterprise which earlier
historians thought typical of classical science in general.

Neat as this scheme is, both historically and philosophically,
further investigations now lead me to doubt its accuracy for the
fourth century, as evidence shows that science in this period was
already interacting with models and mechanisms, in a way that
compromises its postulated rationalistic 'purity'. If the dialectical
pattern of Hellenic pure rationalism–Near Eastern pure empiricism–Hellenistic empirical science holds historically, the
rationalistic, anti-empirical phase must be limited to about a
century, from the arrival of Anaxagoras in Athens (*c.* 467) to the
compilation of Plato's *Timaeus* (*c.* 367, surely begun earlier).[4] That
lends a new, unappreciated magnitude to the role in Western
intellectual history of such thinkers as Anaxagoras, Archelaus,
Socrates, and Plato in his younger days; for it would be just here
that the essential Hellenic component of the later synthesis appeared, to be gradually weakened in the mid-fourth century, and
synthesized after 323.

But was there such a selective transplantation, separating
'science' in Athens from the empirical strand of the Milesian

3. New interest in, and appreciation of, the Near Eastern contribution was
initiated by O. Neugebauer's work (e.g. *The Exact Sciences in Antiquity* (Copen-
hagen 1951)). For an account of the respective contributions and the confluence of Near Eastern and Hellenic 'science', see, for example, Derek J. Price,
Science Since Babylon (New Haven 1961). I have no intention of denying that a
change of emphasis resulted from the new cultural contacts opened by Alexander; I am denying the sharp dialectical antitheses that oversimplify the picture
of the 'Hellenic' stream.

4. 467 B.C. is the date of the meteorite that directed public attention to the
astronomy of Anaxagoras, attention which may account for his invitation to
come to Athens. I think there is general agreement that the *Timaeus* was completed by about the time of Plato's first trip to Sicily. That it is 'impure' science
if absence of models or detailed observations is the test of 'purity' is argued
in my article, 'Plato and the History of Science', *Studium Generale* IX (1961),
520–2.

tradition, and giving it another direction?[5] Was a partial compromise being made in the fourth century, as the 'purity' of this scientific thought was modified by importations of equipment from Italy and Asia Minor? Interesting as this would be – and, in a way, plausible – it seems to me it did not happen.

The evidence here presented for my view is primarily the role played by 'stagey' scientific properties and mechanisms in Aristophanes' *Clouds*. There is throughout the play an intrinsic association of 'new learning', atheism, and mechanical apparatus; and an audience is presupposed already familiar enough with that association to appreciate the grotesque properties hung about in the *Phrontisterion*, and the way Strepsiades misinterprets them.

Since my focus of attention here is the fifth century, I will relegate to a note my reasons for insisting on the 'impure', 'mechanized' character of 'science' in the latter three-quarters of the fourth century, and center on Aristophanes' evidence that the same idea – apparatus interaction held in 423 B.C.[6]

There are four points about the *Clouds* that I think brief citation can establish clearly. First, that the connection of science and hardware is pervasive in the imagery and plot of the play itself, not merely the subject of a few contrived jokes. Second, that the unscrupulous intellectual – typified by Socrates – uses this equipment to intimidate and dazzle the uninitiate. Third, that Aristophanes rejects all such appeals to models as a *non sequitur*; he finds them no more plausible evidence for giving up traditional belief than the pots of a kitchen posing as celestial hemispheres would be. Fourth, that Aristophanes recognized that the appeal of

5. It seems quite clear that the Milesians – coming from a city which, as Burnet pointed out, was noted for its engineers – were designers of instruments and builders of models. In particular, the doxographical reports of Anaximander's cosmological ring model, his map, star-map, and gnomon, and Anaximemes' 'vortex' model of the cosmos make this point.

6. See my *Ancient Greek Gadgets and Machines* (New York 1966). It is suggested there that enough is presupposed about use of models in psychology and cosmology by Plato's *Republic* to justify the assertion that 'pure science', if it existed earlier, had already become considerably less pure by about 385. The hypothesis of a continuing development of techniques, mechanisms, and models without benefit of a literary record is confirmed, for fourth-century Ionia at least, by the identification of a coin reverse as a detailed relief map (A. E. M. Johnson, 'The Earliest Preserved Greek Map: A New Ionian Coin Type', *JHS* 87 (1967), 86ff.).

'gadgetry' was dangerous. Part of the education he undertakes that does rub off on Strepsiades is the notion of using gadgetry as an 'art of mischief', to further injustice. Thus the destruction of the *Phrontisterion* by fire includes, implicitly, the notion of its equipment melting as part of the happy ending.

(To anticipate the objection that this dependence on models may have been only an idiosyncrasy of Socrates, not an attribute of the new system of ideas he represents, we can look at another of Aristophanes' plays. The walk-on bit played by Meton as 'mad scientist' in the *Birds*, with his equipment for staking out lots in upper air, has this same strong thematic association of typical new intellectual and cumbersome new mechanical gear. This combination is therefore proper to the type specimen Meton and Socrates resemble, not just an eccentricity of the latter.)

The whole tone is set at the outset of the Thought-Shop scene by Socrates in his elevated basket. More usually, it would be a god who rode aloft on the theatre's machine, and Aristophanes does not let the audience miss the connection of 'higher-thought' mechanism and Socratic *hybris*. 'Why dost thou call me, O Mortal?' asks Socrates in l. 223:

Σω: τί με καλεῖς, ὦ 'φήμερε;

Strepsiades shortly comments, 'Then it is from the basket that you show contempt for the gods', l. 226:

ΣΤΡ: ἔπειτ' ἀπὸ ταρροῦ τοὺς θεοὺς ὑπερφρονεῖς.

We were already partially prepared for this by Strepsiades' hearsay account of the wise men in the school, who say that 'we are coals beneath the cooking-bell of heaven', ll. 95–7:

οἳ τὸν οὐρανὸν
λέγοντες ἀναπείθουσιν ὡς ἔστιν πνιγεύς,
κἄστιν περὶ ἡμᾶς οὗτος, ἡμεῖς δ' ἄνθρακες.

This homely hearsay paraphrase introduces the two notions that the new Shop has some sort of cosmological model, and that it is really trivial.[7]

7. The 'cooking-bell', with these lines of Aristophanes as caption, is illustrated in B. Sparkes and L. Talcott, *Pots and Pans of Classical Athens* (1958), and discussed by Sparkes in *JHS* 82 (1962), 128f. See also K. J. Dover, *Aristophanes Clouds* (Oxford 1968), *ad loc.*

The suspended basket (κρεμάθρα) at l. 218 is the climax of the initial tour in which the Disciple recounts the ingenuity of his Master, and points out the 'cult objects' that characterize the new sciences. One of Socrates' subtle masterpieces is recounted that sets up the initial association of apparatus and injustice, at l. 179. To get food, Socrates bends a skewer into a compass, pretends to be studying geometry, and hooks his neighbor's sacrificial meat from the altar with it.

> κατὰ τῆς τραπέζης καταπάσας λεπτὴν τέφραν,
> κάμψας ὀβελίσκον, εἶτα διαβήτην λαβών,
> ἐκ τῆς παλαίστρας θυμάτιον ὑφείλετο (177–9).[8]

The gaudy map (περίοδος) of l. 206 anticipates the more sinister model of l. 380. Merry is surely right in envisaging the stage set: 'placed about the School are sundry philosophical instruments, such as some sort of celestial globe to designate *Astronomy*, an *abacus* to represent *Geometry*'.[9]

At l. 380, ὁ Δῖνος, 'The Vortex' appears; he rules instead of Zeus:

> ΣΤ: Δῖνος; τουτί μ' ἐλελήθει,
> ὁ Ζεὺς οὐκ ὤν, ἀλλ' ἀντ' αὐτοῦ Δῖνος νυνὶ βασιλεύων.

(Cf. ll. 828, 1471.) Impiety on the part of Socrates, imbecility on that of Strepsiades, and topical commentary by Aristophanes all intersect in this stage-property. A clay jar symbolizing physical process is the patron deity whose statue stands here in the school (Aristophanes chooses the masculine Δῖνος in preference to Δίνη because the former at once suggests personification more strongly and makes the confusion of the two meanings, vortex and goblet, easier). The scale and function of this model are established by its balanced contrast with the statue of Hermes, to which Strepsiades turns for counsel near the end of the play.[10] The 'thing here of clay' has misled him; he mistook it for a god, ll. 143–74:

> οἴμοι δείλαιος
> ὅτε καί σε χυτρεοῦν ὄντα θεὸν ἡγησάμην.

8. Reading in l. 197 Hermann's θυμάτιον with W. W. Merry (*The Clouds*, Oxford 1879).

9. Merry *ad* 183.

10. And of course making the *dinos* masculine brings out this antithesis of the two 'religious' statues more sharply. Cf. Merry *ad* 380 and Dover *ad* 380 and 1473.

Strepsiades, who is stupid and a non-scientist, sees before him only a gigantic tapered goblet or jar when Socrates points out the cosmic model; but his ambition and gullibility lead him to take *that* as the shape of the new father of gods. Aristophanes invited his audience to share his notions that cosmic models are ridiculous but intimidating to the uninitiate, and that they have an evil power in the hands of the new thinkers of the day. (His property man, if he provided a black or red tapered jar on the same scale as the statue of Hermes, would have given visual emphasis to the point.) A consideration of what must be presupposed about an audience able to appreciate Socrates' addiction to his model, Strepsiades' enthusiastic misunderstanding of it, and Aristophanes' sardonic personification of this odd artefact, underscores my central thesis.

But it requires nothing so grandiose as cosmic models to make mischief; even relatively 'neutral' tools turn to evildoing devices in the play. We have already heard of Socrates' ingenious transformation of compass to skewer, and his theft from the nearby altar, under cover of pretending to study geometry. Strepsiades, trying at Socrates' urging to think in the new way, finds a similar solution to the problem of evading his debts. His first impulse (749f.) is to 'hire a witch', who will steal the moon from the sky, and so by magic postpone indefinitely the date the interest is due. But then, to escape a lawsuit, he hits upon the notion of taking a 'burning-glass' (ὕαλον, l. 768), and using it to melt the wax from the legal tablets. He is inept: the gadgetry is far-fetched, unlike Socrates' geometrical compass, and the intended result involves simple injustice without impiety. But the contagious character of the scientific association of ideas and new tools is well brought out in the 'burning-glass' theme.

> ΣΩ.: τὴν ὕαλον λέγεις;
> ΣΤΡ.: ἔγωγε (768–9).

Strepsiades' final rejection of the new higher learning, at line 1472 (after his son has just repeated that 'the Vortex reigns instead of Zeus', l. 1471 repeating l. 828), again has the model Vortex as its focus. Repenting his folly in mistaking this thing of clay for an immortal god, he turns to Hermes for advice.

> ΣΤΡ: οὐκ ἐξελήλακ᾽, ἀλλ᾽ ἐγὼ τοῦτ᾽ ᾠόμην
>   διὰ τουτονὶ τὸν Δῖνον (1472–3).
>   ἀλλ᾽, ὦ φίλ᾽ Ἑρμῆ, μηδαμῶς θύμαινέ μοι (1477).

(The literal identification of god and goblet was of course Strepsiades' own; for Socrates, it is clearly a *model* of a new atheistic cosmic power; but Aristophanes keeps insinuating that its credibility as a model is no greater than its credibility as a literal sacred object to be worshiped.)

Another association of ideas is the equation of the apparatus with the cult-objects of the Mysteries. 'These must be held as Mysteries', says the Disciple who opens the *Phrontisterion* door (l. 143). The air of the Disciple, as he points out 'that is astronomy...this is geometry', is that of the hierophant explaining a tableau. The resemblance is emphasized by beginning with the students as a group prying into 'things under the earth', and ending with Socrates riding the god-machine.

These are some of the passages that one can cite to show that the association between science and its trappings is treated as intrinsic in the play, presupposing an audience for whom that association is already familiar. And I am sure that anyone charged with designing sets and properties for a production of the *Clouds* would find himself quickly convinced of the crucial part played by the scientific gear in the spectacle.

This is not the only evidence, of course, for the contention that there was no discontinuity in the history of science between phases that depend heavily on concrete models and tools (the sixth century, the period after 323, and I think the scientific work from about 387 to 323), and a fifth-century phase in which science disregarded them; but it does offer one footnote to support the thesis that the partnership of new ideas and new apparatus was in effect and generally recognized in 423.

The further implications of this for studies of the history and nature of Western science are highly complex problems of interpretation; but we must begin by having our facts correct, if we are to understand them.

Phaedra and the Socratic paradox[1]

DAVID CLAUS

Τροζήνιαι γυναῖκες, αἳ τόδ' ἔσχατον
οἰκεῖτε χώρας Πελοπίας προνώπιον,
ἤδη ποτ' ἄλλως νυκτὸς ἐν μακρῷ χρόνῳ   375
θνητῶν ἐφρόντισ' ᾗ διέφθαρται βίος.
καί μοι δοκοῦσιν οὐ κατὰ γνώμης φύσιν
πράσσειν κάκιον· ἔστι γὰρ τό γ' εὖ φρονεῖν
πολλοῖσιν· ἀλλὰ τῇδ' ἀθρητέον τόδε·
τὰ χρήστ' ἐπιστάμεσθα καὶ γιγνώσκομεν,   380
οὐκ ἐκπονοῦμεν δ', οἱ μὲν ἀργίας ὕπο,
οἱ δ' ἡδονὴν προθέντες ἀντὶ τοῦ καλοῦ
ἄλλην τιν'· εἰσὶ δ' ἡδοναὶ πολλαὶ βίου,
μακραί τε λέσχαι καὶ σχολή, τερπνὸν κακόν,
αἰδώς τε· δισσαὶ δ' εἰσίν, ἡ μὲν οὐ κακή,   385
ἡ δ' ἄχθος οἴκων· εἰ δ' ὁ καιρὸς ἦν σαφής
οὐκ ἂν δύ' ἤστην ταῦτ' ἔχοντε γράμματα.
ταῦτ' οὖν ἐπειδὴ τυγχάνω φρονοῦσ' ἐγὼ
οὐκ ἔσθ' ὁποίῳ φαρμάκῳ διαφθερεῖν
ἔμελλον, ὥστε τοὔμπαλιν πεσεῖν φρενῶν.[2]   390

FOR REASONS that are closely related the opening lines of Phaedra's central speech (E. *Hipp.* 373–90) are of considerable importance for both the history of Greek thought and the criticism of Euripidean tragedy. Snell[3] has twice argued extensively that the words καί μοι δοκοῦσιν... οὐκ ἐκπονοῦμεν δέ are intended as a direct response to the Socratic equation of virtue and knowledge

1. I am indebted to both E. A. Havelock, who elsewhere in this volume provides a fuller view of fifth-century evidence for the teachings of Socrates, and Christopher Gill for many helpful criticisms and suggestions at an early stage in the preparation of this paper.

2. The text is that of W. S. Barrett, *Euripides' Hippolytus* (Oxford 1964).

3. Snell's opinions were originally put forward in 'Das früheste Zeugnis über Sokrates', *Philologus* XCVII (1948), 125–35 which he now considers 'superseded' by chapter III of *Scenes from Greek Drama* (Berkeley 1964), in which see p. 59, n. 15 for literature on the Socratic reference prior to 1964.

and that they therefore provide our first contemporary evidence for the teaching of Socrates. His most recent treatment of the text envisages a sequential dialogue between Medea, who admits to knowledge of her wrongdoing but asserts that her θυμός is stronger than her βουλεύματα, Socrates, who replies that 'if the nature of one's insight and knowledge is in order the right kind of thinking will produce the right kind of action', and finally Phaedra, who with the words above replies to this Socratic 'general validity that helps one to come to terms with evil'. Vital to this interpretation of the text is the belief that Phaedra's crisis is an internal one – an inner conflict of purely human drives like that apparently undergone earlier by Medea whom Snell considers a portrait of the first human being 'so completely on his own that the only motive he knows for his action is his passion and reflection' – as well as a 'moral phenomenon' in which words like πράσσειν κακίον[α] and χρηστός must be 'taken ethically in the strictest sense'.[4] On these last points Snell is in agreement with many literary critics, particularly those inclined to psychological readings of Euripidean plays, since they find in Phaedra's words an unusually frank assertion for Greek tragedy of sheer human responsibility for one's thoughts, actions, and situation by a character who assesses her own behavior as morally inadequate and responsible for her downfall. To Conacher,[5] for example, Phaedra is 'struggling with a guilty passion which she can conquer only by her death'; her speech is therefore 'an effective dramatization of the warring elements in Phaedra's soul', and it is 'in this mortal struggle between reason and passion that the whole point of her characterization lies'. The interpretations of both Snell and Conacher, who may be said to reflect the commonplace critical opinion of the passage,[6] share the belief that Phaedra is confessing an acute sense of personal moral wrongdoing occasioned by her feelings of sexual passion for Hippolytus and her apparent realization that she owes her inability to resist those desires to certain flaws in her moral character.

4. Snell, *Scenes*, pp. 56–61 (quotes from pp. 58, 60, 56, and 63).

5. D. J. Conacher, *Euripidean Drama: Myth, Theme, and Structure* (Toronto 1967), p. 16 and p. 35.

6. E.g. E. R. Dodds, *CR* xxxix (1925), 102–4; R. P. Winnington-Ingram, 'Hippolytus: A Study in Causation', *Entretiens Hardt* vi (1960), 173–80; W. S. Barrett, *Euripides' Hippolytus* (Oxford 1964), pp. 227ff. (discussed below).

Recently, however, C. W. Willink[7] has attempted to read the passage as a simultaneous admission and justification of simple 'failure' in life rather than moral wrongdoing, noting that for the Greeks 'success' and 'morality' were never completely separable. Although I believe Willink is right in his rejection of the traditional interpretation of the passage and on several crucial points of Greek, his understanding of the passage as a whole seems to me implausible and preserves several important mistakes of the past. My plan in this paper, therefore, will be to summarize the present state of the textual discussion, propose an interpretation of the passage different from that of both Willink and more traditional readers of the lines, and then relate briefly my view to both the alleged Socratic reference and the familiar 'psychological' interpretation of the play. My own opinion, which I shall state at the outset, is that the speech can only be read intelligibly if we do not regard it as a confession of anything, and that we are therefore led to conclusions about Phaedra's morality and conception of self that undermine both the possibility that she is engaged in a meaningful dialogue with Socrates and the suggestion that she possesses an unusual and guilty awareness that her inability to control her inner life makes her morally responsible for her situation.

Barrett's recent commentary contains the most detailed treatment of the speech as a confession of moral wrongdoing and, following Willink, I shall use his remarks as representative of the traditional view. Barrett differs significantly from Snell primarily on the matter of Phaedra's intent: for Snell Phaedra's purpose is to excuse her moral failure as the predictable outcome in human life of an inner struggle between reason and passion, while Barrett believes Phaedra is trying to gain the sympathy of the chorus by the candor with which she admits to a specific weakness – αἰδώς or, as Barrett translates, 'this indecisiveness, this lack of resolution [which] prevents her from fighting down her love as she knows she should' (p. 230). Barrett's translation of lines 375–90 is therefore the following:

> I have pondered on the downfall of men's lives, and it seems to me that it is not the bent of men's minds that makes them go wrong, for they are many of them right-minded enough;

7. 'Some Problems of Text and Interpretation in the *Hippolytus*', *CQ* xviii (1968), 11–43.

no, this is how we must look at it: we understand what is right and realize it, but we fail to carry it out, some out of laziness, others instead because they set some pleasure in front of virtue; and there are many pleasures in life – long hours of talking, and idleness (a pleasant evil); and shame-fastness. Of this there are two kinds: one no ill thing, but the other a burden on a house. If we could be sure of what was in place, then there would not be two of them spelt with the same letters. Since then these are in fact my views, there is no charm that could have made me pervert them and be reversed in what I thought.

This translation rests on several important points. (1) Words which imply moral values are to be taken in an ethically absolute sense: e.g. τὸ καλόν as 'virtue'; πράσσειν κακίον[α] (reading Schmid's emendation of κακίον' for κάκιον) is 'do wrong', not 'fare badly'; the γνώμη is the seat of volition as well as knowledge; τὰ χρήστ' and διέφθαρται βίος imply respectively moral good and moral corruption based on Phaedra's guilty desires. (2) ἡδονὴν... ἄλλην τιν' is an example of the 'something else, namely...' idiom found for example in Pl. *Phd.* 110e: καὶ λίθοις καὶ γῇ καὶ τοῖς ἄλλοις ζῴοις τε καὶ φυτοῖς. (3) αἰδώς is Phaedra's moral flaw and αἰδώς... οὐ κακή recalls the Hesiodic description of αἰδώς (*Op.* 318) as that which both 'greatly harms and helps men'. There is there-fore a break in Phaedra's syntax at the beginning of 385 when she turns from the listing of pleasures (μακραί τε λέσχαι καὶ σχολή, τερπνὸν κακόν) to αἰδώς τε, which is not a pleasure but merely something wrongfully preferred to τὸ καλόν. (4) εἰ δ' ὁ καιρὸς ἦν σαφὴς / οὐκ ἂν δύ' ἤστην ταῦτ' ἔχοντε γράμματα refers to the difficulty human beings have in distinguishing between the two kinds of αἰδώς: 'The distinction is blurred and the two shade into one another, and so perforce we must use the same name for both' (p. 231).

Willink's main objections to this translation and interpretation are the following: (1) Words like καλός and χρηστός in fact imply for the fifth century the idea of 'success' or the 'good life' rather than abstract ideas of moral right and wrong. Thus, although he admits that the γνώμη embraces 'our notion of moral principles', he believes 'it would be natural for a Greek to evaluate different people's γνώμης φύσις, and variations of an individual's γνώμη in terms of efficient functioning rather than abstract moral values'. Willink therefore insists upon retaining the vulgate πράσσειν κάκιον 'fare badly'. (2) Since ἄλλην τιν' is emphatic, ἡδονὴν... ἄλλην τιν' can only mean that τὸ καλόν is a pleasure, and that men go wrong because they prefer some other pleasure to it. (3) αἰδώς must be included syntactically in the list of pleasures dependent upon ἡδοναὶ πολλαί. (4) It is impossible for αἰδώς to be understood as a cause of wrongdoing. (5) The phrase beginning εἰ δ' ὁ καιρός therefore refers to the difficulty men have in distinguishing between types of pleasure, not types of αἰδώς. Phaedra's ostensible purpose is then, according to Willink, not so much to confess but to justify her 'failure' in life as the unavoidable result of having given priority to one good – αἰδώς in the sense of 'modesty' – over another good – τὸ καλόν in the sense of 'success'.[8]

Willink translates as follows:

> I pondered...upon the manner in which the life of mortals has become imperfect, and it seems to me that they fall short of the good life in a manner unrelated to (their) innate quality of apprehension. At any rate, many people have sound ideas. No – you must view this matter in the following way: good things which we know and apprehend we fail to accomplish, some out of laziness (but) others through having given priority, not to τὸ καλόν, but to some other pleasure. And there are many pleasures in life – long conversations (or 'gossiping') and leisure (or 'time-wasting') and αἰδώς; but pleasures are of two sorts: one is consistent with the good life (οὐ κακή), another (or, 'the other sort') is a handicap; if only we could define the right time-and-place, we should not use the same word for both. This view of life (viz. that failure is to be attributed to goods being mutually irreconcilable) I formed long ago; I hope you will conclude that my γνώμη is

8. I omit reference, for the sake of brevity, to Willink's theory of a persistent *double-entendre* or non-rhetorical level of meaning in the speech which imputes to Phaedra the thought that had she only been able to suppress her αἰδώς she might have had Hippolytus and gotten away with it. For my purposes it is only the surface thought of the speech that matters. To accept Willink on this point, in any case, one must be able to read φαρμάκῳ διαφθερεῖν (389) as 'pervert my (immoral) γνώμη with (salutary) drugs', a meaning for which διαφθείρω is somewhat unsuitable.

δικαία, and that I was unlikely to pervert it in such a way as to become a shameless adulteress.[9]

This interpretation is right, I believe, on two important points. First, ἡδονὴν...ἄλλην τιν' cannot be an instance of the 'something else, namely...' construction. In addition to Willink's point that the use of ἄλλος in an emphatic and following position as here is unexampled in other such constructions, a check of instances[10] shows that the idiom is not used to make direct oppositions or comparisons between things, but only to acknowledge incidentally, so to speak, that a series of things that is different in one respect is alike in others. In this case, therefore, if it is Phaedra's purpose to differentiate ἀργία from ἡδονή, as it must be and as Barrett himself acknowledges, this use of ἄλλος is not simply improbable for stylistic reasons, but contradictory to her intent.[11] Secondly, Willink has rightly rejected the endless and ingenious efforts of scholars to justify Phaedra's choice of αἰδώς as the moral flaw which has brought her to ruin.[12] The Hesiodic αἰδώς describes the stunting of male ambition by the shame of poverty; it is specifically opposed to the θάρσος of a prosperous man. If Phaedra's chief concern in the passage is to protect her chastity the αἰδώς that inhibits male ambition to do bold things cannot be understood as a threat to her in any sense except, remotely, that she has so far lacked the courage to end her troubles by ending her life. But it is difficult to believe, if that failure is the specific self-accusation that Phaedra has in mind, that we find elsewhere in the play no stress on her inability to kill herself, or that she can give such a sense of αἰδώς the peculiar designation of

9. I have used Willink's paraphrase rather than translation of the last sentence in order to provide his exact interpretation at the rhetorical level of these lines.

10. E.g. LSJ II 8, Passow–Crönert v (refs. from Barrett) and Kühner–Gerth 405, n. 1.

11. In defense of Barrett's unexplained rejection of ἀργία as a ἡδονή, it seems obvious that unless Phaedra intends to make (at least for her point here) a categorial distinction between ἀργία and all forms of ἡδονή, she cannot explicate the latter by σχολή without making the already inherent redundancy intolerable. But the attributive use of ἄλλος in a mixed series does not imply such intentional categorical exclusion but its opposite, i.e. that in some sense felt but not expressed by the speaker things which we naturally perceive as different are in fact alike. Thus (*Od.* 1. 132) Telemachus sits apart not from 'the other suitors' but from 'the others [in the hall with him], namely the suitors'.

12. E.g. Dodds (above, n. 6), p. 103, Winnington-Ingram (above, n. 6), p. 178.

ἡδονή. Even in Hesiod, moreover, there are not two kinds of αἰδώς, one of which causes us to do right, the other wrong: there is only one kind, but it is one which, under certain conditions, may make us fail in our ambitions and therefore 'harm' us.

I cannot accept, however, Willink's attempt to construe the text as an assertion of inevitable conflict between the opposing goods of αἰδώς as 'modesty' and τὸ καλόν as 'success'. In effect Willink is repeating the error which he has corrected in the case of the usual treatment of αἰδώς as Phaedra's flaw. The conflict of 'modesty' and 'success' is not a conflict of goods universal in its application like, say, that of respect for society and respect for family in *Antigone*. It is, instead, a conflict that can only have meaning for an ambitious man, not a retiring woman whose consuming interest is to protect her chastity and reputation. It seems implausible, therefore, that Phaedra, who later implies that the γνώμη is the place of justice (427: γνώμην δικαίαν κἀγαθήν) – which in Euripides means primarily reverence for the written and unwritten laws of society – could be advancing the opposition of 'modesty' and 'success' as a conflict beyond the powers of the γνώμη to resolve. Or that she could expect to gain the sympathy of the timid and reputation-conscious chorus by doing so, particularly since 'success' cannot be separated in her case from fulfilling her desires for Hippolytus.

As their translations show, both Barrett and Willink ignore an important problem in Phaedra's logic, one which must be resolved, in my opinion, if we are to understand the text. If Phaedra means by the words εἰ δ' ὁ καιρός and following that she is unable to distinguish between either good and bad use of αἰδώς, or good and bad indulgence in ἡδονή, why does she begin her reflections by saying that most men fail, either morally or otherwise, in a manner not related to their γνώμης φύσις? If, when she says 'many men', her implication is 'I myself and almost everyone else', why does she specifically attribute her difficulties in these subsequent lines to a problem of knowledge? The contradiction cannot be ignored since it reappears at the end of the entire speech, when, as her next to last thought, she offers with seeming approval the *sententia*

μόνον δὲ τοῦτό φασ' ἁμιλλᾶσθαι βίῳ,
γνώμην δικαίαν κἀγαθὴν ὅτῳ παρῇ (426–7).

Once again, if her premise was that no matter who you are life or human nature is such that the quality of your γνώμη has little to do with the outcome of your affairs, why this pious conclusion about the value of a just and good γνώμη?

The only explanation able to remove this difficulty, I believe, is that Phaedra does not include herself among those whose moral success in life is unaffected by the quality of their γνῶμαι. She must regard herself as having succeeded where 'many men' have not, and her speech must therefore be treated as a vindication of the efforts of her γνώμη, not as a confession of their inadequacy. There is only one basis on which Phaedra could make such a claim: she must regard moral success as indistinguishable from preserving her reputation and she must look on herself as so far nearly successful in her efforts to do so despite her destructive passion for Hippolytus. The text supports both ideas and therefore justifies an attempt to read the speech in light of them. First, despite the early despair of the chorus (368) Phaedra's first cries of anguish over her public disgrace come only *after* the nurse has approached Hippolytus. Secondly, εὔκλεια is in fact Phaedra's overwhelming concern in life, as a mere glance at the remainder of the present speech will show. Her earliest concern was silence, not self-correction; she hates, and presumably envies, not women who have obscene passions, but those who succeed in indulging their desires while preserving reputation (413–14); she fantasizes illicit love-making in terms of exposure – τέραμνά τ᾽ οἴκων μή ποτε φθογγὴν ἀφῆ – and points out that nothing could make her take such risks (415–19); she fears the effect of her threatened disgrace on the lives of her children (420–5); and she ends her speech by hoping never to be 'seen' among the evildoers whom time exposes (428–30). Almost nowhere in the remaining lines of this speech does Phaedra speak of her moral responsibilities except in terms of her obligation to defend her reputation.[13] It is, moreover, difficult to imagine words that could place Phaedra more explicitly in the context of a shame culture than those spoken at 403–4:

ἐμοὶ γὰρ εἴη μήτε λανθάνειν καλά
μήτ᾽ αἰσχρὰ δρώση μάρτυρας πολλοὺς ἔχειν.

13. 398–9 must be excepted from this generalization. But εὖ φέρειν, like ἐνέγκαιμ᾽ in 393, shows that she is even here thinking not so much of curing her disease as of controlling her actions.

If we now attempt to apply these two ideas – that Phaedra equates morality with preserving a reputation for chastity and that she believes, therefore, that she has so far committed no wrongs – as assumptions to the opening lines of the speech, it will be seen that they impose three things on the text. First of all, the four terms of value in the early part of the text must now be colored primarily by concern for reputation: διέφθαρται βίος as 'ruin one's reputation in life'; πράσσειν κάκιον as 'fare badly' in the sense of 'do what is bad for reputation'; τὰ χρήστ' as 'what is good for reputation'; and τὸ καλόν as essentially 'good name' itself, an idea well supported by the use of καλός elsewhere in the play, e.g. 487, 706, 709. These connotations have the desirable effect of eliminating the problem of the volitional or moral aspect of the γνώμη, emphasized by Phaedra herself when she describes the γνώμη as δικαία. For these terms of value are now able to embrace a 'moral' problem appropriate to the volitional responsibility of the γνώμη without acquiring absolute moral values of a kind unsuitable for the fifth century, and without at the same time employing the awkward expedient of having the chastity-minded Phaedra describe her morality in terms of male ambition for conspicuous 'success' in life. Secondly, the sentence beginning εἰ δ' ὁ καιρός must be translatable in a way that does not indicate an admission of mental or moral confusion on Phaedra's part. Thirdly, if τὸ καλόν implies to Phaedra a 'good name' based on avoiding public disgrace, it is evident that αἰδώς can in no way conflict with τὸ καλόν. This implies that we do not have in μακραί τε λέσχαι καὶ σχολή...αἰδώς τε, as Willink holds, a list of good and bad pleasures all of which are opposed to τὸ καλόν in the sense of the 'good life' or 'success', but a list of good and bad pleasures defined as good or bad by whether or not they contribute to τὸ καλόν or 'good name'. In making the distinction between the two kinds of pleasure Phaedra's tone of voice thus becomes almost didactic and assertive rather than confessional. In effect, she is giving us a simple version of the attempt by late-fifth-century thinkers to define ἡδονή and to distinguish between true and false pleasure, as attested for example in Democritus (Β 207: ἡδονὴν οὐ πᾶσαν, ἀλλὰ τὴν ἐπὶ τῷ καλῷ αἱρεῖσθαι χρεών) [14] and, significantly for this passage I believe, in fragment Α 19 of Prodicus where,

14. Cf. Β 189.

according to Aristotle, Prodicus attempts to differentiate names for pleasure.[15]

It is this topical discussion of the nature and definition of ἡδονή to which Phaedra applies herself, I believe, from οἱ δ' ἡδονὴν προθέντες to ταῦτ' ἔχοντε γράμματα. Her point is not that she is bewildered by the nature of true ἡδονή but that she is quite certain what it is – τὸ καλόν in the sense of 'good name'. If the distinction between names were clear (hence the importance of the alleged discussion of ἡδονή by Prodicus) the term ἡδονή would only be applied to those things that are 'morally' right. Phaedra's thought is thus somewhat associative and indirect, a pattern typical of passages constructed like this one on gnomic sayings, but nevertheless sensible. (1) Most people know what is right (i.e. they have a 'just' γνώμη that is able to make moral as well as intellectual discernments) but they still come to ruin because they lack the ability to do what the γνώμη tells them, either from sloth, or because they succumb to self-indulgent forms of pleasure. (2) It is a fact – which most people presumably know – that the term ἡδονή embraces both things that are good for us (and our reputations) and things that are utterly destructive. (3) It would be appropriate therefore not to apply the same term ἡδονή to things as diverse as self-indulgence and reputation. (Whether or not her implication on the last point is that people use the inconsistency of language to excuse their lapses, she in any case wants us to be clear that she herself has always been concerned for the real ἡδονή of life – a 'good name'.) (4) Therefore, she was not likely to take morally harmful drugs (assuming φάρμάκῳ is not metaphorical) or in any way allow her virtuous ideas to be corrupted on falling in love with Hippolytus, because to do so would permit her reputation to be ruined. (5) Her γνώμη placed a number of alternatives before her as ways of avoiding disgrace (391ff.), all of which she has faithfully tried, even to the point, now, of taking her own life. (6) In concluding (420ff.) her chief desire in life is to leave her children the memory of a mother who was εὐκλεής. Since she expects to do so no one can deny that a just γνώμη, if you are able to adhere to it, enables one to contend with disasters like hers.

15. Cf. also Pl. *Prot.* 358a where Prodicus is mocked by Socrates for distinguishing between ἡδύς, τερπνός, and χαρτός.

With some freedom, in order to illustrate my interpretation, I translate these opening lines of the speech as follows:

> Women of Trozen...under other circumstances I pondered how men's lives (and reputations) are ruined. They seem to me to fail and be disgraced out of proportion to their powers of judgement. For many people have good intentions. No, we must look at it as follows. We know and understand what is good for us, but we fail to do it – some from laziness, some because they put some other 'pleasure' in front of reputation. There are many 'pleasures' in life (that is, many things can be called 'pleasures') – for example, long hours of leisure and gossip (a vice that is merely agreeable) [16] – modesty as well. But 'pleasures' are of two kinds – the one not harmful, the other a burden upon a house. If distinctions between words were clear there would not be two (different) things described by the same letters. Since I happened to recognize this in advance (reading προγνοῦσ') I was not likely to corrupt my outlook by any method, so as to fall into a different state of mind (and thus succumb to false 'pleasures').

One final point. Confessional readings of the text, including confession of failure rather than moral wrong, have never been able to see the logical development of Phaedra's last three lines. If her general point is that we are foredoomed to failure in the struggle against our passions or in the conflicting 'goods' of life, why should she conclude by saying that since she recognized this fact she did nothing to indulge herself? If she had said that despite her recognition of the inevitability of failure she had done nothing we could perhaps understand what she meant. The difficulties which these words present as part of a confession are shown by the extraordinary sensibility imputed to Phaedra by Barrett who (p. 232) believes she is saying that she will not engage after the fact in the intellectual dishonesty of using charms to quiet her sense of guilt for her illicit desires. Most editors write φρονοῦσ' but in fact, as Willink correctly points out, A's reading of προγνοῦσ' is an

16. This list of pleasures is, of course, a curious one. If we regard τὸ καλόν as reputation then it is possible that they are selected as particular instances of 'pleasures' in which one is tempted to reveal things about oneself detrimental to reputation. To perform these lines successfully the actor should presumably pause for a moment after κακόν.

unlikely corruption and the relationship of τυγχάνω φρονοῦσ' to ἔμελλον is awkward. If Phaedra's point is, as I believe, that she has always known what is right and in addition has always *done* what is right with respect to her reputation then προγνοῦσ' is now not only a workable but an essential reading. The logic of her view is simply that a virtuous woman who has always realized the importance and difficulties of protecting her reputation is not likely even under the duress of passion to have taken drugs or used charms capable of corrupting her honorable intent.

Insofar as these arguments are correct it is apparent that in this speech Phaedra believes herself to have acted in a morally proper fashion and that her conception of morality must therefore be primarily concern for εὔκλεια. This seems, furthermore, a dramatically feasible interpretation of the speech, since neither her protestations of innocence nor her failure to respond directly in her generalizing statements to the immediate crisis of exposure that surrounds her is unconventional in a tragic protagonist under stress. Although I do not wish to undertake an interpretation of the entire play, objections to this explication of the speech based on other lines of the play must be briefly mentioned – most notably Phaedra's reply (317) to the nurse, who asks whether she has blood on her hands, that χεῖρες μὲν ἁγναί, φρὴν δ' ἔχει μίασμά τι, and her plea to the nurse later not to speak things that are αἰσχρά or she will be caught by exactly that which she is trying to flee (505–6). For Phaedra to apply the terminology of pollution to her φρήν is unusual to say the least, and Adkins[17] notes that this passage and the approximate repetition of it in E. *Or.* 1604 are the only occurrences of the idea in Greek tragedy. Although the line obviously cannot be dismissed as irrelevant to the present inquiry it is extremely difficult to know what precisely is meant and to what degree the phrase indicates a new awareness of ideas like conscience and internalization of guilt. Until we can say what kind of inner or abstract moral self is defined by the metaphor of religious pollution – which can, of course, occur involuntarily and be removed through acts of ritual – we must be reluctant to base much of our understanding of the play on it.[18] Phaedra's demonstrated

17. A. W. H. Adkins, *Merit and Responsibility* (Oxford 1960), p. 114, n. 29.
18. As in three passages that might be taken to imply inner guilt: ἔα μ' ἁμαρτεῖν· οὐ γὰρ εἰς σ' ἁμαρτάνω (323), and two uses of ψυχή (159–60 and

fear of succumbing to her desires in 505–6, on the other hand, merely points out that at the time of the great speech she has *not* yet done wrong in her own eyes, and that even when she considers moral failure an imminent possibility she still talks of it in terms of reputation, not abstractions. Indeed, whenever Phaedra talks of right and wrong in the rest of the play it is in terms of reputation (e.g. 487, 499, 715–21); and in 488–9 she appears to recapitulate the precise language of her speech with a pun on καλός, but this time to the effect specifically that words that are not truly καλοί, i.e. concerned with reputation, allow one to follow mere τερπνά into δύσκλεια. The play as a whole cannot be said to show that Phaedra regards herself as a morally divided person or that her values should be thought to go beyond a conventional respect for εὔκλεια. If anything, what Phaedra says elsewhere tends to reinforce the simpler view of her which we have taken on the basis of her speech.

To return now to the question of the alleged Socratic reference from which we began, it must be said that although Phaedra's words follow the form of a response to the Socratic paradox, and are thus, in a limited sense, an answer to it (no longer, of course, a dialogue proper since Phaedra is proposing herself as a model of one who both knows and *does* what is right) her statement that people often fail in a manner out of keeping with the quality of their γνῶμαι is so rooted in a non-Socratic conception of morality and the self that Socrates cannot reasonably be seen as its inspiration. While Socrates would assume that, properly informed, Phaedra's γνώμη ought to forestall her destructive passion for Hippolytus, Phaedra, if our analysis of her speech is correct, thinks only that it ought to prevent her passion, for which she admits neither guilt nor responsibility, from producing tangible results like harm to her reputation. The difference between these views can hardly be considered insignificant. Phaedra's tendency to identify the reputation for virtue with the substance of it – something that can only have seemed grotesque to Socrates – necessarily ties her to a traditional view of the self in Greek literature that

504–5). The context of the first shows that the 'sin' Phaedra has in mind is suicide, not passion, and both instances of ψυχή refer to it as the seat of erotic passion, a usage familiar in Greek from Sappho (LP 62. 7–8) on, and therefore of no exceptional importance in this play.

extends back ultimately, of course, to Homer. As has been repeatedly discussed, figures in the Homeric poems lack as a self-conception the sharply defined idea of a single psychological or volitional self, frequently look upon violent or erroneous impulses as other than self-generated, and objectify mental processes in a way that weakens their predictability with the result that the 'self' tends to be defined by highly tangible things – by what actually happens to one irrespective of intent, by possessions, by an extraordinary physical or mental characteristic, and most importantly by the opinion of others.[19] Although scholars have largely accepted these aspects of psychological self-conception in Homer they have tended to ignore their persistence in the later literary tradition.[20] I would suggest that with her demonic view of ἔρως,[21] her temporary insanity, her sometime interest in curative drugs, her emphatic denial of responsibility for her passion (e.g. 319), and above all her concern to mask rather than overcome her disease, Phaedra is not altogether distant from the psychologically volatile Homeric warrior activated by unstable and unpredictable forces like μένος, θυμός and ἄτη. And if, like him, she is obliged to base her conception of self on the more stable reality of deeds and the opinion of others, her obsession with her good name is understandable. Aphrodite's assertion of her limitless power in the prologue, usually dismissed as a mere framework for the true psychological drama, is thus bound to the substance of the play by the reiterated theme of εὔκλεια.

In this context of unstable, unpredictable, and sometimes demonic psychological forces it is obvious that the Socratic para-

---

19. M. P. Nilsson, 'Götter und Psychologie bei Homer', *Arch. f. Rel.* XXII, 363ff. H. Fränkel, *Dichtung und Philosophie des frühen Griechentums* (New York 1951), E. R. Dodds, *The Greeks and the Irrational* (Berkeley 1951), ch. 1, B. Snell, *Discovery of the Mind* trans. T. G. Rosenmeyer (Cambridge, Mass. 1953), ch. 1, and more recently E. L. Harrison, 'Notes on Homeric Psychology', *Phoenix* XIV (1960), 63–80, as well as J. Russo and B. Simon, 'Homeric Psychology and the Oral Epic Tradition', *Journal of the History of Ideas*, XXIX (1968), 483–98.

20. E.g. Dodds, *Greeks and the Irrational*, pp. 28ff.

21. See A. Rivier, 'L'élément démonique chez Euripide jusqu'en 428', *Fondation Hardt, Entretiens* VI (1960), 45ff. who traces ἔρως as a frequent motif in plays of the years 440–430 and sees it portrayed as both human and divine, that is, 'demonic'. It is difficult to face moral responsibility by halves, however, and in terms of the Socratic demand for a responsible moral self any infection of human judgement by non-human forces is surely inadmissible.

dox – however, precisely, we understand it from Plato – can have little or no meaning. Only if we define the 'self' as a single, finite, and continuous psychological entity capable of containing the interaction of reason and emotion, thereby giving us responsibility for the control of our emotions, can we begin to place moral success in something as intangible as the condition of the psychological life, something internal and personal as opposed to external and social, and thus allow Phaedra to examine herself in Socratic terms. To the extent that Phaedra's view of herself remains traditional, reason and passion must appear to her mind as forces that either are, or are capable of becoming, discontinuous. In her view her problem is not that her reason is insufficient to overcome her passion, and that she is unavoidably responsible for that deficiency, but that, as Agamemnon pleads in *Iliad* xix, it does not even engage her passion in a genuine contest. Of course this position can be overstated even for Homer, but it represents a potential model on which the psychological self-conceptions of any pre-Socratic Greek mind could fix, and to the degree that it is accepted by Phaedra – and her preoccupation with εὔκλεια indicates that that degree is considerable – she is surely incapable of a meaningful dialogue with Socrates. If Euripides did, in fact, have Socrates as his inspiration when he wrote these lines we must ask why he placed his 'response' in such a traditional and inappropriate context.

Finally, to turn to the question of 'psychological' drama as described at the outset, the fact that Phaedra probably does not assume a proportional relationship between reason and passion or define her moral success in terms of a psychological 'self' must also undermine the belief of critics that she provides us with a particularly blatant statement of human responsibility for the events of life, and in particular for the disastrous events of drama. Not only do we now have in Phaedra's defense of her actions an explicit statement by her that she does *not* consider herself to have done any 'wrong' at the time of her speech, it is clear, as Rivier (above, n. 21) has pointed out and as the argument of the preceding paragraphs has suggested, that her supposedly guilty desires are something for which Phaedra cannot really feel responsibility in the sense desired. And since she does not she can be said to be the subject of psychological drama – that is, a play in which the tragic

situation is thought to arise from psychological forces in the protagonist that are entirely human and therefore culpable – only if
we are willing to assign to the play as a whole or to its author,
somewhat ironically perhaps, an attitude towards the human
personality that is essentially antithetical to that of Phaedra herself. Her world, if we have read her words correctly, is one of
shame, not guilt, and accordingly her story must invite us to consider once again how things happen ἀέλπτως.

Euripides' *Iphigenia in Aulide* 1–163 (in that order)

BERNARD M. W. KNOX

WHEN MURRAY,[1] following England's example,[2] printed the iambic trimeters before the anapaests in what was to become the standard text, and so presented generations of students with two incomplete prologues (imposing on the nonconformist much page-turning and mental gymnastics) he was simply reflecting the almost unanimous consensus of European scholarship. Even since Musgrave in 1762 expressed doubts about the anapaests[3] and suggested that two and a half lines cited by Aelian (*Hist. Anim.* VII. 39) from 'Euripides' Iphigenia' came from a genuine, lost prologue, the great figures of European scholarship had wrestled with the problem in languages ancient and modern. Musgrave's championship of the Aelian fragment as part of a lost prologue was soon (for obvious reasons)[4] abandoned,[5] but his attack on the form of the

1. G. Murray, *Euripidis Fabulae* III (Oxford 1909).
2. E. B. England, *The Iphigenia at Aulis of Euripides* (London 1891), p. xxv. 'I have in the arrangement of the text endeavoured to restore the "erratic block" to its original position though I cannot hope to remove all traces of its long sojourn on foreign soil, nor to efface the scars which its intrusion has left in its unnatural position. That is, I have printed the iambics first and left a lacuna in the middle of the anapaests.' Hartung (*Euripidis Iphigenia in Aulide*, Erlangen 1837) had previously rearranged the text of the prologue, but in a more eccentric manner: 49–109, 1–48, 110–14, 115–63 with minor transpositions and lacunae.
3. S. Musgrave, *Exercitationum in Euripidem Libri Duo* (Leyden 1762), pp. 25ff.
4. Musgrave himself realized that such a speech made by Artemis to Agamemnon in the prologue would make nonsense of the subsequent action; he offered the rather feeble suggestion that 'fieri...potest ut quae citavit Aelianus ad Agamemnonem vel absentem vel non audientem dicta sint' (26).
5. It is difficult to see how it could have formed part of an epilogue either, unless the whole of the final messenger speech in our text is a later addition. However, Page's brilliant discussion (*Actors' Interpolations in Greek Tragedy* (Oxford 1934), pp. 196–9) shows that even the last part of the speech (1578ff.), which is usually dismissed as Byzantine forgery, contains enough good whole lines and left-hand line beginnings to suggest that it is rather a Byzantine attempt to restore a faded and damaged page of an ancient codex (though Page thinks the original was fourth-century or later, not Euripidean). He dis-

traditional opening was pressed home by other scholars with new and sharper weapons. Explanations varied (two editions,[6] two separate plays,[7] a manuscript left unfinished by Euripides and completed by his son[8]) as did tastes (some saw Euripides' hand in the trimeters and some in the anapaests) but agreement was almost universal[9] that the prologue in its traditional form could not be Euripidean, that the same man could not have written both anapaests and iambics to run in their present sequence.

Since Murray's text was published, this point of view has been reaffirmed (with some new arguments and a judicious pruning of the old) by two acute and learned critics, D. L. Page[10] and E. Fraenkel.[11] Their two independent discussions – Fraenkel (1956) does not mention Page (1934) – present what may be regarded as the definitive indictment of the prologue; it seems unlikely that

misses the lines quoted by Aelian as non-Euripidean; his main reasons are that 'φίλαις is the adjective of a much inferior poet' and that 'there are only two parallels to σήν prospective at the end of an iambic in Eur., Alk. 658, Hik. 1010...in each of these two the sequent noun follows immediately at the beginning of the next verse' (p. 200). It must be conceded that φίλαις is weak and tasteless but the second argument will not hold water. W. Morel in *Ph. W.* (1935), 401ff. produced a parallel to the Aelian passage with ἐμήν, but closer parallels lie ready to hand. *Hec.* 405 and *IA* 1202 both end with prospective σόν not followed immediately by its noun and *Alc.* 1072 ends with a σήν which looks forward to its noun (γυναῖκα) at the beginning not of the next trimeter but the one after that.

6. A. Boeckh, *Graecae Tragoediae Principum etc.* (Heidelberg 1808), pp. 214ff.

7. One by Euripides and one by Euripides junior (H. Zirndorfer, *De Euripidis Iphigenia Aulidensi*, Marburg 1838).

8. A. Matthiae, *Euripidis Tragoediae et Fragmenta* vol. VII (Leipzig 1823), p. 326. 'Hanc fabulam quae non vivo Euripide sed post eius mortem demum acta sit, ab auctore imperfectam et inchoatam relictam esse, ita ut nonnulla quidem cum cura elaborata essent, alia vero secundis curis relicta, nonnulla etiam fortasse bis diverso modo scripta, quae deinde auctor retractans ea eligeret quae maxime probaret; quae reperiri poterant, ea deinde ab Euripide minore ita coagmentata esse ut iusta fabula agi posset.'

9. Two outstanding exceptions to the general trend were Henri Weil, *Sept Tragédies d'Euripide* (Paris 1879) and C. G. Firnhaber, *Euripides Iphigenia in Aulis* (Leipzig 1841). Weil's defense of the prologue (309ff.) is rather dogmatic and he falls back on an inane explanation of the contradiction he thought inherent in 105ff. and 124–5 (on which see below). Firnhaber (xxivff.) gives an excellent summary of the argument up to his time. More recently the prologue has been defended by W. H. Friedrich, 'Zur Aulischen Iphigenie', *Hermes* 70 (1935), 86ff.

10. *Actors' Interpolations*, pp. 138–40.

11. 'Ein Motiv aus Euripides in einer Szene der Neuen Komödie', *Studi in Onore di Ugo Enrico Paoli* (Firenze 1956), pp. 293–304.

even the most careful scrutiny will discover fresh grounds for con-
demnation.[12] The prosecution may well rest content with its case;
what follows is a plea for the defense, which in the course of a
critical examination of the arguments against authenticity, draws
attention to some significant structural features which seem to have
been overlooked.[13]

The counts against the manuscript prologue, old and new, great
and small, may be conveniently summarized and listed as follows,
numbered from 1 to 11.

(1) There is no parallel in fifth-century tragedy for a prologue
which opens with anapaestic dialogue.

(2) There is, *a fortiori*, no parallel for a prologue consisting of
anapaestic dialogue with an expository iambic speech inserted
in it.

(3) The transition from anapaests to iambics (48–9) is extremely
clumsy.

(4) The text contains major corruptions which come close to
producing unintelligibility (especially 107).

(5) The anapaests and iambics are incoherent (107 and 124
especially irreconcilable).

(6) Anapaests and iambics repeat the same material (35–48 ∼
107–14).

12. H.-M. Schreiber, *Iphigenies Opfertod* (Dissertation, Frankfurt-am-Main
1963), discusses the prologue at some length and rejects it in its present form,
but apart from polemic against Friedrich and Page does not add anything to
the argument. M. Imhof, *Bemerkungen zu den Prologen der sophokleischen und
euripideischen Tragodien* (Winterthur 1957), rejects the iambic passage as post-
Euripidean because it does not measure up to the artistic standards he discovers in his valuable analysis of the Euripidean prologues. 'Es fehlt ihr die
lebendige rhythmisch gegliederte, in Wellen an die Gegenwart heranführende
Gedankenbewegung. Das ist ein rein erzählende, sachlich vorbereitende,
exponierende Prologrede, schon stärker aus der Illusion herausfallend als bei
Euripides' (104). But this criticism has point only if the iambic passage is
treated as a separate unit (in which case it also has to be considered incomplete);
as a narrative speech inserted into 'einer dialogisch-anapästischen Szene von
stark stimmungshaftem Charakter' (105) it cannot and should not be judged by
criteria appropriate for complete iambic prologues.

13. The argument on both sides is limited to internal evidence; early citations
are rare. The anapaests were known to Chrysippus and Machon. Murray's
apparatus cites Arist. *Rh.* III. 11 for v. 80 in the trimeters but Fraenkel
(p. 302, n. 3) reminds us that τοὐντεῦθεν οὖν in that passage was introduced by
Victorius from the Euripides line; the rest, as Fraenkel judiciously remarks,
'may, with slight lapse of memory, refer to *IA* 80, but certainly does not have to'.

(7) Crude imitation of other Euripidean passages betrays the interpolator's hand in the iambics (73ff., 112ff.).

(8) The opening lines of the iambics are clearly intended as the opening lines of the play.

(9) Agamemnon's decision to read the letter to the old man is unmotivated (contrast *IT* 76off.).

(10) The text of letters in tragedy should be given in iambics, not, as in 115–16, 118–23, in anapaests.

(11) Unusual vocabulary, especially μεταγράφω 108.

This is an impressive bill of attainder, but it is not as damning as it at first appears, for Fraenkel and Page, though they have added new items to the list, have seriously weakened, if not destroyed, the cogency of some of the old arguments.

(i) THE UNPARALLELED ANAPAESTIC DIALOGUE OF THE OPENING LINES

This is what originally aroused Musgrave's suspicions.[14] He rejected the obvious answer, that *Rhesus* has such a prologue,[15] with a reference to the *hypothesis* of that play which speaks of not one, but two, iambic prologues, now lost.[16] There is in any case some ground for thinking that the *Rhesus* we possess may not be the play Euripides wrote;[17] to rely on this parallel would clearly be a desperate resort. But there *is* a firm parallel for a Euripidean anapaestic prologue in dialogue form: the *Andromeda*, produced in

14. Loc. cit. (n. 3), p. 26, 'Accedit etiam quod systema Anapaesticum nusquam alibi ab Euripide in initio Tragoediae positum sit.'

15. Similar, but not, as W. Ritchie (*The Authenticity of the Rhesus of Euripides*, Cambridge 1964, pp. 102f.) points out, comparable.

16. The hypothesis attributed to Aristophanes of Byzantium however clearly refers to the text we have: ὁ χορὸς συνέστηκεν ἐκ φυλάκων Τρωικῶν, οἳ καὶ προλογίζουσι.

17. Ritchie's careful and instructive examination of the whole problem leads him to the conclusion that the play we have is indeed the *Rhesus* of Euripides and that it was written very early in his career, in fact before the *Alcestis* (438). His analysis of style and vocabulary demonstrates that many of the objections along these lines were ill-informed or purely subjective; the demonstration still retains much validity after the searching criticism of this part of the book by E. Fraenkel in *Gnomon* 37 (1965), 228ff. His book has put the question of authenticity on a sounder, more objective basis, but it has not settled it. Even if it had, the *Rhesus* would not be a relevant parallel for the *IA* prologue, for even Ritchie believes that it started with a trimeter prologue, now lost.

412. The Ravenna scholiast to Aristophanes' *Thesmophoriazusae* informs us that the anapaestic lines ὦ νύξ ἱερά κτλ.[18] were the beginning of the prologue, τοῦ προλόγου 'Ανδρομέδας εἰσβολή.[19] G. Dindorf first cited this passage in connection with the *IA* prologue,[20] and Welcker accepted it, but, as Fraenkel points out, the great authority of Wilamowitz (who to the end of his life defended his friend Carl Robert's support of Hartung's idea that *Andromeda* must have begun with an iambic prologue spoken by Echo)[21] had such overriding influence that 'for many representatives of modern research' the fact revealed by the Aristophanic scholium 'ceased to exist'.

Fraenkel has rightly reasserted its validity and he justly remarks, on the idea that Echo could speak the prologue, that 'a Greek knew Echo all too well to imagine that one whose nature is such that she is incapable of saying anything except to answer could once for a change speak first'.[22] He emphasizes the vital point that Andromeda's opening anapaests were not a 'monody' (as they are sometimes described)[23] but part of 'an anapaestic duet'; the fact that Echo's part in the exchange was limited to repetition does not alter the fact that the play began with anapaestic dialogue and so gives us a precedent for the anapaestic dialogue of *IA*. It is as a matter of fact a much bolder experiment than the dialogue between Agamemnon and the old man; the Andromeda–Echo dialogue must have walked along the bare edge of the ridiculous and Aristophanes did not have to push it very hard to produce the hilarious parody scene in the *Thesmophoriazusae*.

18. They appear to be 'melic' anapaests (for which see the excellent description in A. M. Dale, *The Lyric Metres of Greek Drama*[2] (Cambridge 1968), pp. 5off.).

19. Fraenkel (p. 304) rightly rejects suggestions that εἰσβολή may not mean 'the opening line' and refers to Λ. *Fr.* 143 N.[2] Further confirmation of his point is to be found in the Venetus scholia to Ar. *Ran.* 1 (p. 274, l. 27 Dübner) εὐθὺς ἐν τῇ εἰσβολῇ διαβάλλει τούς τε κωμῳδούς κτλ. and 1219 Σθενεβοίας δὲ ἡ ἀρχή. διαβάλλει δὲ τὴν ὁμοειδίαν τῶν εἰσβολῶν τῶν δραμάτων.

20. According to Firnhaber (xxvi) it was E. Müller (1838), but Fraenkel points out that the third volume of the Dindorf edition of Euripides (in which the parallel is cited) has a preface dated 1837.

21. For references to Welcker, Hartung, Robert and Wilamowitz see Fraenkel's notes 3 to 6 on p. 303.

22. 'L'idée est plaisante' says Weil (p. 309, n. 2) of Hartung's proposal.

23. E.g. England (p. xxii) 'This passage is a monody'. The incredible proof he gives is that Mnesilochus in the Aristophanic parody says ὦ 'γάθ' ἔασόν με μονῳδῆσαι to Euripides.

(2) THE LACK OF PARALLEL FOR A PROLOGUE
    CONSISTING OF ANAPAESTIC DIALOGUE INTERRUPTED
    BY AN IAMBIC SPEECH

It cannot be denied that there is no parallel at all for an
anapaestic dialogue interrupted by an iambic speech and then
resumed, all this in the prologue. Hermann referred to the delayed
expository prologues in Plautus[24] (*Cistellaria, Miles*) and of course
the same thing occurs in Aristophanes (*Equites, Vespae* etc.) and
Menander (*Perikeiromene*). The parallels from Aristophanes may
be discarded at once, for they involve a characteristically Aristophanic rupture of the dramatic illusion, a specific reference or
appeal to the audience, unthinkable in tragedy. The Menandrian
and Plautine instances are not contemporary, nor are they cogent
parallels;[25] they present a prologue speech delivered in a separate
scene by a new speaker, whereas the Euripidean opening involves
not only a movement from dramatic exchange to expository narrative and back again in one short scene but also a corresponding
alternation of meters. It should be frankly admitted that there is
nothing in the extant remains of fifth-century tragedy which will
make it easier for us to accept the uncompromising novelty of this
experiment. If it is genuine Euripides, it is a bold departure from
'the form of opening he consistently employed, whose stereotyped
use is attested by the ancient witnesses'.[26]

However it is a departure for which in this particular case
compelling motives can be adduced. If Euripides planned to begin
the play with an anapaestic dialogue designed to reveal the
torment in Agamemnon's soul by dramatic rather than expository

---

24. *Euripidis Iphigenia in Aulide* (Leipzig 1831), p. x, 'Neque ea res sine
exemplo videtur fuisse quum etiam in Plauti fabulis, quae ad mediae sunt
comoediae similitudinem factae, quaedam prologum non habeant in ipso
initio.'

25. For a discussion and defense of the use of parallels from comedy see
Friedrich, pp. 92–3 and M. Andrewes, 'Euripides and Menander', *CQ* 18
(1924), 8–9.

26. W. Nestle, *Die Struktur des Eingangs in der Attischen Tragödie* (Stuttgart
1930), p. 133. He is discussing the *Andromeda* prologue, which he does not
believe can have begun with anapaests. (He does not attempt to discuss the
opening of *IA*, 'weil die sich auf die Form ihres Eingangs beziehenden Fragen
nur in Zusammenhang mit den übrigen Schwierigkeiten des Stücks erörtert
werden können' (p. v).)

technique, he was faced with the problem that this play, above all others, needed a full expository speech as well.[27] Not only was it based on a myth known to the audience in many different versions, it also presented a fast-moving complicated plot which was kept in motion by a succession of sudden changes of mind in the principal characters[28] and depended for its effect, in some of the most exciting scenes, on the participants' knowledge or ignorance of the real situation in which they were acting. Euripides had to make sure that the audience was given, right at the start, a complete and precise understanding of the initial situation; an expository speech of some length was indispensable. If the experimental anapaestic dialogue of the *Andromeda* was to be repeated, this time to reveal the dilemma of Agamemnon, only Agamemnon could deliver the expository speech. To put it first would destroy the dramatic and poetic power of the anapaests;[29] to put it after them was clearly impossible, since the scene must end with Agamemnon's new instructions to the old man, and the old man's exit with the letter. There was only one place to put the expository speech – where it is.

There are some significant structural features of the prologue (discussed below) which suggest strongly that the present arrangement is the work not of a clumsy interpolator but of a conscious artist who took great pains to reinforce and normalize the unprecedented form which he invented to answer his dramatic needs. And after all, we cannot be sure that it *was* unprecedented; we have only a remnant of fifth-century tragedy. 'For one who works in a ruin', says Grooneboom, discussing a similar problem, 'it is extremely dangerous to "correct" the scant remains of the building.'[30] The objection has been made that Euripides, though an

27. For an eloquent presentation of this point see Friedrich, pp. 87–8.

28. Cf. B. Snell, *Aischylos und das Handeln im Drama*, Philologus Suppl. xx, 1, pp. 148ff., A. Lesky, *Die griechische Tragödie*[2] (Stuttgart 1958), p. 246, B. M. W. Knox, 'Second Thoughts in Greek Tragedy', *GRBS* 7. 3, 229ff.

29. M. Pohlenz, *Die griechische Tragödie*[2] (Göttingen 1954), ii, p. 183: 'Diesem [i.e. the anapaestic dialogue] noch eine Prologrede nach dem üblichen Schema vorauszuschicken war dann kaum möglich. Hätte Agamemnon selbst zuerst in ruhig-sachlichem Tone zum Publikum gesprochen, musste die folgende Schilderung seine Seeleszustandes ihre ganze Wirkung verlieren.'

30. P. Groeneboom, *Aischylos' Perser* (Göttingen 1960), Part 2, p. 30. He is discussing O. Müller's widely followed transposition of 93–101 to a position after 102–13. 'Es mag auf den ersten Blick verlockender erscheinen die Mesodos nicht nach zwei, sondern – in der Form einer Epode – nach drei Strophenpaaren

innovator in many ways, was a conservative in dramatic form, at least in the larger forms;[31] but this observation stands contradicted by many features of the late plays. If the *Orestes* had not survived intact, who would have dared surmise that one of the most stereotyped, routinely regular of Euripidean dramatic forms – a messenger speech – was in this case couched in astrophic lyric metre and dithyrambic language and put in the mouth of a Phrygian slave?

(3) THE AWKWARDNESS OF THE TRANSITION FROM ANAPAESTS TO IAMBICS (48–9)

This was singled out for criticism as early as Bremi and Welcker and has been a favorite target ever since; the objection finds its most pungent formulation in Fraenkel (p. 298). 'When the king is asked (43ff.) "What is troubling you? What new turn in your affairs? Come, share the story with me..." he cannot possibly (unless of course he exists in a world not of thinking and feeling human beings but of marionettes) reply with the words (49): "Leda daughter of Thestios had three girls..."'

This criticism however ignores the fact that there are many occasions in Greek (and especially in Euripidean) tragedy when the characters seem to modern readers to be speaking more like marionettes than living, feeling human beings. Later in this same play Clytemnestra anxiously demands from Agamemnon detailed information about the pedigree of her prospective son-in-law. 'I know the name of the boy to whom you have given your consent', she says, 'but I would like to know who his father is and where he comes from' (695–6). The answer she gets is: 'Aegina was born daughter to her father Asopus' – an answer beginning *ab ovo* in the same fashion as Agamemnon's answer to the old man. But such

folgen zu lassen, weil drei Strophenpaare in der älteren Dichtung des Aischylos oft ein Ganzes bilden; entscheidend ist dieses der äusseren Form des Liedes entnommene Argument jedoch bei dem spärlichen Vorrat an Vergleichsmaterial nicht: für den, der in einer Ruine arbeitet, ist es äusserst gefährlich die geringen Reste des Gebäudes zu "korrigieren".'

31. Max Imhof (above, n. 12), p. 106: 'Auch die Iphigenie in ihrer dramatischen Beweglichkeit und Lebendigkeit zeigt den neuen Geist, den neuen letzten Stil. Aber in den grossen Formen ist dieser gerade nicht neuernd, sondern archaisierend.'

stichomythic catechisms[32] are not the only type of what appears to us stilted formalism; there is also the beginning of the messenger speech. In the *Orestes*, for example, Electra, informed by the messenger that she and Orestes have been condemned to death, begs him to tell her how they are to die – by stoning? Or will she be allowed to commit suicide? This rather urgent question receives an answer which begins: 'I happened to be just inside the gates on my way in from the countryside...' (866); Electra finally learns that she has narrowly escaped death by stoning some eighty lines later (946). This is, of course, routine technique in Euripidean messenger speeches; no matter how anxious and pressing the inquiry, the messenger begins at the beginning with a narrative sentence that makes it clear he has plenty of time and intends to use it.[33] The regularity of this phenomenon shows that this was a dramatic convention, perfectly familiar to Euripidean audiences, for dealing with a situation in which a direct question required a long narrative answer. But that is precisely the situation created by the insertion of a narrative prologue-type speech in a dialogue. When Euripides decided to open his play with a dramatic dialogue which included an expository narrative a familiar, well-understood convention lay ready to hand.

In any case, the transition is not quite as abrupt as Fraenkel suggests. For the old man continues speaking after asking his question and mentions (46) the name of Tyndareus, which affords a natural transition to Agamemnon's 'Leda' (49).

32. A more extended (and by modern standards of realism even more absurd) example is A. *Supp.* 290ff., where the chorus, challenged to prove its claim of Argive descent, asks the king a series of leading questions to which he supplies unnecessarily full answers; he finally volunteers information without being asked (311) before he himself turns questioner.

33. Cf. e.g. *Ba.* 1041–3, *El.* 772–4, *Andr.* 1083–6, *Hipp.* 1171–3. This abrupt opening which, with no concern for dramatic illusion, ignores the interlocutor's question and insists on telling the story from the very beginning is strictly Euripidean technique. In Sophocles in every case where a long narrative answers a question, there is a preliminary passage (sometimes only one line) which provides a transition from dialogue to narrative. The most striking example is *OT* 1237 (the chorus' question is answered at once, out of time sequence) but cf. also *Aj.* 284, 748, *El.* 680, *Ant.* 1192ff., *Tra.* 749, 899, *OC* 1586.

(4) MAJOR CORRUPTIONS PRODUCING UNINTELLIGIBILITY

The biggest problem is vv. 106–7. 'We alone among the Achaeans know how this matter stands, Calchas, Odysseus and Menelaus.' As Jackson remarks:[34] 'Since not even the shyest of men can
omit himself when tabulating the subjects of a plural verb in the
first person, it is necessary to introduce ἐγώ.' That is not difficult
and the remedy is paleographically acceptable; it was done by
Vitelli, but Murray (following England) reported the emendation incorrectly and Jackson revived the original version:

Κάλχας ᾽Οδυσσεὺς Μενέλεως ⟨ἐγώ⟩ θ᾽· ἃ δ᾽ οὐ
καλῶς τότ᾽, αὖθις μεταγράφω καλῶς πάλιν.[35]

Besides this corrupt passage in the iambics there are two in the
anapaests. In vv. 149–51 sense is restored by the corrections of
Bothe and Blomfield–Wecklein. At 115ff. it seems clear that
Reiske's transposition must be adopted; the old man's λέγε καὶ
σήμαιν᾽ must follow immediately the end of Agamemnon's iambic
speech.

This gives us three passages in 163 lines where the text has to be
restored or rearranged. But in a play which depends solely on LP
(or rather, as Zuntz has shown, on L alone in an intermediate
stage of Triclinian recension),[36] this is not a figure which should
raise doubts about authenticity. The first 81 lines of *Ion*, for
example, have an omitted pronoun (81, cf. *IA* 106) and two lines
(1 and 3) which set textual problems not yet solved – Murray
marks both passages with the obelus. The first 177 lines of *IT*
(which contain anapaests and iambics in roughly the same proportion as the *IA* prologue) make sense and meter in Murray's
text only with the aid of two excisions (142, 146), two insertions
(150, 154), conjectures (omitting obvious and minor corrections)
by Badham (3), Scaliger (58, 118), Canter (62), Markland (125),
Heath (172), Sallier (98), Murray (156–7) and Porson (176) and
the bracketing of 38–9 and 59–60. As if that were not enough,

34. John Jackson, *Marginalia Scaenica* (Oxford 1955), p. 209.
35. 'Neither the enjambement nor αὖθις πάλιν nor the quasi-zeugma (ἃ δ᾽
οὐ καλῶς τότ᾽ – sc. ἔγραψα – αὖθις μεταγράφω) needs any vindication',
Jackson, loc. cit. (n. 34).
36. G. Zuntz, *An Inquiry into the Transmission of the Plays of Euripides* (Cambridge 1965).

Murray labels 134–5 *vix sani*. Compared with these two typical examples from 'alphabetic' plays, the text of the *IA* prologue seems remarkably healthy; as an argument against authenticity, textual corruption is clearly irrelevant.

(5) THE INCOHERENCE OF 107FF. IN THE IAMBICS WITH 124FF. IN THE ANAPAESTS

In 87ff. Agamemnon describes the causes of the agony of indecision which the old man has asked him to explain. Calchas demanded the sacrifice of Iphigenia to Artemis as the price for favorable winds. Agamemnon at first refused and was ready to disband the army but Menelaus persuaded him to obey. Agamemnon sent a letter to Clytemnestra summoning Iphigenia to Aulis on the pretext that she was to marry Achilles. 'Alone among the Achaeans', he says, 'Calchas, Odysseus, Menelaus and I know how this matter stands' (ὡς ἔχει τάδε 106). And now Agamemnon has changed his mind again, and intends to send the old man off with a second letter, countermanding the first.

What exactly is meant by ὡς ἔχει τάδε? The four conspirators share a secret of which the rest of the army and in particular Achilles are ignorant. Clearly the most important thing that has to be kept secret is that the proposed marriage is merely a pretext (ψευδῆ...γάμον 105). But what about the rest of the story? At this point it is not clear from what Agamemnon says whether Achilles and the army think that Iphigenia is coming to Aulis but do not know that the marriage is a mere pretext or whether Achilles and the army do not know anything at all – that they are not even aware Iphigenia has been sent for. Of course it later becomes clear that the second alternative is the correct one, but at this point, for the audience, Agamemnon's words are utterly ambiguous.

And yet one critic after another has assumed the words are clear as day and mean the second and only the second alternative, that Achilles and the army were completely in the dark. Consequently, when the old man, informed of the contents of the new letter, bursts out that Achilles will rise up in anger against Agamemnon because of the loss of his bride, these same critics find an intolerable incoherence, a fresh proof of clumsy patchwork – or else try to defend the passage on the grounds that Agamemnon says 106–7

as an aside (Hermann)[37] or that the old man 'manque un peu
d'attention ou d'intelligence' (Weil). But there is no ground for
such an assumption.[38] At v. 106 some members of the audience
may well have thought that Achilles knew of the proposed marriage, others that he did not, while still others may have realized
that Agamemnon had not committed himself on the point; most
of them, in all probability, did not give the matter a moment's
thought.[39] But the old man's question directs the audience's full
attention to this matter; all of them, those who share the old man's
misunderstanding, those who did not but perhaps now wonder if
they were wrong, those who realized that the question had been left
in the air and those who had not thought about it at all, wait im-
patiently to hear Agamemnon's answer. It is unequivocal this time,
clear as crystal: 'Achilles contributes not his action, just his name;
he knows nothing of the marriage, nothing of what we are doing.'

37. *Euripidis Iphigenia in Aulide* (Leipzig 1831), p. xii 'Agamemno...ea quae
arcana sunt aversus ab sene et submissiore voce ut ille non audiat putandus est
dicere.'

38. W. Friedrich (see n. 9) defends the present form of the prologue but
admits 'Inkonsequenzen' – in particular the clash between 106–7 and 124ff.
However he explains this as a result of the fact that Euripides wavers throughout the play between two different versions of the saga. Here the old man's
question 'hängt...in der Luft' (p. 79) because 'der Dichter hat ihn unwillkürlich
mehr wissen lassen als er wissen kann. Der Alter fragt aus einer un- oder vor-
euripideischen Situation heraus, jedenfalls, um ganz vorsichtig zu reden, aus
einer Situation, die dem Dichter so nahe lag, dass er sich ihrer offenbar
mit Selbstverständlichkeit bediente wenn er sie brauchte.' But this theory of a
different 'Sagenversion die ab und zu in das Drama hineinspukt' (p. 80) merely
explains one inconsistency (for so Friedrich thinks it) by pointing to others and
claiming that the poet is inconsistent throughout; a reference to Tycho von
Wilamowitz' book on Sophocles inevitably follows (p. 81). M. Pohlenz, in his
second edition, came round to the opinion that both anapaests and iambics
were written by Euripides, but finding these two passages 'sachlich unverein-
bar', fell back on the theory that Euripides composed an anapaestic prologue,
then realized that a more complete exposition was needed and composed the
iambics: 'doch ist er nicht mehr dazu gekommen, diese organisch mit dem
ersten Entwurf zu verbinden und innerlich auszugleichen'.

39. Weil's full comment is revealing. 'En disant, au vers 106 sq., que Calchas,
Ulysse et Ménélas étaient seuls dans le secret, Agamemnon entendait que tout le
reste de l'armée ignorait non seulement que le projet de mariage fût un vain
prétexte, mais encore qu'il fût question d'un tel projet et que le roi eût mandé
sa fille. Ceci est évident pour quiconque lit la narration d'Agamemnon avec une
attention réfléchie.' Apart from the fact that even a reading 'avec une attention
réfléchie' does not settle the question at all, the phrase shows that Weil was
thinking of the scholar in his study, not of the audience at the Dionysia.

This is a fact of the utmost importance for Euripides' play and had to be impressed on the audience by the most striking means available. The ground had to be laid for the brilliant scene which was to come later – the meeting of Clytemnestra and Achilles, a scene of Menandrian comedy based on *agnoia* which would have missed its mark, in fact been unintelligible, if the audience had not been made fully aware that Achilles had never heard of the marriage project. Of course, Euripides could have made Agamemnon say explicitly at 106ff. that Achilles knew nothing. But what he has done is to make the point by dramatic exchange rather than expository explanation and so drive it more effectively home.[40]

The temporary ambiguity is not by any means alien to the spirit of Euripidean dramaturgy, for in the prologue scenes of *Hippolytus* and *Ion* Euripides 'is not straightforward...' but 'is concerned...to mislead and mystify without outright misstatement' as Barrett puts it.[41] And the particular technique of this passage, the creation of ambiguity, even possible misapprehension, to produce, by correction, full clarity on a major issue is to be found also in the intellectual dramas of Plato. 'The dramatic misapprehension by the interlocutor is one of Plato's methods for enforcing his meaning', says Paul Shorey, '...the dramatic misunderstanding forestalls a possible misunderstanding by the reader.'[42]

In any case, it speaks volumes for the dramatic viability of the traditional text in this passage that even so severe a critic as Page finds no difficulty in the coexistence of 98ff. and 124ff. – though he does not admire the technique and dismisses 105ff. as an interpolation on other grounds.[43]

40. C. Headlam, *Euripides, Iphigenia in Aulis*[4] (Cambridge 1922) speaks of 'an artistic device for restating a fact on which he wishes to lay special stress'.

41. W. S. Barrett, *Euripides Hippolytos* (Oxford 1964) on v. 42. (The *Bacchae* prologue also 'misleads', cf. vv. 50ff.)

42. P. Shorey, *The Republic of Plato* (Loeb Classical Library, Cambridge, Mass.), vol. II (1935) on 523b and 529a. (He compares also *Lg.* 792b–c.)

43. His reasons for this are given on p. 138. They are: '(1) impossible omission of ἐγώ from 106–7; only violent emendation can restore it. (2) μεταγράφω; word here only in poetry. (3) Indicative εἰσεῖδον very rare in Euripides (v. England). (4) 112–13 owe much to *IT* 760–1. (5) Weak redundancy of ἃ δὲ κέκευθε δέλτος with τἀγγεγραμμέν'. (6) General lameness of the verses.' On (1) see above, on (2) below. As for (3) England was dead wrong, as a glance at the Allen and Italie *Concordance* will show. On (4) see below. The redundancy condemned in (5) is no weaker than that presented by τἀνόντα κἀγγεγραμμέν' in the *IT* passage.

(6) ANAPAESTS AND IAMBICS REPEAT THE SAME
      MATERIAL (ESPECIALLY 35–48 ~ 107–14)

The end of Agamemnon's iambic speech (107–14) repeats much
of the material and some of the words of the concluding lines of
the old man (35–48) which bring the first anapaestic system to a
close. Fraenkel, who thinks that Euripides wrote a complete
anapaestic prologue (stage 1), that someone else later wrote a
complete, but dull, iambic prologue to replace it (stage 2) and that
a third person cut and combined the two to produce what we have
now, sees in these resemblances a proof that the writer of the iambic
prologue (stage 2) simply transposed, as it were, the brilliant
anapaests into the wooden iambics. It is instructive to compare the
analysis of Page. He too posits three authors for the prologue:
Euripides, X and Y. Euripides wrote a complete iambic prologue
(of which we have only part – and 106–14 is not by Euripides), X
(a good poet of the fourth century – 'one thinks of the romantic
atmosphere of Chaeremon') wrote an alternative complete anapaestic prologue (of which we have only part) and Y ('an excellent
editor, no doubt, but a bad poet and a worse dramatist') combined
them in the form preserved in LP, removing some superfluous
anapaests and writing vaguely connective iambics in imitation of
the anapaests (e.g. 110 deliberately copied from the sense of 38,
114 from 45).

There are obviously subjective judgements at work here, but
both critics agree that the verbal resemblances are suspicious. But
it does not seem to have been noticed that the repetitions can be
fully justified; they perform a necessary function. The repetition,
at the end of an expository narrative digression, of the subject
matter and very often the actual words with which the digression
began – ring-composition – is a well-known feature of archaic
style which has been fully explored in Homer, Herodotus and
Aeschylus in a series of publications by W. A. A. van Otterlo.[44]

44. (1) *Beschouwingen over het archaïsche element in den stijl van Aeschylus* (Utrecht
1937) gives examples from Sophocles and Euripides on pp. 23–6 and discusses
the technique in Aeschylus on pp. 76–105. (2) *Untersuchungen über Begriff,
Anwendung und Entstehung der griechischen Ringcomposition* (Amsterdam 1944) is
concerned mainly with Herodotus and Homer. (3) *De Ringkompositie als Opbouw-
principe in de Epische Gedichten van Homerus* (Amsterdam 1948) (with French
résumé pp. 87–92).

His examples from tragedy, however, all consist of single speeches in which the closing repetition and the initial statement which is repeated are both pronounced by the same speaker. This is of course not the case in the passage which concerns us here. But a type of ring-composition in which the closing words of the digression echo the words and matter of the immediately preceding speech which gave rise to it is also to be found in tragedy. In the prologue of Sophocles' *Electra* Orestes ends his long discussion of his mission and his plans for its fulfilment with the words καιρὸς γὰρ ὅσπερ ἀνδράσιν / μέγιστος ἔργου παντός ἐστ᾽ ἐπιστάτης (75–6) which echo the closing lines of the preceding speech of the *paidagogos*: ὡς ἐνταῦθ᾽ ἐμὲν / ἵν᾽ οὐκέτ᾽ ὀκνεῖν καιρός, ἀλλ᾽ ἔργων ἀκμή (21–2).[45] Similarly, in Euripides' *Orestes*, the speech of Apollo which, interrupting action at a point of high excitement, announces the fate and future of the participants, ends (ὅς νιν φονεῦσαι μητέρ᾽ ἐξηνάγκασα 1665) with an echo of the last line of Menelaus' preceding speech (αἷμα μητρὸς μυσαρὸν ἐξειργασμένος 1624). There are many more such passages[46] but these two will suffice to make the point. In both of them the repetition restores dramatic continuity, returning the action to the point at which it was abandoned for exposition. So the last words of Agamemnon's speech, recalling the closing words of the old man, mark the end of the static exposition, the resumption of dramatic action. Once again Euripides solved the technical problem raised by his insertion of an expository speech in a dramatic dialogue by adapting a familiar convention, this one as old as Homer.

(7) REPETITIONS AND IMITATIONS WHICH BETRAY THE HAND OF THE INTERPOLATOR

Fraenkel cites in particular two passages in the iambics: 71ff. and 112ff. The first, a description of Paris (ἀνθηρὸς μὲν εἱμάτων στολῇ / χρυσῷ τε λαμπρὸς βαρβάρῳ χλιδήματι) has often been

45. This repetition seems to have escaped the notice of commentators (even of Kaibel); the only remark on it I have found is G. Schiassi, *Sophoclis Electra* (Firenze 1961): 'La chiusa del discorso di Oreste fa eco a quella del discorso del pedagogo; ritorna il motivo del "momento buono" che è quello dell'azione.'

46. E.g. E. *IT* 258–9 ∼ 337–9, *Ph.* 1087 ∼ 1196, *Tro.* 633 ∼ 681, 352 ∼ 405, *HF* 1254 ∼ 1310, *Supp.* 406 ∼ 425, S. *OT* 582 ∼ 615, *Ant.* 1032 ∼ 1047, 1063 ∼ 1090, A. *P.* 352 ∼ 431, *Ag.* 280 ∼ 316, 550 ∼ 581.

compared with the description of the same person which appears in _Troades_ 991ff. (βαρβάροις ἐσθήμασι / χρυσῷ τε λαμπρόν) but for Fraenkel the relationship between them is dependence, not resemblance. The description of Paris and of the excitement his appearance aroused in Helen is, as Fraenkel says, fully appropriate in Hecuba's speech, 'but', he goes on, 'when the prologue-speaker in _IA_, in his summary of the preceding events, descends to such details as these...the broad depiction of things that are utterly inessential here is completely at odds with Euripidean narrative prologue style'.

It could be argued that since the play's dilemma will finally be solved by Iphigenia's decision to die willingly and so unite the Pan-Hellenic fleet in its determination to sail against the barbarians, this detail is not inessential at all, but rather the first statement of a theme, the contrast between Greek and barbarian, which is given repeated and increasing emphasis throughout the play[47] to prepare our minds for Iphigenia's _coup de théâtre_. But Fraenkel's real objection is that the _IA_ passage is a mere imitation of the lines in _Troades_: 'For the man who wrote εἱμάτων στολῇ etc....the attractiveness of βαρβάροις ἐσθήμασι etc....was irresistible, and that man was certainly not Euripides.' To which the simple answer is that combinations of these words χρυσο-, στολή, λαμπρός and χλιδή in various forms constitute a regularEuripidean cliché – they turn up together again and again (_Ba._ 154 Τμώλου χρυσορόου χλιδᾷ, _Andr._ 2 σὺν πολυχρύσῳ χλιδῇ, 147 κόσμον μὲν ἀμφὶ κρατὶ χρυσέας χλιδῆς, στολμόν τε, _El._ 966 στολῇ λαμπρύνεται, _Hel._ 423–4 λαμπρά τ' ἀμφιβλήματα χλιδάς τε, _Fr._ 688 στολὴν ἰδόντι λαμπρός).[48]

The second passage, vv. 112–13

> ἃ δὲ κέκευθε δέλτος ἐν πτυχαῖς
> λόγῳ φράσω σοι πάντα τἀγγεγραμμένα,

is almost identical with _IT_ 760–1

> τἀνόντα κἀγγεγραμμέν' ἐν δέλτου πτυχαῖς
> λόγῳ φράσω σοι πάντ',

47. Cf. 52, 65, 71, 74, 77, 80, 92, 190ff., 272, 295ff., 308, 324, 350, 370, 410 etc.

48. _Fr._ 7 (N.²) κρεῖσσον δὲ πλούτου καὶ βαθυσπόρου χθονός (from Orion) turns up in Stobaeus with the ending πολυχρύσου χλιδῆς. Cf. also _Rh._ 305–6 πέλτη...χρυσοκολλήτοις τύποις ἔλαμπε.

and for Fraenkel the explanation is simple: the lines in *IA* were 'skrupellos geplündert'. But this judgement overlooks the fact that the language of Attic tragedy from Aeschylus to Euripides uses these same words whenever writing is mentioned: δέλτος, πτυχαί, ἐγγράφω etc. are words which can hardly be avoided, as the following passages make clear: A. *Supp.* 946 πίνακιν...ἐγγεγραμμένα, 947 ἐν πτυχαῖς βίβλων, *Eum.* 275 δελτογράφῳ...φρενί, *PV* 789 ἐγγράφου...δέλτοις, S. *Tr.* 157 δέλτον ἐγγεγραμμένην, 683 ἐκ δέλτου γραφήν, *Fr.* 144 γραμμάτων πτυχάς, E. *IT* 727 δέλτου διαπτυχαί, 763 τἀγγεγραμμένα, 787 τὰν δέλτοισιν ἐγγεγραμμένα, 793 γραμμάτων διαπτυχάς, *IA* 324 τἀγγεγραμμένα, *Fr.* 506. 2–3 ἐν Διὸς δέλτου πτυχαῖς γράφειν. And even λόγῳ φράσω seems to be common Euripidean formula, as appears from *Fr.* 621 φράσαι λόγῳ and *Fr.* 1083.10 λόγῳ φράσαι.

(8) THE OPENING LINES OF THE IAMBICS SUGGEST THAT THIS IS THE BEGINNING OF A PLAY

This argument, often advanced and often rejected, is forcibly restated by Page (p. 139): 'the detail of 49–51 implies that nothing had gone before, e.g. the self-announcement involved in ἐμὴ ξυνάορος is wholly superfluous, especially after τῇ σῇ τ' ἀλόχῳ 46'. But in fact nothing in the way of necessary information *has* gone before; all we know at v. 48 is that Agamemnon is at Aulis, that it is almost dawn and that he has been writing and rewriting a letter in great distress. The opening anapaests have done their job brilliantly – they have created a mood; the speech which now begins will give us the information we need. In any case, the 'self-announcement' involved in the phrase ἐμὴ ξυνάορος, if it is to be the first hint we are given of Agamemnon's identity, is not in line with normal Euripidean practice. In his prologues the opening speakers are identified by this inferential method only when like Medea's nurse (δέσποιν' ἐμὴ Μήδεια 6–7) or the farmer in the *Electra* (ἡμῖν δὲ δὴ δίδωσιν Ἠλέκτραν ἔχειν / δάμαρτα 34–5) they have no name of their own.[49] The phrase is not a 'self-announcement' but (with the following line) the first identification of the imposing and important lady who is to bulk so large in the action of the play.

49. Apollo in *Alcestis* and Silenus in *Cyclops* are identified by inferred self-announcement but in both cases their identity was clear from their costume.

Page's further objections, that in the iambic speech Agamemnon is not addressing the old man and in any case tells him nothing he does not know, apply too rigid a standard of stage realism. Deianira's long prologue speech in *Trachiniae* shows just as little consciousness of the presence of her nurse, who has however listened to it, as her first lines show; Iolaos in the *Heraclidae* tells his children (whom he finally addresses at v. 48) a great many things they must know already, and Amphitryon's account of the woes of Heracles' family in the *Heracles* prologue can scarcely have been news to Megara.

(9) AGAMEMNON'S DECISION TO READ THE LETTER TO THE OLD MAN IS UNMOTIVATED

This objection is as old as Dindorf but is most forcibly stated by Fraenkel. In the corresponding passage in *IT*, he points out, there is an excellent motive for Iphigenia's reading of her letter: Pylades must know the contents in case the letter is lost with the ship at sea – if that were to happen he could keep his solemn oath to deliver the letter only if he knew what it said. 'Here the motivation is fully established', says Fraenkel, ' …but of such a meaningful motivation there is in the corresponding passage of the trimeter prologue not the slightest trace' (p. 301).[50]

No motive is stated but one leaps to mind. The old man is ordered to deliver to Clytemnestra a letter which will surprise and shock her; her questions will be many, sharp and urgent, for the letter gives no reason for Agamemnon's change of plan. If the old man does not know the contents of the letter he may be driven to indiscretions; Agamemnon does not want him to reveal that the marriage of Iphigenia was a fraud, still less that she was to be sacrificed. The mission is a delicate one; the old man, when questioned, must say just what is in the letter, no more, no less – consequently, he must know what it says.

50. Fraenkel's objection unfortunately applies also to the hypothetical complete anapaestic prologue he tries to reconstruct. 'Der Dichter der Anapäste lässt…den alten Mann sagen: "lass mich den Inhalt des Briefs erfahren, damit ich ihn genau wie du ihn geschrieben hast wiedergeben kann (falls der Brief verloren geht)".' But why on earth should the old man be afraid of losing the letter? Unlike Pylades, he is not going by sea; he is supposed to intercept Clytemnestra's chariot (149ff.).

There is a passage in Xenophon's *Cyropaedia* which provides a parallel situation and even some verbal parallels. It was cited by Markland long ago, and England saw its significance, but it is worth quoting again since another relevant passage, further on in Xenophon's text, was overlooked. After a victory of Cyrus over the enemy, won while his commander, King Cyaxares, is feasting, the King sends a messenger to Cyrus rebuking him for his independent action and ordering the recall of his troops. Cyrus detains the messenger and sends a trusted man of his own back with the answer; since he intends to continue independent action the letter calls for diplomatic skill – it has to be conciliatory in tone and firm in purpose. The messenger will have a difficult embassy; the King is angry and he is in any case ὠμός... καὶ ἀγνώμων (IV. 5. 9). Cyrus reads his letter to the messenger (*Cyr.* IV. 5. 26): ἀναγνῶναι δέ σοι καὶ τὰ ἐπιτελλόμενα, ἔφη, βούλομαι, ἵν᾽ εἰδὼς αὐτὰ ὁμολογῇς ἄν τί σε πρὸς ταῦτα ἐρωτᾷ. And then after reading the letter, he says: ταύτην αὐτῷ ἀπόδος, καὶ ὅ τι ἄν σε τούτων ἐρωτᾷ, ᾗ γέγραπται σύμφαθι (ibid. 34). The messenger of Cyrus had a delicate and dangerous mission; it was vital that when questioned he should take the same line as the letter he carried. This is exactly the case of the old man, and the words he uses – ἵνα καὶ γλώσσῃ / σύντονα τοῖς σοῖς γράμμασιν αὐδῶ – correspond to Xenophon's ἵν᾽ εἰδὼς αὐτὰ ὁμολογῇς and still more to ᾗ γέγραπται σύμφαθι.

(10) LETTERS IN TRAGEDY ARE GENERALLY PHRASED IN IAMBIC TRIMETER

This is a new argument, developed by Fraenkel in support of his contention that there was once a complete iambic prologue in existence.

> The composer of the trimeters cannot possibly have intended to have the reading aloud of the letter in anapaests. If there is any form of communication in drama for which according to Greek and for that matter Roman feeling for style the character of plain everyday speech must be preserved and for which accordingly that metre is preferable which, as Aristotle says, partakes most of the nature of τὸ λεκτικόν – it is the letter form (p. 300).[51]

51. Fraenkel refers to his *Iktus und Akzent im lateinischen Sprechvers* (Berlin 1928), p. 93. The examples given there are of course all from Roman comedy.

17   PSI

It follows, he goes on, that the writer of the iambics must have written a complete prologue, containing the reading aloud of Agamemnon's letter in iambic trimeter.

This argument seems to turn in its user's hand, for of course the anapaests, which Fraenkel attributes to Euripides, do contain the text of the letter and Fraenkel, in his reconstruction of the lost anapaestic prologue, retains these lines. It seems to follow that Euripides was perfectly willing to have a letter read aloud in anapaests, but the writer of the trimeters was not: unfortunately the reason given for his reluctance is so general that it would surely have restrained Euripides as well.

But in any case, how many letters are read aloud in extant Greek drama? There seem to be only two certain examples: the anapaestic letter in *IA* and the iambic letter in *IT*.[52] Possibly (though it does not seem to have been suggested) Theseus at *Hipp.* 855–6 is quoting Phaedra's letter; if so we have another iambic letter (two lines long). But the more one considers these two lines, the more they look like what Barrett and other editors assume them to be – the words of Theseus. Clearly the evidence for Fraenkel's generalization, as far as Greek tragedy goes, is slim.

(11) μεταγράφω (108) OCCURS HERE ONLY IN POETRY

This is one of Page's arguments for rejecting 106–14. But it is not cogent. If the occurrence of a word which is found elsewhere only in prose is to be reckoned as a count against authenticity one trembles to think of the fate of e.g. Sophocles, *Trachiniae* 873–91. It contains three words which occur elsewhere only in prose (and late prose) if at all; καινοποιηθέν 873 does not reappear until Polybius, διηίστωσε 881 is found nowhere except as a conjecture of Grenfell and Hunt at Pindar, *Paeans* VI, 96 (rejected by Bowra

---

52. G. Monaco, in an interesting article on the use of letters in ancient drama ('L'espistola nel teatro antico', *Dioniso* 39 (1965), 334–51), points out that the letter in *IT* is not read aloud by Iphigenia (she couldn't write as is clear from 584ff. so presumably she couldn't read either) and that in fact part of what we hear is her memory of what she dictated to the prisoner who once wrote it for her and part paraphrase adapted to the dialogue with Pylades. 'Il messaggio...è esposto in forma diretta (cioè com'è stato dettato al volenteroso prigioniero poi ucciso) ma inframezzata da qualche riferimento che non sembra testuale (come τοῖς ἐκεῖ del v. 771...)...Dopo la parte in forma diretta, che occupa i vv. 770 sg., 774–776, 778 sg., il resto è parafrasato' (p. 347).

and not recorded by Snell) and χειροποιεῖται 891 does not seem to turn up again until it is used by Epiphanius,[53] Bishop of Constantia in Cyprus, who died in 403 A.D. Agamemnon's μεταγράφω is much easier to defend. It is a good fifth-century word (Thucydides uses it of the same circumstances and in the same sense – a change in the text of a letter)[54] and it is used by Xenophon of changing the text of treaties and by Demosthenes of changing the text of judicial verdicts.[55] If Euripides wanted his Agamemnon to speak of revising the text of a letter, what other word was there to use?

To sum up: the case for the defense states that the objections to vocabulary (11), style (7) and meter (10) are invalid, the appeal to textual corruption (4) irrelevant, the allegations of incoherence (5) and lack of motivation (9) short-sighted, the claims that the opening anapaests cannot (1) and that the opening iambics must (8) constitute the beginning of a play unfounded, and the complaints about awkward transition (3) and repetition (6) a failure to recognize the dramatist's adaptation of existing tragic conventions for a prologue which, it has to be admitted, has no formal parallel (1).

The case for the defense, then, requires further only that the reader entertain the possibility that Euripides, for understandable dramatic reasons, experimented with a new form of prologue: an anapaestic dialogue enclosing an iambic expository speech. If this seems a large demand it should be remembered (though it seems to be generally forgotten) that the prosecution's demands on the reader's imagination are incomparably greater. They ask us to believe that Euripides wrote a complete anapaestic (or iambic) prologue, that someone else later wrote a complete alternative iambic (or anapaestic) prologue and that still a third person cut pieces off both prologues and fitted the bits together to form what we have now (perhaps writing some dull verses himself to bridge the gaps he had created). There is no doubt which of these two

---

53. And even there only in the active voice. *Haer.* II. lxiv 31. 32 (p. 633 Dindorf II).

54. I. 132. 5 παρασημηνάμενος σφραγῖδα ἵνα, ἢν ψευσθῇ τῆς δόξης ἢ καὶ ἐκεῖνός τι μεταγράψαι αἰτήσῃ, μὴ ἐπιγνῷ, λύει τὰς ἐπιστολάς. Cf. *IA* 37ff. γράμματα...σφραγίζεις λύεις τ' ὀπίσω.

55. Cf. LSJ *ad v.* But the entry cites the *IA* passage under the meaning 'copy, transcribe'. It should come below under 'rewrite, alter or correct what one has written'. (The new supplement does not note this error.)

explanations would have appealed to William of Occam. But the three-hand theory, apart from its assumption of pluralities, creates some problems its champions do not attempt to answer.[56] Why did the third man, faced with two perfectly good prologues, mutilate and combine them to create something which both Page and Fraenkel regard as a sorry product? What on earth was his motive? And secondly, if someone so perverse and stupid really existed, why is it that his version of the prologue and his alone has survived?[57]

But there is a much graver objection to the theory of triple authorship. Leaving the question of his purpose aside, it does not seem beyond the bounds of possibility (though Friedrich finds it so)[58] that the third man could have carved and glued the two prologues so skillfully that the resulting amalgam would contain all the information necessary for the audience's understanding of the subsequent action. What does seem incredible is that he should have done so and at the same time created the remarkable formal symmetry which distinguishes the prologue in its present form. It does not seem to have been noticed, but it is a fact, that the anapaestic systems on either side of the iambic speech are of exactly the same metrical length.[59] Further (and this seems to have been

56. The three-hand theory also presents us with the *disiecta membra* of two once-complete prologues. Fraenkel offers us the hacked remnants of a splendid Euripidean prologue in anapaests, Page the truncated corpse of a (possibly) Euripidean prologue in trimeters embedded in two pieces of a fine fourth-century anapaestic prologue. Both, when they have separated the wheat from the chaff, are forced to appeal to presumably lost lines for completeness. Our present prologue is at least complete; if it could take voice it might say to us, adapting the words of a recent American President, 'I'm the only prologue you've got.'

57. The play was famous in the fourth century and often produced. The Alexandrians knew that there were in existence three different prologues to *Rhesus*; it seems strange that if there were three versions of the prologue of *IA* no Alexandrian comment on the fact survives.

58. P. 91, n. 2, 'Man bedenke, mit welcher Häufung von Zufällen man rechnen müsste: Zufällig enthalten die Trimeter, wie zugegeben wird, gerade das, was den Anapästen fehlt. Zufällig fangen die Trimeter genau an dem Punkte an, wo die Mitteilungen erwartet werden, die Agamemnon in seiner Rede macht usw.'

59. This is obscured by Murray's colometry (which departs from that of Barnes but retains his numbering). But the important point is that counting paroemiacs (more frequent in the second system because of Agamemnon's melic anapaests) as dimeters, there are exactly 88 anapaestic dimeters on each side of the trimeters.

overlooked, too), Agamemnon's speeches in the first half of the second anapaestic system, and there only, are melic anapaests; this medium for expressing heightened emotion, especially sorrow, is used for his reading of the letter (115–16), his assurance that Achilles is ignorant of the proposed marriage (128–32), his desperate regrets (137–8) and his urgent command to the old man not to delay *en route* (141–2). This change of meter, coming immediately after the iambic speech in which Agamemnon confides in the old man the full desperation of his situation, is in exactly the right place.

It does not seem likely that such formal symmetry and such precise metrical organization can have resulted from the activities either of Fraenkel's 'Bearbeiter' who 'pasted up (zusammenge-klittert) the product that has been preserved for us', for he was a fast and careless worker ('er hat hastig gearbeitet'), or of Page's editor who was 'a bad poet and a worse dramatist'. It seems much more likely that the two anapaestic systems were written to stand exactly where they are, fore and aft of the iambics, and if so there seems no good reason to doubt that the poet who arranged the three elements of the prologue so artfully also wrote them or that the poet in question was Euripides.[60]

60. This article had already been in the editor's hands for some time before the appearance of Gudrun Mellert-Hoffmann's *Untersuchungen zur 'Iphigenie in Aulis' des Euripides* (Heidelberg 1969). The second part of this work, pp. 91–155, contains a vindication of the *IA* prologue in its present form with a careful consideration of all the objections which have been advanced against it and an especially valuable examination of the attacks on its language and style. Naturally enough some of the material of the present article is there anticipated but it also presents new arguments which, if generally accepted, will serve to reinforce Mellert-Hoffmann's impressive demonstration.

Notes on Sophocles' *Trachiniae*

HUGH LLOYD-JONES

1. 122–3:

> ὧν ἐπιμεμφομένας ἀ-
> δεῖα μέν, ἀντία δ' οἴσω.

Kamerbeek's defence of L's ὧν ἐπιμεμφομένας against the ὧν ἐπιμεμφομένα σ' of Laur. xxxii 20 and other later manuscripts is rightly approved by Page, *Gnomon* 32 (1960), 318. More questionable is his retention of the manuscript reading ἀδεῖα against Musgrave's αἰδοῖα, which has been accepted by Jebb, Pearson, Masqueray and Dain–Mazon. Hermann pointed out long ago that ἀδεῖα as neuter plural was not Attic, and Kamerbeek's parallels are not relevant.

But Musgrave's αἰδοῖα is hardly more satisfactory. The expression ἀντία οἴσω is equivalent to a single verb (cf. ἀντιφερίζω, etc.), so that ἀντία could hardly be so far disjoined from οἴσω as to be made antithetic to a second neuter plural adjective governed by that verb. Further, one may say ἀντία οἴσω, but it is far less easy to say αἰδοῖα οἴσω. For the antithesis yielded by Musgrave's conjecture I see no real parallel.

Hermann and Campbell both took ἀδεῖα as nominative singular and supplied εἰμί. Ellipse of the first person is rarer than ellipse of the third, but Denniston on Euripides, *Electra* 37 and Fraenkel on Aeschylus, *Agamemnon* 806 give instances; Aeschylus, *Choephori* 412, Sophocles, *OC* 207 and Euripides, *Cyclops* 503 are all good ones. Ellipse is particularly common with adjectives like ἕτοιμος or πρόθυμος, and ἀδεῖα would resemble these in signifying readiness to accept the other's point of view. But can the word bear this sense?

'In a pleasant vein', Jebb objected, 'must mean "suggesting thoughts of comfort"; as in *OT* 82 "pleasant" = "bringing good news".' But since ἀντία expresses remonstrance against D.'s despair, there is no proper antithesis with ἀδεῖα. If ἀδεῖα can only mean 'pleasant' or 'comfortable', there is much force in this argument. We should expect the sense here to be, 'I am kindly disposed towards you, but I shall offer a remonstrance'. Can ἡδύς mean 'favourably disposed'? The only passage in tragedy where it seems to have this meaning is Euripides, *Phoenissae* 771. Eteocles wishes to consult Tiresias, but because of a past quarrel he asks Creon to approach him on his behalf. σοὶ μὲν γὰρ ἡδὺς εἰς λόγους ἀφίξεται, he says to Creon, and in this context ἡδύς can only mean 'kindly', as Powell thinks. One could wish that there were more examples of the sense in question; but the *Phoenissae* passage seems to indicate that the view of Hermann and Campbell is likelier to be right than any other that has so far been put forward.

Pearson in his commentary renders it by 'gladly', comparing Demosthenes XXIII. 64 ἡδίους ἔσεσθε ἀκούσαντες. But in that place the sense is not 'You will be the gladder for having heard it', but 'You will be in a sweeter temper, a better state of mind, for having heard it'; and in the *Phoenissae* passage the presence of the pronoun σοί clearly limits the operation of the word to the relation of Tiresias to Creon. LSJ gives as sense II. 2 of ἡδύς 'well-pleased, glad'. The only instances given besides the passage of Demosthenes already dealt with are two passages of Plutarch. At *Vita Camilli* 32 ἡδίους...ταῖς ἐλπίσιν means 'more optimistic'; but we could extract this sense from 'sweeter in their hopes' without taking ἡδύς to mean 'glad'. At *Vita Fabii* 5 τὴν γνώμην ἡδίω πρὸς τὸ μέλλον ποιεῖν yields no evidence for such a meaning.

2. 216 ff.:

> ἀείρομ' οὐδ' ἀπώσομαι
> τὸν αὐλόν, ὦ τύραννε τῆς ἐμῆς φρενός.
> ἰδού μ' ἀναταράσσει
> εὐοῖ ⟨εὐοῖ⟩ μ'
> ὁ κισσὸς ἄρτι βακχίαν
> ὑποστρέφων ἄμιλλαν.

Jebb and Kamerbeek take ὑποστρέφων to mean 'whirling a little'. The word could certainly bear this meaning, but when one considers it in this context, it is hard not to agree with Pearson (*Cl. Rev.* 39 (1925), 2) that this view is 'not attractive'.

Others – for example Brunck, Hermann, Wunder, Campbell – have taken the sense to be 'turning me round'. Pearson (loc. cit.) objects that in this way the word would have to mean 'turning back something which is in process'. This objection has no force. The word may perfectly well mean that the speaker tries to go forward, but is whirled backwards as a ship is driven backwards by a contrary wind.

This is confirmed by what seems to be the most relevant parallel, which seems not yet to have been adduced. This is found in the words of Cassandra at the beginning of her final outburst of revelation (Aeschylus, *Agamemnon* 1214ff.):

> ἰοὺ ἰού, ὢ ὢ κακά.
> ὑπ' αὖ με δεινὸς ὀρθομαντείας πόνος
> στροβεῖ ταράσσων φροιμίοις...

στροβεῖν is 'an iterative-intensive form of στρέφειν' (see Schwyzer, *Gr. Gram.* I, 720, I. 4) so that ὑπό...στροβεῖ must be equivalent to ὑποστρέφει: Fraenkel rightly translates it 'whirls me round'.

At Aristophanes, *Pax* 174–6, the manuscripts read

> ὢ μηχανοποιέ, πρόσεχε τὸν νοῦν, ὡς ἐμὲ
> ἤδη στροφεῖ τι πνεῦμα περὶ τὸν ὀμφαλόν,
> κεἰ μὴ φυλάξεις, χορτάσω τὸν κάνθαρον.

Coulon and Platnauer both print Dindorf's στρέφει, but I should prefer στροβεῖ.

3. 831 ff.:

> εἰ γάρ σφε Κενταύρου φονίᾳ νεφέλᾳ
> χρίει δολοποιὸς ἀνάγκα
> πλευρὰ προστακέντος ἰοῦ,
> ὃν τέκετο θάνατος, ἔτρεφε δ' αἰόλος δράκων,
> πῶς ὅδ' ἂν ἀέλιον ἕτερον ἢ τανῦν ἴδοι,   835
> δεινοτάτῳ μὲν ὕδρας
> προστετακὼς φάσματι;

'Melted into, glued to the most dread shape of the Hydra' makes no sense, and in consequence innumerable emendations of φάσματι have been attempted. A large collection will be found in

Jebb's appendix on the passage; Dr A. A. Long, the author of a valuable book on *Language and Thought in Sophocles* (London 1968), has just revived θρέμματι, one of several suggestions made by Blaydes (*Greek, Roman and Byzantine Studies* 8 (1967), 275f.).

I am convinced by none of these suggestions; and I believe this to be one of the fairly numerous cases in which a comparatively rare word has been unjustly vexed, while a common and therefore innocent-looking word in the same passage conceals the canker. In this place the common word which I believe to be corrupt is δεινοτάτῳ. Eduard Fraenkel has lately reminded us (*Horace*, p. 20, n. 4 and *S.B. der Bayerischen Akademie* (1957), p. 48, n. 137) how often the endings -τατος and -τερος are confused; in this case the confusion may have been occasioned by a misunderstanding of the sense. I believe that Sophocles wrote δεινοτέρῳ, and meant 'glued to a shape more deadly than the Hydra'.

The Lernaean Hydra Heracles had vanquished; he now found himself locked in combat with a more formidable antagonist, that Ἐρινύων ὑφαντὸν ἀμφίβληστρον (1051–2) which is so vividly personified in the great speech that follows the μέλος ἀπὸ σκηνῆς:

πλευραῖσι γὰρ προσμαχθὲν ἐκ μὲν ἐσχάτας
βέβρωκε σάρκας, πλεύμονός τ᾽ ἀρτηρίας
ῥοφεῖ ξυνοικοῦν· ἐκ δὲ χλωρὸν αἷμά μου
πέπωκεν ἤδη, καὶ διέφθαρμαι δέμας
τὸ πᾶν, ἀφράστῳ τῇδε χειρωθεὶς πέδῃ.

But can φάσμα be used in this way to signify the shirt of Nessus? One might quote l. 508, where Achelous as he comes in bull shape to fight Heracles is called φάσμα ταύρου, but there he may be called 'the apparition of a bull' because he looks like one. But consider Euripides, *Cretes* fr. 82, 23–4 in Colin Austin's *Nova Fragmenta Euripidea in Papyris Reperta* (Berlin 1968). Minos, says Pasiphae, did not sacrifice the sacred bull to Poseidon as he had promised:

ταῦρον γὰρ οὐκ ἔσφαξ[εν ὅν γ᾽ ἐπηύ]ξατο
ἐλθόντα θύσειν φάσμα [πο]ντίω[ι θε]ῶι.

Page (*Greek Literary Papyri*, 74) translates 'that bull, that apparition'. The bull is so called because it is uncanny, strange, mysterious; so, if I am right about the Sophoclean passage, is the shirt of Nessus.

4. 1004–43:

A. H. Coxon in *Cl. Rev.* 61 (1947), 7f. performed a notable service to the text of Sophocles by challenging the arrangement of the μέλος ἀπὸ σκηνῆς proposed by Seidler, *De versibus dochmiacis tragicorum graecorum*, 1811–12, pp. 311f., and accepted by all editors down to and including Pearson. Dain and Mazon in their Budé edition (vol. I, 1955) without knowledge of Coxon's article took the same view as he that the strophe extends from 1004 to 1017 and the antistrophe from 1025 to 1043, against Seidler who had adopted the following unusual scheme:

> (Heracles): str. α′, str. β′, hexameters, antistr. α′.
> (Old Man, then Hyllus): hexameters.
> (Heracles): str. γ′, antistr. β′, hexameters, antistr. γ′.

Dain and Mazon's arrangement is somewhat different from that of Coxon. Indeed, the text is so corrupt that there is room for some difference of opinion about its proper constitution; and though I wish to put forward a third arrangement that differs in some respects both from that of Coxon and that of the Budé editors, I hardly suppose that I shall say the final word on this difficult problem.

I shall start by giving my own version of the text and then try to justify it in a line-by-line commentary:

1004–17 = 1023–43

ἐέ,	ὦ παῖ, ποῦ ποτ᾽ εἶ;
⟨– – – ∪ –⟩	τᾷδέ με, τᾷδέ με
ἐᾶτέ μ᾽, ἐᾶτέ με	πρόσλαβε κουφίσας. 1025
δύσμορον εὐνάσαι 1005	ἐέ, ἰὼ δαῖμον
ἐᾶτέ με δύστανον.	θρῴσκει δ᾽ αὖ, θρῴσκει δειλαία
πᾷ ⟨πᾷ⟩ μου ψαύεις; ποῖ κλίνεις;	διολοῦσ᾽ ἡμᾶς
ἀπολεῖς μ᾽, ἀπολεῖς.	ἀποτίβατος ἀγρία νόσος.
ἀνατέτροφας ὅ τι καὶ μύσῃ.	(hexameters ending with ὦ γλυκὺς ῎Αιδας,
(hexameters)	transposed by Seidler from 1041, after
	αὐθαίμων)
ἐέ,	
οὐδ᾽ ἀπαράξαι ⟨μου⟩ 1015	ὦ Διὸς αὐθαίμων 1041
κρᾶτα βίου θέλει	εὔνασον εὔνασόν μ᾽,
⟨– ∪∪ –⟩ μολὼν τοῦ στυγεροῦ; φεῦ φεῦ.	ὠκυπέτᾳ μόρῳ τὸν μέλεον φθίσας.

1004 ante hunc versum lacunam posuit   1015 ⟨μου⟩ post Blaydes addidit Pearson
      Coxon   1017 ⟨παυσίπονος⟩? ⟨λυσίπονος⟩?
1005 εὐνάσαι A: εὐνᾶσαι L   1023 ὢ παῖ LG: ὢ παῖ πᾶι L cett.
1006 ὕστατον Σʸᵖ·: εὐνάσαι (-ᾶσαι L) post   1025 ἰὼ rec.: ἰὼ ἰὼ L
      δύστανον del. Dain   1042 εὔνασον εὔνασόν μ’ Erfurdt: εὔνασόν
1007 ⟨πᾶι⟩ Seidler   μ’ εὔνασον codd.
1009 ἀν⟨α⟩τέτροφας Erfurdt

1004–6: Coxon supposes that a dochmiac metron responding with ὢ παῖ, ποῦ ποτ’ εἶ (1023) has dropped out before ἐᾶτέ μ’. Dain and Mazon suppose that ἐᾶτέ μ’ responds with ὢ παῖ, ποῦ, that between ἐᾶτέ μ’ and ἐᾶτέ με a cretic has been lost and that ἐᾶτέ με δύσμορον responds with τᾷδέ με τᾷδέ με. So far there can be no doubt that Coxon's view is likelier to be right, since ἐᾶτέ μ’, ἐᾶτέ με and τᾷδέ με τᾷδέ με very probably respond with one another.

Coxon makes δύσμορον εὐνάσαι (1005) respond with πρόσλαβε κουφίσας (1025). Dain, having used up δύσμορον already, has to place in the text the ὕστατον which appears in L's margin as a variant on δύσμορον, so that ὕστατον εὐνάσαι is made to respond with πρόσλαβε κουφίσας. Here again one must prefer Coxon's view. It is not likely that ὕστατον belongs in the text; it may have originated as a corruption of δύστανον in l. 1006, as Seidler thought. It is just worth contemplating the possibility that the stanza began with ἐὲ ἐᾶτέ με responding with ὢ παῖ, ποῦ ποτ’ εἶ; : in that case one would have to fill up the space by inserting a third ἐᾶτέ με or by accepting Dain's insertion of ὕστατον. But Coxon's way of dealing with the difficulty is to be preferred.

1006: Here Coxon follows Triclinius and several modern scholars in holding that the manuscript reading ἐᾶτέ με δύστανον εὐνάσαι is 'a simple variant of ἐᾶτέ με δύσμορον εὐνάσαι which has displaced an exclamation metrically equivalent to ἐὲ ἐὲ ἰὼ ἰὼ δαῖμον'. But Dain obtains response simply by deleting εὐνάσαι, so that ἐᾶτέ με δύστανον answers to ἐὲ ἰὼ δαῖμον. This responsion is perfectly legitimate; εὐνάσαι could easily have got in from the line before; and in this place Dain's solution is to be preferred.

1016–17 = 1041–2: In the manuscripts the words ὢ γλυκὺς Ἀΐδας (thus L: some others have Ἄιδας) appear after ὢ Διὸς αὐθαίμων. Seidler transposed them to fill a gap at the end of the hexameters, in l. 1040; he has been followed by all modern editors, and also by Coxon. Dain prefers to suppose that the end of l. 1040 has been lost, to keep ὦ γλυκὺς ᾽Αίδας after ὦ Διὸς αὐθαίμων and to suppose that ὦ γλυκὺς ᾽Αίδας responds with κρᾶτα...θέλει (1016). Does the actual sense of ll. 1015–17 make Dain's solution likely?

In l. 1016 almost all modern scholars have accepted Wakefield's alteration of βίου to βίᾳ. Kamerbeek is an exception; his fear of departing from the manuscripts occasionally leads him to prefer the right reading.[1] If it is true that strophic responsion is present here, something must be missing from this stanza; and once that is admitted, the rashness of altering βίου is obvious. Kamerbeek has observed that a scholion written against l. 1016 in L gives a distinct indication of what the sense of the complete stanza may have been: οὐδεὶς ἐκείνων, φησί, βούλεται ἐλθὼν τὴν κεφαλήν μου ἀποτεμεῖν καὶ ἐλευθερῶσαι τοῦ μοχθηροῦ βίου.

What, then, is likely to have dropped out? Dain, who keeps γλυκὺς ᾽Αίδας (*sic*) where it is in the manuscripts, thinks – ∪ ∪ – ∪ × is missing in l. 1016 after θέλει. At the beginning of l. 1017, he thinks a choriamb is missing; so that ὠκυπέτᾳ μόρῳ τὸν μέλεον φθίσας responds with – ∪ ∪ – μολὼν τοῦ στυγεροῦ · φεῦ φεῦ.

Coxon accepts Seidler's transposition of ὦ γλυκὺς ῎Αιδας (*sic*) to the vacant space at the end of l. 1040; so he does not suppose that – ∪ ∪ – ∪ × is missing at the end of l. 1016. But in l. 1017 he accepts Erfurdt's transposition τοῦ στυγεροῦ μολών, deletes φεῦ φεῦ, and prints the line like this: τοῦ στυγεροῦ μολὼν – ∪ ∪ – × .

Working backwards from l. 1017, it is clear that Coxon had no good reason to accept Erfurdt's transposition, or to cut out φεῦ φεῦ. For we have only to suppose a choriamb is missing at the beginning of the line to get responsion; in other words, ὠκυπέτᾳ μόρῳ τὸν μέλεον φθίσας may well have responded with ⟨– ∪ ∪ –⟩ μολὼν τοῦ στυγεροῦ · φεῦ φεῦ. Can we hazard any guess at what the sense of the missing four syllables may have been? Let us look back at the text of the scholion which Kamerbeek and I agree may furnish a clue to the missing part of this stanza. Kamerbeek's effort at a supplement may be found on p. 215 of his commentary. It might, I think, have been more convincing had he not accepted without

1. Bergk, it is true, kept βίου; but as he postulated no lacuna in this line, it is hard to see what sense he made of it.

question Dain's view that ὦ γλυκὺς Ἅιδας stands in its proper place in the manuscripts. For suppose for the sake of the argument that Dain is wrong, and that Seidler's transposition is correct. Then one could easily fill the space and bring the sense of the text into line with the paraphrase in the scholion by supplying before μολών a single compound adjective; something like παυσίπονος (Eur. *IT* 451, Ar. *Ran.* 1321), λυσίπονος (Pindar, *Pyth.* IV. 41; fr. 131. 1), παυσανίας (Soph. fr. 887 P.), λυσανίας (Ar. *Nub.* 1162), ῥυσίπονος (anon. *AP* IX. 525. 18). The sense is so neatly supplied by such an insertion that I feel the case for Seidler's transposition is considerably strengthened by these observations.

ADDENDUM In the second of these notes, I ought to have explained that I take μ' to be the object both of ἀναταράσσει and of ὑπο-στρεφων. Βακχίαν...ἅμιλλαν I take to be an accusative limiting the action of the verb, so that the words mean, 'whirling me around in the Bacchic race'.

By using the word 'race', I do not mean that there is any suggestion of a competition. ἅμιλλα, like 'race', may imply simply rapid movement, without any suggestion of 'racing' in the competitive sense. At Euripides, *Or.* 456, for instance, Di Benedetto rightly says that in the phrase γέροντι δεῦρ' ἁμιλλᾶται ποδί the verb means not 'contendere', but 'affrettarsi'. Kannicht on Euripides, *Helen* 546 says that in such instances the basic meaning of 'certare' is still present, because the movement in question has to overcome a resistance; he quotes also Euripides, *Hypsipyle* fr. 764 (p. 24 Bond).

In his article on 'Der Einzug des Chors im *Prometheus*' (*An. Scuola Norm. Sup. di Pisa*, serie ii, vol. xxiii (1954), 269 f. = *Kleine Beiträge zur kl. Philologie* I 389 f.), Eduard Fraenkel tried to show that the Oceanids entered not in a 'celestial omnibus', but each in her separate winged car. He proved that the separate winged car was not a prerogative of Triptolemus, as earlier scholars had supposed, and went on to argue that the words πτερύγων θοαῖς ἁμίλλαις (l. 129) showed that each Oceanid had her separate car, or they could not have raced each other. When his article first appeared, Sir Denys Page pointed out to me that, since ἅμιλλα need not imply a 'race', the proof was not complete.